T0003948

PRAISE FOR
THE NEW SCIENCE OF NARCISSISM

"Narcissism is both widely discussed and widely misunderstood—which is why the world desperately needs a book like *The New Science of Narcissism*. Campbell and Crist explode the myths around narcissism and, in its place, build a solid understanding of what narcissism really is and how it displays itself across so many realms, from relationships to the workplace to social media. *The New Science of Narcissism* will give you what you need to better manage narcissism no matter where or how you experience it. "

> JEAN M. TWENGE, PhD,
> author of *iGen: Why Today's Super-Connected Kids*
> *Are Growing Up Less Rebellious, More Tolerant, Less*
> *Happy—and Completely Unprepared for Adulthood*

"This is a fascinating journey into research and theory on narcissism, from one of the world's leading experts on the topic. Although there is plenty of science, there are also concrete and useful tips on how to work with narcissists on a practical level. Most surprising is that they also consider the beneficial sides of narcissism, with suggestions on how to work with rather than against the narcissists who are an unavoidable part of the social world."

> KRISTEN NEFF,
> author of *Self-Compassion*

"This book provides a comprehensive, clear, and easy-to-read account of what we know and don't know about narcissism, guided by both influential theoretical accounts as well as the increasingly large and sophisticated research literature. Keith Campbell, a leading researcher in narcissism, presents this information in a down-to-earth, funny, and easily digestible manner that makes for a fun and breezy read on this important topic."

> JOSHUA MILLER, PhD

"This is an incredibly timely book given the prevalence of narcissism in politics, boardrooms, and social media platforms in the world today. This book arms you with the latest science to not only understand narcissism in its many forms—from the trait to the disorder—but also to apply it to your own life so that you can live your best life. This book is for everyone interested in learning more about this fascinating and often misunderstood topic."

SCOTT BARRY KAUFMAN,
author of *Transcend: The New Science of Self-Actualization*

"*The New Science of Narcissism* offers a comprehensive understanding of narcissism, a personality disorder that wreaks havoc on relationships. With historical examples, pop cultural references, and other sources that give insight into this malignant phenomenon, this fascinating and important book is also peppered with Campbell's down-to-earth wit and humor."

KARYL MCBRIDE, PhD,
author of *Will I Ever Be Good Enough? Healing the Daughters of Narcissistic Mothers* and *Will I Ever Be Free of You? How to Navigate a High-Conflict Divorce from a Narcissist and Heal Your Family*

THE NEW SCIENCE OF NARCISSISM

THE NEW SCIENCE OF NARCISSISM

Understanding One of the Greatest
Psychological Challenges of Our Time—
and What You Can Do About It

W. KEITH CAMPBELL, PHD
Carolyn Crist

sounds true
BOULDER, COLORADO

Sounds True
Boulder, CO 80306

© 2020, 2022 W. Keith Campbell and Carolyn Crist

Sounds True is a trademark of Sounds True, Inc.

All rights reserved. No part of this book may be used or reproduced in any manner without written permission from the author(s) and publisher.

Published 2020, 2022

Cover design by Jennifer Miles
Book design by Happenstance Type-O-Rama
Photo of W. Keith Campbell by Jason Thrasher
Photo of Carolyn Crist by Jordana Dale

FSC
www.fsc.org
MIX
Paper | Supporting
responsible forestry
FSC® C103098

Printed in the United States of America

BK06551

978-1-64963-011-7

The Library of Congress has cataloged the hardcover edition as follows:
Names: Campbell, W. Keith, author. | Crist, Carolyn, author.
Title: The new science of narcissism : understanding one of the greatest psychological challenges of our time-and what you can do about it / W. Keith Campbell, Carolyn Crist.
Description: Boulder : Sounds True, 2020. | Includes bibliographical references and index.
Identifiers: LCCN 2019058215 (print) | LCCN 2019058216 (ebook) | ISBN 9781683644026 (hardback) | ISBN 9781683644033 (ebook)
Subjects: LCSH: Narcissism. | Personality disorders.
Classification: LCC BF575.N35 C357 2020 (print) | LCC BF575.N35 (ebook) | DDC 155.2/32—dc23
LC record available at https://lccn.loc.gov/2019058215
LC ebook record available at https://lccn.loc.gov/2019058216

10 9 8 7 6 5 4 3 2 1

*To those trying to
understand narcissism
for any reason,*

and for Murphy

CONTENTS

PREFACE:
Why You Need This Book
ix

PART I. DEFINING NARCISSISM TODAY

CHAPTER 1:
Defining Narcissism
3

CHAPTER 2:
Measuring Narcissism
23

CHAPTER 3:
Basic Traits and the Narcissism Recipe
45

CHAPTER 4:
Narcissists' Goals and Motives
63

CHAPTER 5:
Narcissistic Personality Disorder
79

CHAPTER 6:
Narcissism's Cousins: The Four Triads
97

PART II. OBSERVING NARCISSISM IN THE WORLD AROUND YOU

CHAPTER 7:
Relationships and Narcissism
113

CHAPTER 8:
Leadership and Narcissism
135

CHAPTER 9:

Social Media and Narcissism

153

CHAPTER 10:

Geek Culture and the Great Fantasy Migration

171

PART III. DEALING WITH NARCISSISM TODAY AND IN THE FUTURE

CHAPTER 11:

Using Narcissism Strategically

185

CHAPTER 12:

Reducing Another's Narcissism

197

CHAPTER 13:

Reducing Your Own Narcissism

211

CHAPTER 14:

Psychotherapy for Narcissism

223

CHAPTER 15:

Future Science Around Narcissism

237

EPILOGUE:

Facing the Future with Hope

251

QUICK-START GLOSSARY

255

NOTES

257

SUGGESTED READINGS

265

ABOUT THE AUTHORS

25

PREFACE

WHY YOU NEED THIS BOOK

You don't need to go far to find narcissism. It shows up in news headlines about our political leaders, commentary about social media influencers, and online discussions about manipulative relationships among friends, family, romantic partners, coworkers, and organizations. The term *narcissist*—generally defined as those who have excessive interest in or admiration of themselves—garners up to 1 million monthly searches online, and tens of thousands of us are searching for information about "narcissistic traits," "narcissistic behavior," and "signs of a narcissist." Hundreds more specifically want to know if they're "married to a narcissist" and how to "deal with a narcissist." *Narcissism* is a household term these days, and we want to know what it means in our lives. The good news is that in the research world, we understand so much more about narcissism than we did twenty, ten, and even five years ago.

At the same time, when I'm talking to people about narcissism and how it affects their lives, I see that there is a large gap between the way I think about narcissism, as someone who does scientific research on the topic, and the way the term is often used. Narcissism is more complex and nuanced than people expect, and the way we talk about it in daily conversations and news stories can get confusing. The term *narcissism* can mean several different things, such as a basic personality trait that most of us exhibit to some extent or a full-blown personality disorder that is severe, diagnosable, and should be treated. When we have mixed definitions like these, no one in a conversation about the topic quite knows what the other person is saying, and it creates confusion. My hope is that this book will give you the knowledge to understand narcissism in its multiple forms. You will learn how narcissism works in the world and how it applies to your life. I want to empower you to understand and deal with narcissism in the world today, using the most cutting-edge scientific research I can share with you.

In fact, our conversations about narcissism have become more nuanced and confusing because the science around narcissism has also become more nuanced and confusing. I purposefully put "new science" in the title of this book because the research on narcissism has exploded during the past decade, and psychologists at universities across the United States—and the world—understand far more about it as both a personality trait and a disorder than before. You deserve to know the latest thinking in the field. To describe the latest science on narcissism, I also provide some background on personality science and personality disorders, so if you wonder why you stumbled into an "Introduction to Personality" lecture early on, I apologize in advance.

In this book, I'll talk about narcissism in a variety of ways, but for the most part, I'll talk about it as a personality trait, not a disorder, though details about narcissistic personality disorder appear in chapter 5. You may be surprised that the beginning of the book is so focused on personality. That's quite intentional; much of what we know now considers narcissism to be a personality trait that spans a spectrum, which is not entirely good or bad. Ultimately, I believe we need to study narcissism to better understand it in ourselves and others and the reasons it may be useful or harmful. People sometimes fear narcissism and want to eliminate it. I understand that feeling, especially from the many people who have been harmed by narcissism. But the reality is, narcissism is here, and we can accept it and work with it (or fight against it as needed). Through this book, you can learn these nuances and strategies for dealing with narcissism.

My own interest in narcissism shows some of these complexities. I didn't grow up wanting to be a narcissism researcher. I wanted to study the self and ego and be philosophical about who we are and what motivates us. When I went to graduate school, I was interested in Buddhist thought and the "non-self," or what exists beyond ourselves and the soul. Growing up in Western society, we aren't often taught to think this way, and I wanted to learn more. In a psychology lab, however, it's difficult to study and measure this idea of the non-self. Instead, you study ego, and so I did. As I delved into the research, my focus on ego moved beyond self-esteem and identity and shifted more and more toward narcissism: What does narcissism mean? How do people use it? What are its social effects?

I've now been studying narcissism for more than thirty years, and as you can imagine, the understanding around narcissism has changed dramatically. I came up in a time when social psychologists, who traditionally studied ego and the self, generally ignored personality. It sounds crazy now, but that was the 1980s. As social psychologists, we used to think that people were generally self-enhancing and self-promoting, and to some extent, that's true. But when I began studying narcissism, I realized that this isn't always the case. For the most part, people are quite generous and kind, especially as individuals. On the other hand, when you encounter someone with narcissistic tendencies, it's a mixed bag. As a trait, it's not good, and it's not bad, but as a disorder, it can be horrific. I wanted to learn more.

As I was studying narcissism, current events began to change our understanding of narcissism as a trait and how it shows up in people. First, while doing my postdoctoral research with psychologist Roy Baumeister at Case Western Reserve University, the Columbine shooting happened. Fellow postdoc Jean Twenge and I were studying social rejection at the time, and we started looking at this case. We realized that, wow, these shooters were using narcissistic language. They wanted a movie made about them, and more than that, they wanted Steven Spielberg to produce it. That event sparked us to look at narcissism and group aggression.

A few years later, social media took over our lives. I remember standing in the lab with my student Laura Buffardi while she showed me Facebook on the desktop computer. I knew that this was the biggest cultural change I had ever seen (Facebook has dwarfed Woodstock, for instance), and that it would be deeply tied to narcissism. I told Laura to figure out how to study it, and she put together a wonderful early study on Facebook that we published in 2008, which showed that narcissism predicted higher levels of social activity on the site, and narcissism was linked with posting more self-promoting content.

After that, people became interested in cultural change, which Jean and I had been looking at for years in various ways—from changes in baby names to pronoun use—especially related to individualism. We wrote a 2009 book called *The Narcissism Epidemic*, which captured the early rise of smartphones in the 2000s, as well as financial, educational, and social factors that play a role in cultural narcissism. Overall, it seemed that our culture (at least in the United States) was shifting toward a more narcissistic and individual-focused mentality. YouTube said to "Broadcast Yourself," and Netflix began creating customized suggestions just for us. It seemed like younger generations were shifting toward more narcissistic outlooks and attitudes (though that's beginning to change, as I'll explain later).

During these thirty years, especially during the past decade, the science about narcissism has progressed rapidly. When I began, we had a basic scale, called the Narcissistic Personality Inventory, that measured narcissistic traits. It worked pretty well for one aspect of narcissism, but it missed the vulnerable side of narcissism completely and wasn't particularly well-made. As interest in narcissism research grew, we had various academic squabbles, but over time, social personality psychologists like me began meeting with clinical psychologists, organizational psychologists, measurement and assessment specialists, and experts in many other fields, and we started working together to understand the nuances of narcissism, both as seen in therapy and in everyday life. My own understanding of narcissism is now largely informed by the work I have done with my colleague Josh Miller and his lab at the University of Georgia. I'll talk about these new findings throughout this book and what they mean about how narcissism operates in many facets of our lives.

As you'll see, I start the book with a conversation about personality, personality traits, and the recipe that makes up narcissism. Of course, you can read the chapters as you wish, but I believe it's important to know the foundational aspects of narcissism so that you can see how it operates in the "real life" chapters that follow about leadership, social media, and relationships. Once you know the ingredients, you can learn how to change your own tendencies or help others in your life. Knowing the narcissism recipe will also help you keep up with future research as it's presented in the public sphere.

In addition, research psychologists in personality and clinical areas have finally come to an agreement on the basic personality ingredients of narcissism in the past few years. Before that, we were arguing about what it was, how to measure it, and what to do about it. As it turns out, both groups were right in our own ways, and now it's come together as a cohesive view of narcissism. This sets us up for a great discussion for the next twenty years. I wrote this book to invite you to be part of that conversation.

But I didn't want that conversation to break off into too many tangents. That's why, at the end of most chapters, you'll find two extra sections: "Nerd Herd" and "Inside Scoop." If you're a nerd like me, you appreciate the finer details behind the scientific concepts, and the "Nerd Herd" sections will give an in-depth look into the research. Similarly, the "Inside Scoop" sections will give a behind-the-scenes peek at my own insights into some of the research out there, including studies I've conducted with students and colleagues, as well as some of the discussions and debates in the psychology research world today.

Before you dive in, I want to make an important point: the goal here is not to dwell on the horror of narcissism, especially the extreme, the pathological, the most malignant form of narcissism. The goal is to understand narcissism itself, which means stepping back and seeing it from a psychological distance. To do that, I use metaphors and plenty of humor. This distance is not meant to be dismissive of intense feeling or personal experience. It is meant to provide a little psychological space to make sense of things and move forward.

Ultimately, I hope you come away from this discussion with more insight and empowerment around narcissism in your life. On a recent fishing trip, I talked with several friends about narcissism in their clients' lives, in politics in several countries, in boardrooms and operating rooms, and on emerging social media platforms. As the conversation and understanding continues to grow in our society, we can better see where narcissism works and where it doesn't—and what we can do about it. I see hope and positivity for the next generation, and I hope you will, too.

W. KEITH CAMPBELL
Athens, Georgia
January 2020

I

DEFINING NARCISSISM TODAY

CHAPTER 1

Defining Narcissism

Narcissism can range from everyday actions to more extreme behaviors. I want to intentionally start with an extreme example that has become familiar to us all—the narcissism-driven mass shooting. It's extreme and harrowing but provides a common starting point to talk about the elements of narcissism that drive certain behaviors. This example is similar to the Columbine shooting in 1999 that I incorporated in my research around social rejection, but it is a more recent illustration that pulls in today's cultural context of social media. Although this case is extreme and pathological, all of us can relate to feeling rejected. And some of these feelings of entitlement may look familiar in small doses in yourself or a friend.

This example focuses on Elliot Rodger, the twenty-two-year-old son of a Hollywood filmmaker who killed six students and injured fourteen others in the college town of Isla Vista, California, in May 2014. Near the University of California at Santa Barbara campus, Rodger stabbed three men—his two roommates and their friend—in his apartment, and then three hours later, he drove to the Alpha Phi sorority house and shot three women outside. Next, he drove past a deli and shot a male student, and then he sped through the small town, shooting and wounding several pedestrians and hitting some with his car. During the chase, Rodger exchanged gunfire with police twice and received a nonfatal shot to the hip. In the end, he crashed his car into a parked vehicle. Police found him dead in the car with a self-inflicted shot to the head.

Authorities later found a video he uploaded to YouTube, called "Elliot Rodger's Retribution," which outlined his upcoming attack and his motives. In the video, Rodger said he wanted to punish women for rejecting him, as well as men who had successfully picked up women. He also emailed a manuscript, called "My Twisted World: The Story of Elliot Rodger," to two dozen people, including his therapist and some family members. What became known as his "manifesto" details his relatively affluent childhood, family conflicts, hatred of women, contempt of couples, frustration about his virginity, and his plans for retribution. In the final section of the document, Rodger said: "I am the true victim in all of this. I am the good guy."[1]

Rodger's case was cited across mainstream media as a heightened example of narcissism-gone-wrong, and psychologists were asked to comment on his grandiose fantasies, twisted motivations, and ongoing YouTube delusions that may have signaled a diagnosable disorder. We'll use this example to unpack what narcissism is, how it motivated Rodger's actions, and how it shows up in our society. First, let's define narcissism, and then we can pull apart the case throughout the chapter to better see the details.

BROACHING THE NARCISSISM CONVERSATION

Narcissism has become an enormously popular term, but we often don't have a clear idea of what the term means. Is it about being arrogant or vain? Is it about being a jerk? Is it about manipulativeness? Is it about insecurity? Is it a normal trait or a psychiatric disorder or something in between? The truth is that the answer to all these questions is "yes," but it is a little more refined than that. Narcissism has nuance and falls on a spectrum of sorts. For example, the following three individuals demonstrate different types of narcissistic traits and behaviors:

- Your favorite blogger talks about the high-status people she meets and the fancy places she goes. She name-drops constantly, and you get the sense that she sees herself as superior to most people. She expertly turns conversations back toward herself and her experiences, no matter the topic. However, she is also charming and entertaining, which makes her likable despite her self-centeredness. You think that you two could be friends.

- An acquaintance of yours is shy and insecure. He seems depressed but at the same time a bit full of himself. He wants everything done his way, doesn't show a lot of compassion for others, and complains that people don't realize how smart he is. You have talked to him about his depression, but he can't take responsibility for it. To him, all of his problems are a result of the unfair treatment the world has given him. If only the world recognized his brilliance, everything would be okay.

- Your coworker uses his Twitter account to brag about his accomplishments at work, although you don't consider them to be as significant as he does. He belittles coworkers and is incapable of showing gratitude to others who help him with his projects. He expects special treatment, and when he doesn't get it, he is mean and vindictive. Some people call him "prickly" because he is so reactive to criticism. Despite all of these flaws, the boss likes him. He is seen as a go-getter, but you see him more as a suck-up.

These three people seem different, but each shows features of narcissism. The first is outgoing and charming, the second is insecure and depressed, and the third is a combination of the two—arrogant but also defensive.

At its core, narcissism is about self-importance, antagonism, and a sense of entitlement. Narcissists believe they matter more than other people and deserve to be treated that way. Each of these three individuals shares this selfish core of narcissism, but they also differ in important ways that the science of narcissism is now beginning to reveal.

The first individual is what we call a *grandiose narcissist*. These are ambitious, driven, and charming individuals. They have high self-esteem and generally feel good about themselves. These are the narcissists you will see most often in your life: you work for them, date them, and are entertained by them. You are often drawn to their boldness but are later repelled by their self-centeredness and lack of empathy. Many fictional characters are grandiose narcissists, including Tony Stark in *Iron Man*, Gilderoy Lockhart in the *Harry Potter* series, Gaston in *Beauty and the Beast*, and Miranda Priestly in *The Devil Wears Prada*. These characters range from humorous, like Ron Burgundy in *Anchorman,* to evil, like Nicole Kidman's character in *To Die For.* Historically, many labels describe grandiose narcissists, including *overt, exhibitionistic,* and *special child.* You might think of this first example most frequently as you move through the book.

On the other hand, you may also start to think about the second example, a person who is considered a *vulnerable narcissist.* These people are introverted, depressed, and easily hurt by criticism. They report having low self-esteem, but despite that, they see themselves as deserving of special treatment. Vulnerable narcissists are harder to see in your life, so much so that psychologists often call them "hidden" narcissists. Vulnerable narcissism is also harder to see in fiction. Woody Allen plays a vulnerable narcissist in many of his movies—neurotic and self-absorbed—with Alvy Singer in *Annie Hall* being a good example. Another character with these qualities is George Costanza in *Seinfeld.* The labels for vulnerable narcissists include *covert, closet,* and *shame child.* Table 1.1 lists the terms that have been historically used to identify grandiose and vulnerable narcissists. You'll begin to understand these narcissists and what motivates them, too.

Table 1.1: Historical Narcissism Labels

GRANDIOSE NARCISSIST	VULNERABLE NARCISSIST
Manipulative	Craving
Overt	Covert
Uncivilized spoiled child	Infantilized spoiled child
Thick-skinned	Thin-skinned
Oblivious	Hypervigilant
Overtly grandiose	Overtly vulnerable
Exhibitionistic	Closet
Special child	Shame child
Arrogant	Shy
Unprincipled	Compensatory

The individual in the third example is a combination of the two types of narcissism. He has the extraverted, ambitious qualities of grandiose narcissism and the more defensive qualities of vulnerable narcissism. Yes, to make things more confusing, some individuals can be both grandiose and vulnerable and live in the "middle zone" of the two types. Former US president Richard Nixon is a good example of combined grandiosity and vulnerability. Another more recent figure who appears to have both high grandiosity and high vulnerability, at least in his public image, is rapper and pop culture icon Kanye West, who is known for having a high opinion of his work but doesn't take criticism with grace. Although we technically don't define the narcissism types on a spectrum, it can be helpful to think about it that way. You may see a bit of grandiosity or vulnerability in yourself; in general, most of us exhibit some measure of narcissism, and it can come out in different ways, both positive and negative.

ONE OR THE OTHER? GRANDIOSE VERSUS VULNERABLE NARCISSISM

Until recently, many psychologists didn't separate these terms and typically researched the grandiose form of narcissism, so the early studies of narcissism focused on its extraverted, arrogant qualities. At the same time, psychotherapists were seeing patients who exhibited more of the vulnerable form of narcissism. As you might imagine, most people seek psychotherapy when they feel bad—anxious or depressed—or they're struggling socially. And not just bad, but bad enough to seek psychological treatment, with its costs and potential stigma. Psychotherapy is usually not plan A in life.

Because of this, psychotherapists didn't often see the grandiose narcissists, who didn't believe they needed help. Grandiose narcissists don't tend to struggle socially, feel depressed about their circumstances, or see distressing behavior in themselves that they need to address through therapy. In fact, they often feel full of self-esteem and are socially successful. Some grandiose narcissists seek treatment for issues outside of depression and anxiety, such as substance use or relational therapy, but still not as often as vulnerable narcissists. As a result of this bias, narcissists in treatment exhibit more vulnerability than the average grandiose narcissist. And since people are encouraged to express themselves or "open up" in therapy, grandiose narcissists who do seek treatment may be more likely to discuss personal weaknesses in therapy than they would otherwise. In essence, therapists were likely to see more vulnerability in grandiose narcissists than the outside world did, including in the studies we were conducting in psychology labs.

This is where the new science comes in. When psychologists and psychiatrists met in recent years to define and discuss narcissism, they wanted to include both sides of what the researchers and clinicians were seeing. We knew that having two forms of narcissism was a problem, and it was odd for one term to describe two different personality structures.

Grandiose and Vulnerable Narcissism

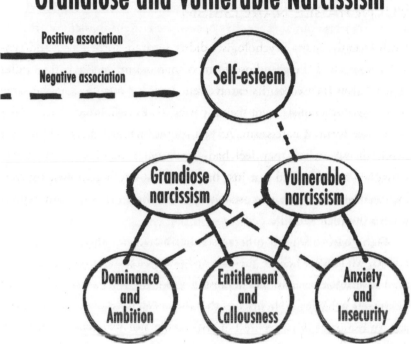

At first, the grandiose/vulnerable distinction was resolved by assuming that grandiose narcissists feel vulnerable deep down, having a vulnerable core with a grandiose mask, which is sometimes called the "mask model" of narcissism. Under this interpretation, however, it would mean that when President Donald Trump goes home at night and looks in the mirror, he sees Woody Allen staring back at him. This is a neat idea, but like many neat ideas, it doesn't hold up to scrutiny. Researchers (myself included) have tried to find this hidden vulnerability in grandiose narcissists with the available tools, including word association tests, projective tests, neuroimaging, and the wonderfully named "bogus pipeline," which is essentially a fake lie-detector test. There are some hints of grandiose narcissists' hidden vulnerability, but it remains a bit like Bigfoot—hard to locate and probably just a human in an ape suit. What we find is that grandiose narcissists become reactive in the face of a threat. In addition, they don't typically feel sad or depressed, but instead, aggressive and angry. They lash out at those they believe are criticizing them or treating them unfairly.

As research psychologists and clinical therapists pieced their theories together, we found that each group was right in its own ways, so we developed a cohesive model that combines everything and creates a solid foundation for discussion. This new model, called the Trifurcated Model of Narcissism, connects grandiose and vulnerable narcissism as two related but separate traits. Both share a core of disagreeableness, self-importance, and a sense of entitlement, but they differ a great deal on what additional traits they blend with that core. With grandiose narcissism, you see confidence, boldness, and self-esteem, but with vulnerable narcissism, you see low confidence, anxiety, and low self-esteem.

Looping back to the story about Elliot Rodger, you can see elements of vulnerable narcissism. He felt social rejection and wrote a manifesto about his frustrations and what he believed he deserved. You may also note aspects of grandiose narcissism and entitlement, which were tied in some ways to his privileged upbringing and affluent background. Throughout the book, I give examples of both forms of narcissism so you can see how the new model has changed our understanding. As we clarified and united the two concepts of grandiose and vulnerable narcissism, we saw a major increase in understanding the workings of narcissism in everything from violence to selfies. This new understanding should change the cultural conversation around how narcissism operates in our society.

HOW DID PSYCHOLOGISTS START STUDYING NARCISSISM?

Since narcissism is often seen as either a personality disorder or a personality trait (and we know now that it's related to both), I want to take a moment to briefly explain how psychologists began to make sense of the overlapping worlds of personality and personality disorders. This lays the groundwork for our insight into narcissism and how it shows up in our lives.

Essentially, personality psychologists observe the world in a few broad ways, which have heavily influenced how we talk about personality and personality disorders in everyday conversations. One of the broadest "old-fashioned" models for thinking about personality is the *psychodynamic model*, which studies the psychological forces that underlie human behavior, particularly the conscious and unconscious. Sigmund Freud, known as the founder of psychoanalysis, talked about this model and the major psychological drives of sex, aggression, and pleasure-seeking. In Freud's model, sexual energy and early childhood experiences—often influenced by your parents—shape your ego and personality. Subsequent researchers, such as well-known psychiatrist Carl Jung, expanded on Freud's ideas by talking about the ways relationships are represented in our unconscious and collective unconscious. With this psychodynamic model, you might say narcissism and narcissistic traits come from our earliest experiences in life. Although research psychologists don't use this model as much anymore, we still think of Freud and Jung often. Many modern theories are based on these ideas, and some clinicians still use modern variants of methods from psychodynamic models.

Another common broad model is the *humanistic model*, which emphasizes empathy and the good in human behavior. In this model, personality is said to grow from basic needs such as food, shelter, love, self-esteem, and self-actualization, and based on that, psychologists focus on the best ways to help people improve themselves and their self-image. You may know about this as American psychologist Abraham Maslow's Hierarchy of Needs theory, which says that we need to take care of our physiological needs first (such as food, water, and sleep) and then safety, friendship, self-esteem, and self-actualization. Related to narcissism, you might talk about self-esteem and how a grandiose narcissist has an overly high sense of self or how a vulnerable narcissist has a wounded sense of self. This model is useful, but like psychodynamic models, humanistic models have either been discarded or absorbed into other ideas.

Today in the United States, popular culture often uses what I call the "standard psychological model" to explain personality, which is a mixture of psychodynamic lite and humanism lite. Essentially, people see their problems as grounded in childhood but also believe in the possibility of greater fulfillment through self-improvement. Not everyone believes this, but it's common in Western culture. Think about the problems that television characters face: They're usually rooted in childhood conflicts and then resolved through confrontation with tough truths. This leads to a path of transcendent growth and a better life filled with more love, authenticity, and joy, which parallels the "hero's journey" that writers often use. To put it another way, these plots rarely revolve around characters who realize that their depressive symptoms or anxiety problems are largely genetic and bio-chemical in origin, ask their parents for detailed family histories of mental illness, and then retool their psychobiology through a combination of dietary, physical, social, cognitive, and pharmaceutical interventions. This process works, but it doesn't lend itself to exciting TV drama.

However, this last example lines up with clinical thinking in today's personality psychology studies and related fields. Clinical areas, such as medicine and clinical psychology, use the *biopsychosocial model*, which says biology, personality, and social dynamics are connected. This is why, if your friend says, "I need meds. My kids are driving me insane, and I hate my job," you nod with understanding. Personality, as well as narcissism, springs from biology, psychology, and society.

Since most models are built for human needs, they tend to focus on treating disease more than adding potential. That's why personality disorders were first studied more than personality strengths, and that's also why we tend to think of narcissism as its most negative form—narcissistic personality disorder—which is discussed in chapter 5. The medical establishment wanted to see what risks personality presented to humans. They developed cut-offs to define the extremes, classified them as disorders, and then treated patients to bring them back to "normal levels" or isolated them from the population in prisons. These same biases apply to work on narcissism, and really, all mental health. The *Diagnostic and Statistical Manual of Mental Disorders*, or *DSM*, formalized a narcissistic personality disorder diagnosis in 1982, along with the rest of the original selection of personality disorders. This clinical interest in narcissism as a personality disorder came before the research interest in narcissism as a trait, which is what we focus on today.

HOW DO PSYCHOLOGISTS STUDY NARCISSISM NOW?

As personality science expanded, researchers moved beyond the broad models mentioned above and transitioned to more focused models to explain how personality works. For instance, trait models focus on personality as a normal part of human nature, and people can range from high to low, which is not a clinical problem. We often think about personality as a giant web of the correlations between traits, more formally known as a *nomological network*, which connects the different personality variables. When studying narcissism, for instance, researchers may look at the association between narcissism and someone's self-esteem or anxiety scores. If someone scores highly on one scale, they may score highly on the other. This nomological network is important to personality science because it is the navigation system. All aspects of personality should relate (or not relate) with every other aspect. If I measure narcissism in a group and find it correlates positively with kindness and memory problems (which isn't typically the case), I know something is wrong with my ideas about narcissism or the measurement or the data.

Another framework that personality researchers use is the *self-regulatory model*, which says that personality is related to goals and achievements.

In essence, our personalities are different because we're wired to chase goals differently, such as being happy, starting a romantic relationship, or avoiding harm. Some people, for instance, are more concerned with the threats in their life. They focus on how circumstances can go wrong and try to avoid those risks, which can display as germaphobia, social anxiety, or a fear of public places. Other people aren't attuned to these fears, and they can eat food a few seconds after it falls on the floor, meet strangers without fear, and watch horror films. This influences how people regulate themselves or act toward events in their lives, which can explain some of the motivations behind narcissists' actions.

A third model of personality, called *evolutionary psychology*, argues that personality evolved to deal with common environmental challenges such as food, shelter, mating, warfare, and social dynamics. For those with fearful or anxious personalities, this has obvious evolutionary benefits. Scared people might be better at avoiding threats. Think about a time when you flew in a plane that hit major turbulence or were stuck in an elevator when it stopped between floors. What you notice in those situations is that people start chatting with each other. They have a natural desire to be close to other humans when danger approaches. As I tell my students, ancestors who ran away from the tribe when lions appeared did not survive to reproduce.

In complement to the evolutionary model, there's also a fourth model that says personality is shaped by *culture*. Often these two models of personality—evolutionary versus cultural—are seen in competition. People are either the products of evolution or culture. In reality, culture and evolution probably work together to shape us.

Each of these four models or approaches can be useful for understanding narcissism, and we use all four throughout this book. A nomological model of traits works well for questions about the structure of narcissism, such as "How does narcissism fit with other traits?" The self-regulatory model is useful for thinking about how narcissism operates, including questions such as "How does someone manage to maintain such an elevated opinion of herself?" At some level, narcissism is also adaptive in an evolutionary sense. This is useful for understanding similarities in narcissism across the world, especially in regard to mating behavior.

Narcissism is related to culture as well, and as my colleague Jean Twenge and I documented in *The Narcissism Epidemic* more than a decade ago, certain cultures support narcissism more than others. In China, for instance, two major historical agricultural practices exist, with wheat farming in the north and rice farming in the south. Of the two, rice farming requires more cooperation among farmers. The water needs to flow from paddy to paddy in a synchronized way for all to benefit. Wheat farming needs less cooperation. Narcissism scores follow the same pattern, with lower narcissism in the rice-farming south and higher narcissism in the wheat-farming north.

Table 1.2 shows how each of these four models might view narcissism.

Table 1.2: Psychological Models and Narcissism

MODEL	DESCRIPTION	EXAMPLE
Nomological network, or trait model	Narcissism is a stable trait that exists in a network with other traits.	Narcissism is linked with psychological entitlement.
Self-regulation model	Narcissism is a trait but needs to be actively maintained by meeting goals.	Narcissism leads to forming friendships, which in turn leads to self-esteem.
Evolutionary model	Narcissism evolved to meet certain fitness goals.	Narcissism predicts short-term mating success.
Cultural model	Narcissism is created, modified, and spread by cultural forces.	Narcissism was formed and spread by the broader focus on individualism.

LET'S PUT THESE MODELS TOGETHER: BACK TO ELLIOT RODGER

Now that you're familiar with the different models, you can think about Rodger's case from a personality scientist's point of view. Based on a general psychological perspective, Rodger's reasoning for killing is complex and uncertain, but a few aspects stand out that this case has in common with several other recent mass shootings in the United States.

First, Rodger felt an ego threat, which can come from narcissistic triggers such as social rejection, being fired from a job, a marriage separation, or a failed academic assignment. As Rodger wrote, "All my suffering on this world has been at the hands of humanity, particularly women." It seems one of his big issues was that women didn't date him, but women dated his Asian roommates. Rodger was biracial and thought that his whiteness should give him a leg up. He was also a good-looking young man who drove a BMW and had a successful parent, which might have boosted his ego further. The challenge, in Rodger's case, is that he appeared to be a vulnerable narcissist. Take this excerpt from his "manifesto" as an example:

> Everything my father taught me was proven wrong. He raised me to be a polite, kind gentleman. In a decent world, that would be ideal. But the polite, kind gentleman doesn't win in the real world. The girls don't flock to the gentlemen. They flock to the alpha male. They flock to the boys who appear to have the most power and status. And it was a ruthless struggle to reach such a height. It was too much for me to handle. I was still a little boy with a fragile mind.

After this epiphany, Rodger decided to move to Santa Barbara and nearby Isla Vista, which he believed was a party town filled with attractive women. According to his document, he saw this in a movie:

> It was all because I watched that movie *Alpha Dog*. The movie had a profound effect on me because it depicted lots of good-looking

> young people enjoying pleasurable sex lives. I thought about it for many months afterward, and I constantly read about the story online. I found out that it took place in Santa Barbara, which prompted me to read about college life in Santa Barbara. I found out about Isla Vista, the small town adjacent to UCSB where all of the college students live and have parties. When I found out about all this, I had the desperate hope that if I moved to that town, I would be able to live that life, too. That was the life I wanted. A life of pleasure and sex.

But when Rodger made it to Isla Vista, he didn't find a life of pleasure and sex, or even a girlfriend. Although he once tried to ask someone on a date, she didn't hear him or acknowledge him. Instead of facing his failure with the ladies, Rodger opted for plan B, "The Day of Retribution." Step one was purchasing a handgun, a Glock 34. The weapon supplied some of the ego hit he needed:

> After I picked up the handgun, I brought it back to my room and felt a new sense of power. I was now armed. "Who's the alpha male now, bitches?" I thought to myself, regarding all of the girls who've looked down on me in the past. I quickly admired my new weapon.

And we know what happened next. This case is an extreme example, but it allows us to think about narcissism and the four models. Under the trait model, Rodger certainly showed the classic narcissistic personality traits of self-importance, antagonism, and entitlement, and his behavior and beliefs were largely consistent over time. He described a basic sense of entitlement and a lack of success or respect (that he believed he deserved) going back to childhood. He documented it so the world could learn about how poorly he was treated.

Under the self-regulation model, Rodger also tried to actively maintain his ego by meeting his self-esteem goals. He moved to Isla Vista in an attempt to lead a life of pleasure and sex. He purchased a handgun to feel powerful. He killed others in an effort to gain alpha male status. He made efforts to attain his grandiose dreams, but he failed.

When it comes to the evolutionary model, this incident highlights the changing dynamics around male social status and sexual access to females in the US and many Western countries, which have included at times a patriarchal system of dominance and control. Although the social norms have changed and continue to change, Rodger felt entitled to attention and adoration, particularly from women. Another version of this story is the grandiose narcissist who feels outcast and rejected and seeks status and revenge against all those who harmed him.

At the same time, this story shows how cultural elements shaped Rodger's narcissism. The Isla Vista party lifestyle lured him there in the first place. He was able to gain access to a weapon. The victims also symbolized a cultural concern. In a more typical homicide, a man (usually) feels shunned or rejected and then attacks that specific person. In Rodger's case, however, he targeted women who were symbolic of those who shunned him. In a sense, it was a terroristic act. It was a cultural and political statement rather than a personal grudge or vendetta.

Which model is the correct one to interpret the narcissistic aspects of Rodger's case? They all add a puzzle piece to understanding his situation, and personality scientists do the same when trying to understand narcissists and how narcissism operates in our world today. In the next chapter, we'll take this a step further and explore how personality scientists measure narcissism—and how they know it's accurate.

NERD HERD: THINK OF MODELS AS MAPS

When psychological models become confusing, I find it helpful to think about personality science with maps instead. In other words, just like maps, personality models are guides to the terrain. While driving, you want a map that highlights roads and traffic, but you likely don't care about altitude. While hiking, you want a map that skips traffic but shows the elevation. While sailing, you need special navigational charts that include reefs and snags. While drilling, you need geological maps. Similar to social science models, you can use many types of maps, and they can be more accurate for some tasks than others. The map that gets you to the ski resort is not the one that helps you go up the mountain.

Predictive models are important as well. This is obvious in the case of maps: they need to predict that the place you are going will be there. Street maps are good at this because streets change slowly, so mapmakers can keep up. But prediction also matters in personality science. If my model says that narcissists become angry when they are embarrassed publicly, I should be able to embarrass a group of people publicly and then measure their anger. The people in this study who are more narcissistic should show the greatest anger. This predictive power of personality psychology is especially important in applied areas, like leadership selection or clinical evaluation to diagnose a disorder.

Just like maps, scientific models should be useful and constantly improving. If you look at old maps of the world, they are typically accurate in some areas, usually closest to the mapmaker's home, and highly inaccurate in other areas. In the oldest maps, the edges become vague, and some even say, "Here there be dragons," with detailed drawings of dragons and beasts. Importantly, maps have improved as measurement and reporting has. When I was a kid, it was impressive to have maps in books that you could flip while driving, and now we have real-time GPS on our smartphones, which is unbelievable. Personality models have improved a great deal as well, evolving from the basic Greek humors to descriptive models and now complex statistical models. These could plausibly become real-time data models in the future.

INSIDE SCOOP: THE RUSSIAN NESTING DOLLS OF NARCISSISM

My grandmother used to have a set of Russian nesting dolls. When you open the wooden doll by pulling it in half, you find another similar but smaller one inside. You open that one and see a smaller doll, and it goes on like that for several layers. At the center is a miniature doll that can't be split. Personality is like these nesting dolls. You can view personality from different layers, and to researchers, these layers are considered *levels of analysis*—the biological, cultural, and ecological.

At the biological level of personality, traits are grounded in genetics, exacerbated by certain molecules, and associated with patterns of neural activation. At the psychological level, traits are involved with emotional and cognitive processing, predictive of decision-making, and integrated into the self. Between two people, among small groups, and in larger teams, personality is predicted and predicated by other variables, including love or leadership. At the organizational level, personality also relates to work behaviors, such as teamwork and customer service. At the cultural level, broader patterns and trends support personality traits, such as workaholism or individualism.

Personality scientists look at narcissism the same way. At the biological level, it may be influenced by testosterone and other molecules. At the psychological level, as you've seen in this chapter, narcissism is related to ego and entitlement. With groups and teams, narcissistic tendencies may emerge with certain leaders. At the organizational level, narcissism is linked to systemic behaviors such as sexual harassment. Culturally, narcissism is related to the rise in plastic surgery and cosmetic procedures and the obsession with selfies, which was a topic of my earlier book, *The Narcissism Epidemic*.

In reality, understanding narcissism—or any personality trait—is hard work. It means understanding it across all of these levels of analysis and how these levels work together. This is a complex, interactive system, and most often, researchers spend time discovering connections at the psychological level, where narcissism predicts personality, attitudes, or emotions. Less commonly, we look at narcissism at lower levels of analysis, like brain circuitry or genetics. When it comes to research funding, though, I can run a full personality study with 250 participants using self-report measures for the same price as a single participant in a neuroimaging study.

What we lack are studies that put these levels together. How do narcissistic personality traits, self-concept, and neurochemistry work together in leadership or love? We have some insight that narcissists are more likely to view leadership and love as places to gain status. This status boost might be linked with the release of testosterone in narcissistic men, which can energize their pursuits, or it might be linked to dopamine and the need to seek rewards. Over time, this might create a feedback loop that increases the desirability of leadership and love, but we don't yet know. This research is possible, but it's expensive and therefore slow in coming.

In general, the lower levels—like hormones or genetics—cause the higher levels, like individual psychology. However, the effects can also go the other way, and a bad relationship or boss can have negative psychological effects and even physiological effects. What this means is that intervention can take place at many levels, which gives us hope. In the case of anxiety, for instance, medications can help the molecular level, cognitive behavioral therapy can help the psychological level, and yoga can help the psychophysiological level. Similar treatments don't yet exist for narcissism, but they may be on the way.

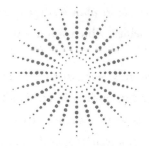

CHAPTER 2

Measuring Narcissism

How do you identify yourself and define yourself? I'm sure you've taken a personality quiz or two—who doesn't love those? Under the Myers-Briggs Type Indicator, you may be an ENTJ (extraversion, intuition, thinking, judging—a natural leader) or an ISFT (introversion, sensing, feeling, thinking—a nurturer). In Harry Potter's world, you might be a good fit for Gryffindor or Slytherin. If you're in *Stranger Things*, you could be similar to Mike, Steve, or Eleven.

Many variations of these personality tests exist, and chances are, many of them have little or no grounding in scientific evidence, especially if they are related to pop culture. These popular tests seem to work for a couple reasons. First, they make *some* sense. If someone takes the "Desired Boyfriend Test" and a question asks, "Do you prefer a partner who wants to tango or read books?" the person who selects "tango" will be matched with the Dancing Lover rather than the Nerdy Academic. The questions tend to pair with obvious answers.

Second, quiz takers often encounter what psychologists call the Barnum Effect, named after P. T. Barnum, the American showman and Barnum and Bailey Circus cofounder who apocryphally said, "There's a sucker born every minute." The Barnum Effect works by giving vague, ambiguous feedback that applies to everyone. With the dating test mentioned above, for instance, an answer might say, "You can commit to a relationship but at times feel that things might not work out in the long run." The Barnum Effect has kept the fortune cookie and horoscope industries in business for ages.

When it comes to personality tests and scales in the field of psychology, the good news is that an entire science and practice around assessment has evolved during the past century. Due to the high demand for assessing people's personalities, these scales have been tested and improved over time. First, let's talk about the evolution of basic personality tests, and then we'll uncover the details of specific narcissism tests used today.

THE BIRTH OF THE PERSONALITY TEST

Personality tests have come a long way. The first formal personality assessment celebrates its milestone one hundredth birthday in 2020. American psychologist Robert S. Woodworth developed it during World War I for the US Army. The Woodworth Personal Data Sheet was designed to test military recruits for their resilience to shell shock, which we now call post-traumatic stress disorder (PTSD). The 116 questions were straightforward and answered with a simple yes/no scale. It typically asked, "Do you get rattled easily?" or "Do you usually feel well and strong?" The Office of the Surgeon General accepted it and established a preliminary screening program that referred recruits to a psychologist for further evaluation if they scored high on the test. Although the test was designed too late to be used during the war, it was influential in later personality tests, particularly ones that measured traits such as anxiety and depression, which we often group under the label *neuroticism*.

During the early years after this, most psychological tests were revisions of Woodworth's work since it had so many questions. Soon personality tests popped up everywhere. Industrialists wanted tests for employee selection, psychiatrists wanted tests to diagnose mental disorders, and academic researchers in psychology and other fields wanted to understand personality. Now with a century of progress, hundreds or perhaps thousands of scientifically based personality measures exist to explain various work styles, social situations, and personality traits. The creators of each one of these personality tests and measures started with some idea of what they wanted to measure—whether resilience to shell shock, extraversion, or impulsivity—which is harder to do than it might sound. Essentially, the definition of a psychological construct and its measurement are intertwined because we can't know exactly what we're talking about until we measure it, but we also can't measure it until we know what we're talking about, so these assessment tests develop in cycles. Similarly, the first narcissism tests had to figure out what exactly to measure.

HOW DO I DEFINE WHAT I'M MEASURING?

When describing personalities, people tend to use "folk psychology," or informal language that conveys a meaning. For instance, to describe antagonism in others, we might call them a-holes. Our language works well for everyday life, but it isn't precise. We also use scientific or professional terms colloquially. In this case, we might say someone is narcissistic, but that might mean "jerk" or "vain" depending on the context. "You stuck-up, narcissistic jerk" captures strong emotion, but it doesn't give a nuanced use of the term *narcissist*.

The science of personality, however, takes a somewhat different approach to defining narcissism that formalizes and blends our everyday approaches. Personality science has three basic steps in measuring a trait: (1) define the aspect of personality that you want to measure, (2) build good tools for measuring it, and then (3) relate that new variable to others of interest. When you or a loved one takes a formal psychology assessment for narcissism, you want to be assured that it's been measured and tested again and again before being used widely.

Let me show you how this works with a relatively simple variable such as self-esteem, which is typically associated with narcissism. If I want to study self-esteem, I first need to define it. This sounds easy since we all know what self-esteem is, at least what it sounds like in everyday discussion. Typically, people use the word *self-esteem* without much confusion. However, the literature on self-esteem, including the historic use, philosophical traditions, and research work, shows that our understanding of the term is a bit of a mess.

Historically, *self-esteem* arose in the seventeenth century when there was an emphasis on adding *self-* to words, marking the rise of individualism during the Enlightenment. However, in the early uses, the word had a range of meanings, according to the *Oxford English Dictionary*. The first recorded use of *selfe esteeme* is a 1619 put-down: "His wit being so shallow, and selfe esteeme of his owne worth and works so great . . ." But not long after that, *Paradise Lost* author John Milton included *self-esteem* in his 1667 epic poem as a positive trait, "grounded on just and right." Already in the 1600s, self-esteem took on a negative form and a positive form, with the difference seemingly based on whether self-esteem is grounded in reality.

In academic psychology, *self-esteem* was first adopted by renowned American psychologist William James in 1890. He described self-esteem more formally, using the formula "self-esteem = actual success / pretensions." What is cool about this idea is that self-esteem could be raised by either having greater success or lowered pretentiousness. James gives the example of a man who lost everything in the Civil War and "actually rolled in the dust, saying he had not felt so free and happy since he was born." James's explanation shows a more paradoxical view of self-esteem here—notably, the highest self-esteem is held by someone with the highest accomplishments and least sense of entitlement to those accomplishments.

Then self-esteem made two additional major historical appearances. The humanists, notably Maslow, placed self-esteem as a central need in human growth. Rather than a mixed blessing or peripheral psychological concept, self-esteem became a core developmental need, and it was right there between belonging and self-actualization in the hierarchy of needs. This placed self-esteem development as a major issue for anyone with a humanistic or growth orientation, which includes many people in education and counseling. In today's culture, for instance, the personal development field relies heavily on building self-esteem and self-actualization of goals.

Then the meaning of self-esteem took yet another direction when psychotherapist Nathaniel Brandon published the first self-esteem book, *The Six Pillars of Self-Esteem*, in the late 1960s. This massively popular work expanded the definition of self-esteem to include taking responsibility for one's own actions, using assertiveness in creating boundaries, and embracing self-acceptance. This view of self-esteem blends the humanistic view with objectivism, a philosophical system developed by writer Ayn Rand that makes our own happiness a goal in life and productive achievement the greatest activity. Brandon's book has a highly action-oriented view, yet it also captures many variables that today's psychologists would place beyond self-esteem, such as mindfulness and self-efficacy.

Ultimately, the definition becomes confusing, right? Measuring self-esteem, or another aspect of personality, sounds easy, but different definitions often take away from the meaning and ability to explain specifics. When things get too out of hand, some researcher will develop a minimalist model, or the simplest way to think about a concept that almost everyone agrees on. In this case, a social-cognitive researcher defined self-esteem as a link between positivity and the self. High self-esteem is simply the strength of the relationship "self = good."

Researchers then debated the structure of self-esteem. Is self-esteem based in a deep spring of well-being, or is it more about repeat positive experiences? Is there one self-esteem or many self-esteems, such as appearance esteem, intelligence esteem, and social ability esteem? Is self-esteem something that we have to be aware of, or can our self-esteem be unconscious? Does the "esteem" in self-esteem refer to feeling warmly about and liking oneself or believing oneself competent and capable? Or is it both? Rather than dismiss these questions or pick a single concept, scientists observe what happens empirically by testing the questions themselves. The process isn't pretty when researchers fall in love with their own measures, fight about the meanings, and sometimes cheat with the definitions, but it's the best system we have in personality science. As I mentioned earlier, personality scientists have fought about the definition of narcissism for decades, and we've come to an agreement around the grandiose and vulnerable aspects under the Trifurcated Model, but we're always testing our theories and improving what we know.

AND THEN, HOW DO I MEASURE WHAT I'M MEASURING?

Measurement is a core issue in every scientific arena. Even the most basic measurements have long histories. Time is key for measurement in many fields, but time measurement had to be invented as well. Early efforts included water clocks that used water movement as a measure of time. We still use sand-based versions of these clocks today. In the Middle Ages, clocks used springs and gears to tell the time. This technique is still used in mechanical clocks and watches, but it doesn't always work that well. For instance, compare the time on a $8,000 Rolex to a $25 Casio: the Casio tells better time because it uses quartz technology. At the scientific level, however, that still isn't enough, and engineers and physicists continue to build better clocks. Some atomic clocks are now so precise that they can be used to measure mass as well as time. If we still used mechanical clocks, we couldn't do much in the field of physics, and we couldn't do much in psychology either, where measurements are often timed to the thousandth of a second.

Think about the different types of measurement in a doctor's office— blood pressure with a cuff, temperature with a thermometer, and blood chemistry through lab work. For centuries, though, people didn't think they could measure mental content or psychology. Although huge breakthroughs took place in other disciplines, mental content seemed too hidden to measure well. Fortunately, that changed when experimental psychologists challenged that idea. German physicist and philosopher Gustav Fechner tested people's ability to notice differences between weights. Imagine you are blindfolded and pick up two weights that are similar in size, say a 10-pound bowling ball and a 10.5-pound bowling bowl. Could you tell the difference? Thus, psychophysics was born with the idea that we could measure psychological content in a similar way to physics.

Researchers then found that if the idea worked for weight, it could work for other aspects such as attitudes and cognitive mental ability. Louis Leon Thurstone, who founded the psychometric laboratory at the University of North Carolina at Chapel Hill in the 1950s, started building scales that could detect small changes in attitudes. You might be familiar with American social psychologist Rensis Likert, who developed the eponymous 5-point scale often used in surveys—Likert or Likert type scales. Here's an example:

I LIKE HONDA.

Agree 1 2 3 4 5 Disagree

I LIKE TRUMP.

Agree 1 2 3 4 5 Disagree

I LIKE MYSELF.

Agree 1 2 3 4 5 Disagree

We now have a large array of personality measures, from broad and comprehensive models of basic traits to more targeted and focused assessments of specific topics such as self-esteem and narcissism. What these personality measures share (assuming they are done correctly) are validity and reliability. *Validity* means hitting the correct target, and *reliability* means hitting the target consistently. Imagine two hunters who go into the woods together to shoot quail. Hunter 1 bags two of the five quail he sees, and Hunter 2 bags five of the five pheasants he sees. Hunter 1 has validity because he hit the right target but not reliability because he missed more than half the time. On the other hand, Hunter 2 has reliability because he hit the target each time but not validity because it was the incorrect target. In science, the best hunter would hit five out of five quail—and would be valid and reliable. We look for both validity and reliability when testing our personality assessments.

In modern personality science, validity is the more challenging target. How do you know you are measuring what you think you are measuring? If I build a new type of thermometer, say one that reads temperature from a person's forehead, I can compare the new one to previously tested thermometers. If the thermometer reads the same temperatures as the others, I can assume it is valid. Personality measurement carries the same idea, but there aren't always already-tested valid measures for comparison. As a result, personality researchers build measures that make sense. For instance, a narcissism measure would ask about feeling superior to others, not about creativity. This is called *face validity*, as in, the scale looks good on the face of it. Popular magazine quizzes about dating styles and online surveys about *Star Wars* characters stop at face validity. They're fun but limited.

Personality science takes a second step by comparing one scale to others, just as the new thermometer would be compared to others. For instance, a new grandiose narcissism scale should relate *positively* with other narcissism scales, as well as narcissism-related measures such as self-esteem and the need for power. The new scale should also relate *negatively* to measures not typically associated with narcissism such as emotional empathy and kindness.

Finally, since people answering questionnaires may report on their own personality incorrectly, the new scale must be tested with others' opinions of those people. This is seen as a process of triangulation. Someone's personality is measured with a self-report scale, and then it is compared to the report from a close friend, parent, or teacher, which should show some agreement. When it comes to clinical narcissism, or the extreme and inflexible kind that can be diagnosed as a personality disorder, a self-report scale may be compared with a formal clinical interview by a professional or study of clinical case files. None of these is the "right" measure of personality, but they all point to personality in some way. The good news is that self-report measures work well. For instance, people who are psychopaths believe their predatory and self-centered beliefs make sense, so they are happy to express those opinions in a low-stakes environment such as a confidential psychology study. A psychopath wouldn't be as forthcoming on a date or during a police interview, but self-report questionnaires often work well.

Compared to validity, reliability is more straightforward in personality science. If a personality scale has ten questions, for example, the answers to those questions should be consistent. Years ago, the first personality tests simply split the questionnaire in half to check whether both halves were answered the same way. Today, those measurements are more sophisticated but work similarly. Testing the same group of people over time is also a test of reliability. If the measure of personality is stable, then the scores should also be stable.

Why am I spending so much time explaining this? Personality measurement is the most important question in personality science, and with narcissism in particular, the measures have changed over time. Before you study a topic, you must know how to measure it. However, with the scientific method, this process can be circular. Scientists might use one measure for years and then begin to see flaws emerge, so they might revise the measure or build a new one. Plus, culture changes and definitions shift, which is what happened in the case of self-esteem. Scientists built a variety of self-esteem measures to capture their ideas, with the most popular being the Rosenberg Self-Esteem Scale. Developed by sociologist

Morris Rosenberg, the ten-item scale asks survey takers to agree or disagree with face-valid statements such as "I take a positive attitude toward myself" or "At times I think I am no good at all." This scale has stood the test of time as a measure of global self-esteem, but many other measures developed as scientists became interested in specific types of self-esteem, including views around athletic prowess or physical appearance. As you can imagine, as measures of self-esteem changed, so did measures of narcissism, which is linked to self-esteem.

Most challenging, researchers tried to develop measures of self-esteem that were unconscious, or implicit. They did, but these measures didn't seem to agree. In a 2000 study, a research team led by Jennifer Bosson tested implicit self-esteem that was measured in three different ways and found little correlation between them. Titled "Stalking the Perfect Measure of Implicit Self-Esteem: The Blind Men and the Elephant Revisited?" the study references a Buddhist story about three blind men who try to identify an elephant by grabbing it. One grabs the ear, one grabs the leg, and the other grabs the tail, so they all come to different conclusions. This is where most trait theories exist. Overall, the result is a range of scales built for specific tasks. A similar process led to the different narcissism scales, but the story is a little more complex, as I'll explain below. Table 2.1 shows the variety of self-esteem measures that have been developed over the years.

Table 2.1: Self-Esteem Measures

ASPECT OF SELF-ESTEEM BEING MEASURED	SAMPLE MEASURE	TYPE OF MEASURE
Global self-esteem	Rosenberg Self-Esteem Scale (1968)	Global 10-item self-report measure
	Single Item Self-Esteem Scale (Robins & others; 2001)	Single self-report statement

ASPECT OF SELF-ESTEEM BEING MEASURED	SAMPLE MEASURE	TYPE OF MEASURE
Specific self-esteem	Self-Attributes Questionnaire (Pelham & Swann; 1989)	10-item self-report measure (to 60)
State self-esteem	State Self-Esteem Scale (Heatherton & Polivy; 1991)	20-item self-report measure (performance, appearance, and social domains covered)
Implicit self-esteem	Implicit Association Test (IAT; Greenwald & colleagues; 1998)	Speed of association of self with positive vs. negative words
Indirect self-esteem	Name-letter effect (Nuttin; 1985)	Rate liking of letters and compare the letters in own name to others

WHAT ABOUT NARCISSISM SCALES?

After observing the process of building a scale around a "simple" concept such as self-esteem, you can likely guess the complexity that underlies the narcissism scales. Any measure of narcissism depends on how the psychologist who created the scale thinks about narcissism. If narcissism is seen as grandiose, the scale will reflect grandiosity, and likewise, if narcissism is seen as vulnerable, the scale will reflect vulnerability. The legendary personality psychologist Henry Murray developed the first scale of what he called "narcism" in the 1930s. This scale contained both vulnerable and grandiose content mixed together. The newer scales are more specific about the type of narcissism being measured. Let's walk through a few of these together.

Grandiose narcissism measures are designed to capture the bold, dominant, and antagonistic face of narcissism. Psychologists who build grandiose narcissism scales tend to include questions about leadership, power, attention-seeking, vanity, a sense of entitlement, and a willingness to take advantage or exploit others. For instance, "Do you like to be the center of attention?" or "Do you find it easy to make people believe what you tell them?"

Today, the Narcissistic Personality Inventory (NPI) is the most popular measure of grandiose narcissism. Robert Raskin and colleagues started working on this measure in the late 1970s, but the NPI scale caught on in 1988 when the 40-item version was published in the *Journal of Personality and Social Psychology*. This scale made most of modern narcissism research possible, although several important improvements were added along the way. You can find the Narcissistic Personality Inventory and others on our website, narcissismlab.com. If you want to take a quick one yourself, see the end of this chapter.

For all its staying power, though, the NPI is quirky. For one, the items were inspired by a previous description of narcissistic personality disorder, which is discussed in detail in chapter 5, but these traits don't always "hang together" as they're observed today. The NPI captures at least two big aspects of narcissism—being bold and outgoing, and then being entitled and manipulative. For the first association, the NPI asks whether respondents agree with statements such as "I like to be the center of attention" and "I like to have authority over other people." For the second association, it asks for agreement with "I can usually talk my way out of anything" and "If I ruled the world, it would be a better place." These statements may reveal a charming jerk or a self-centered and domineering boss, but they are different flavors of grandiose narcissism.

The NPI is also weird because it uses a forced-choice format with two sentences, such as these:

A. I don't particularly like to show off my body.

B. I like to show off my body.

The idea is that both choices are equally desirable, so the NPI score measures the number of times a respondent leans toward the narcissistic choice. Here is another one of the more well-known NPI items:

A. The thought of ruling the world frightens the hell out of me.

B. If I ruled the world, it would be a better place. (Some versions insert *much* before *better*.)

Before the Internet, we used to pass copies of the scales around, and they evolved as different psychology labs retyped them, swapped a word, and passed them along. (Read more about the NPI in this chapter's "Nerd Herd" section.)

For the last item above, I chose answer B. Do I really think if I ruled the world it would be a better place? Now that current events are so screwed up, I actually might, but chances are it would be an absolute disaster. On the other hand, ruling the world doesn't frighten me. In fact, it sounds like it would be a huge, fun, exciting challenge . . . that would likely end in disaster. So, given the two options, I go with B.

But consider if the test question were stated like this instead:

True or False: If I ruled the world, it would be a better place.

I would choose "False" because I don't have that level of confidence in my abilities as a world ruler. Despite this potential weakness, the NPI still works well with the narcissistic items used on a 5-point Likert scale. In fact, there are shorter versions (with the 13- and 16-item options being the most popular) and multiple translations in other countries that work well. The NPI is the trusty hammer of grandiose narcissism measures. A few of the newer measures on the market might be better in some ways, but the NPI has stood the test of time.

Another targeted way to measure grandiose narcissism is with adjectives. The Narcissistic Grandiosity Scale (NGS), developed by Yale University psychopathologist Seth Rosenthal, uses this approach. Participants rate themselves on sixteen narcissistic adjectives on a 9-point scale, where 1 means the adjective doesn't describe them at all, and 9 means it describes them very well. The ratings are then combined for the score.

In 2016, University of Georgia graduate student Michael Crowe validated the scale and extracted the following six key narcissism trait words:

Glorious	Acclaimed	High-status
Prestigious	Prominent	Powerful

People who see themselves as glorious, acclaimed, and powerful also report high scores of more complex narcissism measures. What is cool about the NGS and other trait scales is that they are short and can be given to people on smartphones over several days, or even several times a day, to understand and measure changes in narcissism.

On the other side of the Trifurcated Model, vulnerable narcissism measures capture the more neurotic, suspicious, hostile, and entitled face of narcissism. Psychologists who build vulnerable narcissism scales include questions about susceptibility to blows to the ego, or what the psychodynamic folks call "narcissistic wounds." At the same time, these scales also try to capture the self-centered, entitled qualities found in grandiose narcissism.

The Hypersensitive Narcissism Scale (HSNS) is the most popular measure of vulnerable narcissism. The HSNS was created by taking the vulnerable content from Murray's original 1930s scale and updating it into a modern measure. In addition, the Narcissistic Vulnerability Scale (NVS) measures six trait words associated with vulnerable narcissism:

Underappreciated	Insecure	Ashamed
Envious	Resentful	Self-absorbed

Several newer measures of narcissism capture both grandiose and vulnerable narcissism. These scales all have a different flavor (you can see a summary of some of the most popular assessments in table 2.2), but I will stick with the separate grandiose and vulnerable language in this book. If you've stuck with me this far, you now have a great foundational knowledge of how personality scientists have come to understand narcissism—and how the definitions changed over time as "grandiose" and "vulnerable" nuances were added. With these scales in mind, you can probably see why there's so much confusion around narcissism, the way we talk about it in society, and how the different definitions could apply to you, people around you, and leaders who may show more extreme traits of narcissism than you or I probably do. Now that the basics have been covered, we can talk about the "fun stuff" in the next chapter—the specific traits of narcissism and what I call the "narcissism recipe."

Table 2.2: Measures of Narcissism

NARCISSISM MEASURE	TARGET	SAMPLE ITEM	FLAVOR
Narcissistic Personality Inventory (NPI)	Grandiose	If I ruled the world, it would be a much better place.	Agency and extraversion with grandiosity
Hypersensitive Narcissism Scale (HSNS)	Vulnerable	My feelings are easily hurt by ridicule or by the slighting remarks of others.	Self-centered neuroticism
Narcissistic Grandiosity Scale (NGS)	Grandiose		Six main adjective traits
Narcissistic Vulnerability Scale (NVS)	Vulnerable		Six main adjective traits

(continues)

(continued)

NARCISSISM MEASURE	TARGET	SAMPLE ITEM	FLAVOR
Pathological Narcissism Inventory (PNI)	Grandiose + vulnerable	When others don't notice me, I start to feel worthless. I often fantasize about having a huge impact on the world around me.	Focuses more on vulnerability than grandiosity
Narcissism Admiration and Rivalry Questionnaire (NARQ)	Grandiose + vulnerable	I deserve to be seen as a great personality. Most people are somehow losers.	Focuses on admiration and rivalry
Five-Factor Narcissism Inventory (FFNI)	Grandiose + vulnerable	I often feel as if I need compliments from others in order to be sure of myself. I am extremely ambitious.	Focuses on antagonism, extraversion, and neuroticism

A WORD OF CAUTION: PERSONALITY SCALE LIMITS

Personality scales are fantastic tools, but there are also limits to what they mean. First, the conclusions largely come from patterns of correlations, essentially based on what goes with what and what doesn't go with what. Like the "web" model, or the nomological network mentioned in the previous chapter, psychologists often think of personality traits that "hang together," such as humility and kindness. Don't get me wrong—there's science behind this. The statistical models can get crazy, but the basic idea of "hanging together" is at the center of personality science. What does this concept mean in terms of the predictive power of personality? It means that personality traits arrange themselves in certain ways, on average. That is interesting and important, but it is as predictive as saying, "Well, he's got a pecan tree in his yard. I bet he has some squirrels."

Second, personalities differ quantitatively rather than qualitatively. Few, if any, personality "types" exist in a pure form. Instead, traits fall on a spectrum. For example, your level of narcissism exists on the same scale as Donald Trump's narcissism in the same way that your height in inches exists on the same scale as Shaquille O'Neal's height. This is the case for all traits: Mother Teresa and the Dalai Lama do not represent a kindness "type"; rather, they are examples of remarkably high levels of kindness.

In addition, people tend to fall along the range of most personality scales in a somewhat normal or bell-shaped distribution, with most people in the middle and fewer at the tails, or extremes. A narcissistic leadership scale might place Donald Trump at the high extreme and the Dalai Lama at the low extreme, but all leaders would be spread across the range with an average somewhat closer to the Trump side. Also, the middle of the bell-shaped curve depends on the personality trait being measured. With a trait such as self-esteem, for instance, the average score is close to the top of the scale. Plenty of people exhibit really, really high self-esteem, and fortunately, far fewer express very, very low self-esteem. Narcissism shows an opposite but less extreme pattern, with few people reporting very high narcissism.

In essence, much of personality science is based on determining how a group of people vary on one personality measure compared to another. There is much less effort directed at defining the personality of a specific individual without anchors to the personality of large groups. This was the realm of psychoanalysis and depth psychology, but for better or worse, it hasn't yet resulted in a modern assessment science.

NERD HERD: EVOLUTION OF THE NPI

The Narcissistic Personality Inventory has an unusual history that makes it a messy scale but one that has withstood the test of time. It started as a 223-item scale designed to assess narcissistic personality disorder according to the third edition of the *Diagnostic and Statistical Manual of Mental Disorders* (*DSM-III*). These were whittled down and announced in the late 1970s by Santa Cruz psychologists Robert Raskin and Calvin Hall. Cutting it down to eighty items, I suspect, likely pushed out the assessment of more vulnerable forms of narcissism.

In addition, the NPI was developed as a forced-choice scale. The idea was that both answers were considered equally desirable, and the survey respondent would select one. However, there's a reason you don't see this type of scale often. Forced-choice scales make statistics ugly. Instead, the Likert-type, 5-point scales better capture the range of outcomes and are now typical. Personality psychologist Robert Emmons next published several shorter versions that didn't catch on, but they inspired Raskin to revise his work and publish what became the de facto NPI-40 in 1988.

In the 1980s and 1990s, these scales were typed and shared through hard copies. The original version that I saw was a mimeograph obtained by my doctoral adviser, Constantine Sedikides, at the University of North Carolina at Chapel Hill. As I mentioned earlier, some research labs at this time would change an item or drop a couple of questions, and others would make the positive items true-false statements or ask them on a 5-point scale. They often were passed along to others and in this way evolved over time. Ultimately, the NPI is still useful after all these years, but it isn't enough to capture the full scope and complexities of narcissism, especially the vulnerability aspect. As you know now, I'm talking about narcissism more as a trait rather than a disorder in this book, so the NPI is still valid to use but complicated given its history in measuring a disorder.

INSIDE SCOOP: BACKGROUND OF THE NGS

When Seth Rosenthal created the Narcissistic Grandiosity Scale at Yale University about a decade ago, personality psychologists thought it was pretty cool and got excited. The narcissistic adjectives seemed to be a great way to gauge participants' thoughts about themselves, and the 9-point scale created enough differentiation for a robust statistical analysis.

At the time, Seth didn't publish anything about the scale, but in 2016, Michael Crowe, who was a graduate student at the University of Georgia under my colleague Josh Miller, was intrigued by the possibilities of the scale and wanted to validate it. A team of us worked together to examine the factor structure of NGS and generate an abbreviated version of the scale to use in research. We looked at several short scales as they related to measures of grandiose and vulnerable narcissism, the Big Five personality traits (which you'll learn about in the next chapter), self-esteem, and the *DSM*'s personality inventory. It was also correlated with expert ratings of typical cases of narcissistic personality disorder. Overall, the NGS was found to be a valid measurement of narcissistic grandiosity. The abbreviated version was also reliable and consistent with the full version, and Crowe outlined the six traits listed earlier in this chapter.

In July 2019, Seth published an official assessment paper that positions the NGS as a measure to distinguish between high self-esteem and narcissistic grandiosity.[1] When testing the validity, he and colleagues at other universities in the US and the United Kingdom found that the NGS scores related strongly to phenomena linked to grandiosity, such as competitiveness, overestimating one's attractiveness, and a lack of shame, while the self-esteem scores related more to an individual's well-being, such as high levels of optimism and satisfaction with life, and low levels of depression, worthlessness, and hostility. They concluded that the NGS could be used by researchers to clarify the distinctions between narcissistic grandiosity and high self-esteem, as well as other aspects of narcissism.

Essentially, you'll find research published like this in most fields. People start projects, which get picked up by others who are interested, and then the original research team circles back to provide an update. It's a fun and fascinating aspect of academic research.

Test Yourself: Using the NPI-13

If you'd like to take a quick test of your own (or someone else's) measure of narcissism, try this 13-item version we use at the University of Georgia. As you know, it's not definitive, but it's been tested and validated for years. It's a good place to start.

In each of the following pairs of attributes, choose the one that you *most agree* with:

_____ 1.

    A. I find it easy to manipulate people.

    B. I don't like it when I find myself manipulating people.

_____ 2.

    A. When people compliment me, I get embarrassed.

    B. I know that I am a good person because everybody keeps telling me so.

_____ 3.

    A. I like having authority over other people.

    B. I don't mind following orders.

_____ 4.

    A. I insist upon getting the respect that is due me.

    B. I usually get the respect I deserve.

_____ 5.

    A. I don't particularly like to show off my body.

    B. I like to show off my body.

_____ 6.

    A. I have a strong will to power.

    B. Power for its own sake doesn't interest me.

_____ 7.

    A. I expect a great deal from other people.

    B. I like to do things for other people.

_____ 8.

    A. My body is nothing special.

    B. I like to look at my body.

_____ 9.

    A. Being in authority doesn't mean much to me.

    B. People always seem to recognize my authority.

_____ 10.

    A. I will never be satisfied until I get all that I deserve.

    B. I will take my satisfactions as they come.

_____ 11.

    A. I try not to be a showoff.

    B. I will usually show off if I get the chance.

_____ 12.

    A. I am a born leader.

    B. Leadership is a quality that takes a long time to develop.

_____ 13.

    A. I like to look at myself in the mirror.

    B. I am not particularly interested in looking at myself in the mirror.

Scoring. Give yourself one point per question based on the following key:

1. A = 1	6. A = 1	11. B = 1
2. B = 1	7. A = 1	12. A = 1
3. A = 1	8. B = 1	13. A = 1
4. A = 1	9. B = 1	
5. B = 1	10. A = 1	

Now add up your total. If you score seven or more, you tend to exhibit more narcissistic tendencies, with a higher number being more narcissistic. Remember: High numbers aren't necessarily negative and don't indicate a diagnosable disorder, but this does give an idea of your personality and behaviors that you can now monitor.

CHAPTER 3

Basic Traits and the Narcissism Recipe

B efore we talk about my favorite metaphor—the narcissism recipe—and the components that build narcissism, it's helpful to look at personality traits in general and how they work together. If you're cooking a meal based on a recipe, you need to know the ingredients (in our case, the traits) that you'll mix together. Like any chef, once you understand how fats, salts, and carbs mix and cook differently, you can make almost any meal work, and you can experiment along the way. Similarly with personality, you need to know the traits to create the recipe you're making.

To do this, let's start with an imaginary job interview. I bet you know this familiar prompt: Use three adjectives to describe yourself. What comes to mind? "Hardworking, driven, team-oriented." If you're more honest with yourself, you might also think, "Self-conscious, uncertain, unfocused," though you'd never tell a potential employer that. When people think about adjectives to describe themselves, they tend to talk about them as personality "traits."

A powerful way to think about personality from a scientific perspective is as a collection of traits that serve as the basic building blocks of personality. Think of personality traits as cooking ingredients or chemical elements that can be talked about alone or combined as more complex personality structures.

Numerous traits can be used to understand personality, so it may seem difficult to pinpoint the specific traits that best capture personality from a scientific standpoint. In a dictionary or thesaurus, about four thousand adjectives describe personality as we know it: nice, quirky, cruel, curious, hardworking, creative, dutiful, silly, considerate—with enough remaining to fill thousands of poems.

In fact, language is a good place to start examining personality. More than a hundred years ago, the brilliant British polymath Sir Francis Galton made a key observation: Language evolved to capture these personality traits. If people needed a specific way to describe someone, say, as humble or eccentric, they figured out how to do it.[1]

Further, Galton reasoned, if they needed to use that description frequently, the language created a *single* word to do it. Instead of saying, "John is the kind of person who likes to hoard money and not spend it on others," language evolved so that we could simply say, "John is stingy." With this simple but brilliant insight, known by personality scientists as the *lexical hypothesis*, Galton launched trait models of personality. Personality adjectives are now called *traits* by psychologists, which are also referred to as *personality traits* or *character traits*.

SEEING PERSONALITY TRAITS AS INGREDIENTS

To best understand complex personalities, we'll think of them as recipes with ingredients that make up a dish—like flour, yeast, and water together make a dough. Traits can be blended just like ingredients in a recipe to create a full personality description. You might have a friend who is kind, quiet, quirky, and hardworking. Blending these traits, you have the recipe for a lovable nerd. Similarly, a friend who is kind, loud, exciting, and energetic might be a lovable party animal.

Of course, it would be too complicated to make a personality recipe book out of thousands of independent trait ingredients. As humans, we can only make sense of a few items at a time. Psychologists have estimated this in different ways, and the results seem to range from a high end of seven, such as an old-school phone number without the area code, to a low end of four when looking at objects. In essence, when humans make sense of the world, we like to divide ideas and objects into manageable "chunks." When these chunks are too large to remember, we make even smaller, more precise chunks. Fortunately, ingredients cluster together to form larger groups. The term *pasta* describes hundreds of specific ingredients, such as angel hair, spaghetti, or ziti. Another category includes mini-pasta, ribbon pasta, and wheat and nonwheat pasta like gnocchi. Beyond that, pasta itself is a member of a larger food group, which is "grains" in the US system and "breads, cereal, rice, and pasta" in others. In this chapter, we'll talk about the ways that psychologists categorize traits to describe personalities—and the traits that matter most when researching and measuring narcissism.

UNDERSTANDING THE BIG FIVE

Just as there are the "big three" ingredients in cooking—protein, carbohydrates, fats—that underlie all recipes, the Big Five traits in personality underlie all complex personality traits and personality disorders. When you understand the Big Five, you can understand narcissism from the ingredients on up.

Based on common sense, personality traits can be easy to cluster into groups: *nice, kind,* and *caring* go together, and *mean, callous,* and *nasty* go together. At the same time, all six of these words describe opposite ends of the same bigger trait, which psychologists call *agreeableness.* As another example, the traits *calm, peaceful,* and *happy* group together, and *anxious, depressed,* and *unstable* group together. They also describe opposite ends of a bigger, more encompassing trait, which psychologists call *neuroticism.*

When personality scientists use this clustering technique with the known words for personality traits, they come up with five major traits, which is known in the field as the Big Five. These Big Five traits are meaningful at both ends, where *kind* and *nasty* are part of the same trait spectrum, but they're typically described by just one end. The Big Five traits (and the opposite pole of each) are as follows:

Openness to experience (versus low openness)

Conscientiousness (versus low conscientiousness)

Extraversion (versus introversion)

Agreeableness (versus disagreeableness or antagonism)

Neuroticism (versus emotional stability)

They're easy to remember as a mnemonic because the first letters of the Big Five traits spell OCEAN (or CANOE). The Big Five traits are the ingredients that cover almost all other personality traits. At the same time, a personality recipe loses precision when using the Big Five traits; it's a recipe that lists meat as an ingredient but doesn't specify steak, pork, or chicken. The recipe is simple and straightforward, but vague. Let's dig in to the Big Five to better outline the narcissism recipe near the end of this chapter.

Extraversion is a term we typically use to mean outgoing, friendly, and energetic. In personality science, extraversion also contains the ingredients of drive, ambition, and reward-seeking. Extraversion is like adding spice to a personality; it is energizing. Highly extraverted people include entertainers such as Jimmy Kimmel and politicians such as Bill Clinton. At the other end of the extraversion spectrum, you see less sociability and drive. Introversion, or low extraversion, is a trait that is seen in less-outspoken celebrities such as J. K. Rowling or business leaders such as Bill Gates.

Openness to experience, usually just called *openness*, is a combination of intellectual curiosity, adventurousness, an appreciation of new ideas, and an interest in art, fantasy, and imagination. Artists and entrepreneurs are often high in openness, with examples such as Steve Jobs, Andy Warhol, or John and Alice Coltrane. To see a high openness in media, watch Joe Rogan and Elon Musk discuss the world on YouTube, or watch Ellen and her zany humor or Oprah with her wide-ranging media empire. Those with low openness are generally less curious or aesthetically open. I think of Vice President Mike Pence as someone who comes across as low in openness—at least that is his brand, slow and steady.

Agreeableness is a trait that includes kindness, morality, and trust. Agreeable people play well with others. The low end of agreeableness, which is often called *antagonism* or *disagreeableness*, is particularly important for understanding narcissism. Antagonism includes a sense of superiority to others and a sense of entitlement, which means a person's needs matter more than those of others. Antagonism is also associated with mistrust of others. People who are selfish see their own trait in others. Highly agreeable people include Snow White and Janet on *The Good Place*. At the low end, characters such as Bart Simpson and Coach Sylvester from *Glee* aren't so agreeable.

Conscientiousness is the Big Five trait that encompasses work ethic, a desire for order, cautiousness, and self-discipline. Most tests that employers use to screen workers are looking for conscientiousness. Grit and a willingness to strive for challenging goals is a component of conscientiousness. At the high end of conscientiousness, you see expert managers and administrators (and their assistants who keep them on track). You see diligent workers who follow the rules. Hermione Granger from *Harry Potter* is highly conscientious, as well as Leslie Knope from *Parks and Recreation*. At the low end of conscientiousness, you have The Dude from *The Big Lebowski*.

Neuroticism, the final trait, is associated with anxiety, fearfulness, self-consciousness, and emotional reactivity, which is a fancy way of saying neurotic people often get angry or aggressive when faced with threats. Sometimes it is useful to think of neuroticism as a form of threat detection.

People who are high in neuroticism see many threats in the world, and people on the emotionally stable side see fewer threats. There are plenty of neurotic characters out there. Woody Allen made a career out of neuroticism, as did Callista Flockhart's character in the show *Ally McBeal*. On the other hand, we have an ultra-calm, low-neurotic character such as Professor McGonagall in the *Harry Potter* series, as a more maternal version, and ultra-cool action characters played by Tom Cruise or Denzel Washington.

UNLOCKING THE BIG ONE TO THE THIRTY FACETS

The Big Five traits themselves don't follow the same notion as the atom—that is, they aren't the fundamental building blocks of personality. Traits can always be clumped together into bigger units or broken down into smaller units. At the thirty-thousand-foot view, one major personality trait, really a "meta-meta-trait," is called the Big One. The Big One is the combination of high levels of extraversion, openness, agreeableness, conscientiousness, and low neuroticism. In one view, the Big One represents what we in the United States generally consider a positive or well-functioning person who is outgoing, curious, kind, hardworking, and calm. Although I tend to see all traits as trade-offs, if someone asked me if I wanted my daughters to have high levels of the Big One trait, the answer would be "yes!"

If you glide down for a little closer view, what you see are two meta-traits. Agreeableness, conscientiousness, and low neuroticism hang together as one meta-trait, called *stability* or *alpha*. Extraversion and openness hang together as a second meta-trait, called *plasticity* or *beta*. The Big Two breakdown is useful when thinking about change. Plasticity is energizing and creating. It is related to the reward system in the brain. People who score high in plasticity build social networks, idea systems, art, fantasy, and organizations. Plasticity drives change, and change means the destabilization and even destruction of older realities. When Silicon Valley folks talk about moving fast and breaking things or dump five hundred electric scooters in a town to see what happens, that is the work of high plasticity.

On the other hand, stability solidifies and slows change. People high on the stability scale do this by getting along with others, following rules and tradition, and remaining calm. For example, Elon Musk represents someone very high in plasticity, so high that the SEC and some shareholders want him surrounded by stabilizing individuals. Many entrepreneurs get the boot after they are successful in building an organization because entrepreneurs thrive on plasticity, yet big structures need stability in the form of rules, manualized policies, and laid-out systems. Stability is at work when a company's board of directors tosses out the founder and replaces her with a manager who makes work boring. That is the tension: plasticity wants to create and build, and stability wants to formalize and bolster. This balance is so much at the center of the dynamics in life that many ancient peoples had terms for it: yin and yang, Shakti and Shiva, love and strife.

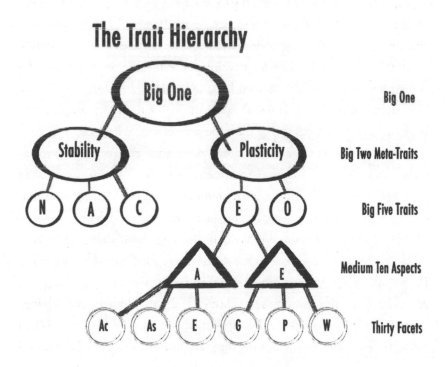

The Trait Hierarchy

In the other direction, the Big Five traits break down into two *aspects* each. I see this as the Medium Ten. In this book, we won't deal much with aspects, but a few are relevant for narcissism. Most importantly, extraversion splits into *enthusiasm* and *assertiveness*. People are drawn to enthusiasm, or a high-positive-energy personality such as personal development coach Tony Robbins or *Today* coanchor Hoda Kotb. In addition, people are moved by assertiveness, or the idea of pushing themselves, goals, or an agenda. Sometimes we respect assertiveness, and sometimes we push back against it. Narcissism correlates with both aspects of extraversion but especially the assertiveness side.

At the most specific levels of personality traits, scientists typically work with personality *facets*, also known as the Thirty Facets. Single facets are only used to answer specific questions about personality, so they aren't often used alone. Where personality facets shine is in building personality profiles. A personality profile is a rating of an individual based on each facet of the Big Five. As you'll see in the next section, these facet-level profiles can be quite useful for understanding narcissism and its specific recipe. Table 3.1 gives an overview of the levels of personality traits, from the highest level meta-traits to the lowest level facets.

Table 3.1: Personality Trait Levels

TRAIT LEVEL	NAME	DESCRIPTION	COMMENT
Meta-trait	Big One	E + O + A + C – N	The "positive" poles of the Big Five
Meta-trait	Big Two	A + C – N E + O	Stability (also Alpha) Plasticity (also Beta)
Trait	Big Five	E, O, A, C, N	All-around most useful but has trade-offs of precision and generality

TRAIT LEVEL	NAME	DESCRIPTION	COMMENT
Aspect	Medium Ten	E, broken into enthusiasm and assertiveness	Useful for more specific questions
Facet	Thirty Facets	E broken into activity, assertiveness, excitement-seeking, gregariousness, positive emotion, and warmth	Useful for building complex profiles

BUILDING THE NARCISSISM RECIPE

A complex personality trait such as narcissism is made up of numerous specific traits and patterns of behavior, which can sometimes seem unrelated. For example, wanting to rule the world and wanting to look good in the mirror may seem quite different at first. Some people want to rule the world, and others want to look hot. In narcissism, however, these traits go together. Throughout history, rulers have not only dressed in incredible finery but also commissioned paintings, statues, and photographs to record their power and success. An ancient city like Rome or Giza showcases the history of one ruler outdoing another.

In Big Five terms, the core ingredient of narcissism, which is the main ingredient considered necessary to make narcissism, is low agreeableness or high antagonism. Antagonism is where we find narcissists' sense of entitlement, lack of empathy, manipulativeness, and belief in their superiority. This core antagonism has been called *entitled self-importance* or *darkness*. Some of the psychodynamic folks use the term *malignant narcissism* to describe cases where the amount of antagonism is especially high in the narcissism recipe.

For grandiose narcissism, a second crucial ingredient is extraversion, which includes sociability, boldness, and drive. With extraversion, a much higher functioning individual compensates for the antagonism with likeability or success. If someone who is powerful or attractive is also energetic and likable, he can also be somewhat mean and get away with it. This extraversion is also what allows narcissism to spread across social media and upward into positions of power.

In vulnerable narcissism, on the other hand, the recipe mixes the core component of antagonism with high levels of neuroticism, which brings in insecurity, anxiety, depression, and hypersensitivity. From this perspective, a vulnerable narcissist is essentially someone who is self-important, self-centered, and entitled but also insecure, depressed, and self-conscious. Vulnerable narcissists are sometimes thought of as thin-skinned: they expect special treatment and are hypersensitive to criticism and "perceived slights," or situations that most of us wouldn't make a big deal out of, such as not being consulted by neighbors painting their house, not being invited to an acquaintance's wedding, or simply not being texted back quickly enough.

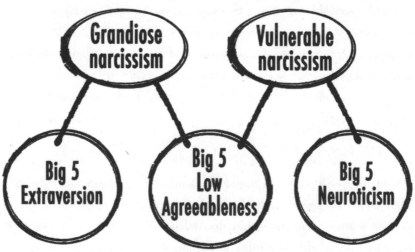

Basic Trait Ingredients of Narcissism

- Grandiose narcissism
- Vulnerable narcissism
- Big 5 Extraversion
- Big 5 Low Agreeableness
- Big 5 Neuroticism

Of course, if the recipe combines low agreeableness with extraversion and neuroticism, the result is a blend of grandiose and vulnerable narcissism. These people are outgoing and driven but also thin-skinned in private or when caught off guard around others. As will be explained in chapter 5, this mixture makes up narcissistic personality disorder.

Although the basic trait recipe for narcissism is simple, many variations exist. Think about a basic cheeseburger, which has three key ingredients: meat, cheese, and a bun. Even with these three ingredients, thousands of varieties can exist by altering the content of the meat, the kind of cheese, and the type of roll or bread, along with different condiments or toppings. The same is true for narcissism. Narcissists share key ingredients, but these can manifest in many ways. Not all narcissists are the same, which is why narcissism can look like many other traits, the same way a sloppy joe looks suspiciously like a hamburger. (Although with narcissism, the sloppy joe would be another disorder, such as psychopathy, as will be discussed in chapter 6.)

Also—and this is important to remember—the recipe is not the same as the dish. A recipe can produce many different results based on the source of the ingredients and the hands of the chef. Plus, different people enjoy different recipes. Some people love bitter flavors, yet others intensely dislike them. Similarly, a person's traits or trait profile is not the same as the person, but they are a useful way to think about how a person is structured. In this sense, a person can have narcissistic tendencies but not necessarily be categorized as a narcissist.

HOOKING THE TRAITS TOGETHER: MORE ON THE NOMOLOGICAL NETWORK

When creating a recipe, personality scientists think about traits hanging together. If I gave a hundred different personality tests to a thousand people, I would find the following correlations: People who score high on extraversion will score high on grandiose narcissism and self-esteem.

People who score high on self-esteem will report high levels of happiness and low levels of depression. People who score high on neuroticism will also score high on vulnerable narcissism and low on self-esteem. Researchers have observed these correlations consistently because personality constructs hang together in regular or lawful patterns. Sometimes this is easier to see graphically, as in the following image.

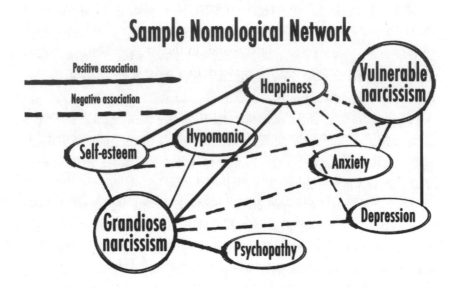

Sample Nomological Network

As briefly mentioned earlier, this huge network of correlations or relationships between traits is called the *nomological network*. It is a mouthful, but it matters because it is our map to all traits. If there were no relatively stable relationships between traits, personality scientists wouldn't have the science to explain their observations. Instead, narcissism would correlate with low agreeableness one day, then high agreeableness the next day. It would be hopeless.

Thanks to the nomological network, researchers can make predictions, or at least reasonable assumptions. For instance, if someone reports low self-esteem and depression, they are more likely to be vulnerably narcissistic rather than grandiose. If someone is happy, they are less likely to be anxious. At the same time, the association might tell us nothing—plenty of constructs don't relate at all or have small, unstable relationships. Scientists can get excited about these observed differences and might consider them new findings, but often they are what the great personality psychologist Paul Meehl called "crud," or the messy way that traits can sometimes hang together.[2] In addition, the nomological network is a well-established idea in Western-based academia but less so in other areas. The truth is, most of our research has been conducted with undergraduate psychology students and, in the last several years, online surveys. The entire nomological network may warp or bend in other cultures and study populations.

As a final note, the nomological network allows us to understand what traits mean. Essentially, traits are defined by their relationships with other traits. Some people find this uncomfortable. It would be great to have a self-esteem bump on our skulls that serves as an objective measure of self-esteem like the phrenologists of old believed, but personality doesn't work that way. This is where the food metaphor breaks down because we do have specific genetic and other descriptive systems for identifying what we eat. However, dealing with human personality is fuzzy and complex. Researchers have the ability now to see reliable patterns in personality in large groups of people, and it improves as more studies are conducted, but personality scientists also need a lot of humility, especially when it comes to predicting behavior based on personality. It goes along with the popular maxim, "The best predictor of future behavior is past behavior." To guess what a person is going to do, look at their past. If I have to guess which of two people will be unfaithful in the future, I am going to guess the one who has been unfaithful in the past. A variant of this rule is that if someone does something, it probably isn't the first time. If you catch someone cheating, stealing, or any other behavior, it is rarely the first time they did it.

But here is another thought: people change. They seek out new experiences and relationships. They grow and learn. The world changes. Even the popular maxim doesn't hold with a high level of certainty. Traits models don't capture this movement or dynamic. In future chapters, we'll talk about how people, including narcissists, can change themselves.

A QUICK CASE STUDY: THE RECIPE INGREDIENTS FOR DONALD TRUMP

Donald Trump has a *big* personality. He puts it out there straight, no chaser. I'm not saying what he says about his personality is true, or false for that matter, but what I'm saying is that he has been a public figure for decades by his choice. His brand is himself. Trump is a good candidate for personality rating from nonexperts. Hundreds of millions of people have seen a great deal of Trump.

Trump is also a polarizing figure. Some people fiercely support him, and others oppose him with a similar passion, so you have to take politics into account when you get someone's take on his personality. Based on common sense, you would guess that people who support him will have a more favorable view of his personality.

We did a 2018 study on this at the University of Georgia, led by graduate student Courtland Hyatt. These can be seen in the following chart—where the facets of agreeableness and conscientiousness are highlighted. We asked Trump and Hillary Clinton supporters to rate Trump based on the Thirty Facets of the Big Five and used those facet ratings to create trait profiles. We then compared these two profiles of Trump's personality—one from Trump supporters and one from Clinton supporters—to each other, as well as to the low agreeableness and high extraversion recipe for grandiose narcissism and the low agreeableness and high neuroticism of vulnerable narcissism.

It turns out that both groups see Trump as having a grandiose narcissistic trait profile. Both groups expressed complete agreement, for example, that Donald Trump is off the charts on assertiveness and grandiosity. However, the big differences occurred in their perceptions about honesty, straightforwardness, and altruism. Trump supporters saw him as working in the interest of others' welfare with integrity, but Clinton supporters saw Trump as self-serving, dishonest, and, to add some spice, lacking in any trait conscientiousness other than trying to achieve his personal goals. Trump does not appear especially vulnerable from either trait profile.

For the purposes of this book, I have no interest in making a political statement about Donald Trump, but I do believe grandiose narcissism is core to his personality structure. What's fascinating is that these facet profiles allowed us to see the range of what narcissism is. Trump supporters might say, "Yeah, Trump can be an arrogant SOB, but we need an SOB to get the job done. Plus, I know Trump cares about the country at a higher level." On the other hand, Clinton supporters might say, "Trump is a highly ambitious, self-serving, untrustworthy, lazy, and wildly incompetent leader who is in it for fame and power. He is a train wreck destroying the democratic system."

If this seems interesting, check out the deep dive into narcissism and leadership in chapter 8. In this quick case study, the point is that studying personality facets can sometimes illuminate how different people see someone. In this case, the different groups believe the same narcissistic individual has brighter and darker shades, or motives, which is the focus of the next chapter.

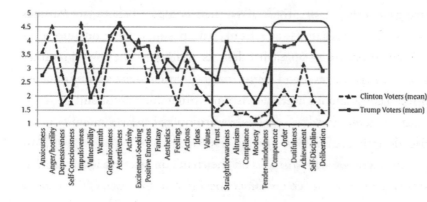

NERD HERD: COMMUNAL NARCISSISM AND GIVING BACK

Another fascinating area of research centers around narcissism in situations that should seem more selfless than selfish. Even while engaged in acts of friendship, philanthropy, and giving back, narcissists are in it for the esteem and the status they gain from doing good deeds. Called *communal narcissism*, the idea is that people can be self-centered about communal traits, thinking of themselves as the greatest friend ever or the best volunteer ever.

This type of narcissism sometimes pops up in nonprofit and religious groups when people proudly talk about how much they give, how much time they spend, and who else they know and associate with among charity ball circles or the PTA crowd. They look down on others because they have a cause or mission, and they often gossip about others who aren't doing as well in the organization. This frequently causes in-fighting and cliquish behavior in charitable groups. For a pop culture reference, think of the character Tahani, played by Jameela Jamil, in the show *The Good Place*. Throughout life, she gave to charities and threw audacious events, but it was meant to show off her giving nature and become closer to celebrities, not to highlight or support the organizations that she helped.

Jochen Gebauer and colleagues at Humboldt University of Berlin in Germany developed the Communal Narcissism Inventory to measure this type of narcissism. They validated it in 2012, and I expect this area of research to blossom. The inventory asks people to agree or disagree on a 7-point scale with statements such as, "I am the most helpful person I know," "I am an amazing listener," and "I have a very positive influence on others." Although we'd all like to think we're helpful and good listeners, narcissists act this way for the love of themselves rather than for friendship or community.

This type of narcissism is also particularly tricky because leaders who are pillars of the community may fall into this category. Although they are devoted to the community and are generally positive in public interactions, their antagonism and self-focused nature hurts their private relationships, which can make it tough for spouses, children, and other relatives to grapple with the reality of their loved one's personality. Gebauer notes, though, that communal narcissists tend to fall out of favor over time, just as "agentic" or typical grandiose narcissists who are motivated by esteem and power become less popular over time.[3] As they pull drama and destructive patterns into their communal relationships or good deeds, people catch on, and they lose favor as others see hints of these narcissists' hypocritical motives.

INSIDE SCOOP: DISAGREEMENT OVER THE BIG FIVE

If you're familiar with the basics of psychology and personality, then you're likely familiar with the Big Five as an overarching theme that's well infused into the research. At the same time, the Big Five is often presented as if there's no debate in the field, but I promise there is. In fact, one group of narcissism researchers like to use the Big Six, also abbreviated as HEXACO, because it breaks up agreeableness more and tries to capture that aspect with more nuance than the Big Five.

In 2005, Canadian researchers Michael Ashton and Kibeom Lee wrote about the sixth factor: honesty-humility.[4] Although straightforwardness and modesty link agreeableness with this sixth factor, they wrote, separating them provided a better prediction of questions about deceit without hostility, such as social adroitness and self-monitoring. They concluded that it was important to assess honesty-humility separately. In fact, they use the HEXACO Personality Inventory to evaluate the six major dimensions of personality (honesty-humility, emotionality, extraversion, agreeableness, conscientiousness, openness).

A decade later, researchers at several universities in Ontario, Canada, led by Angela Book, evaluated how the HEXACO model accounted for "dark" traits such as narcissism. Similar to the Big Five model, they found that the darker traits lined up with low honesty-humility, low emotionality, low agreeableness, and low conscientiousness, with low honesty-humility having the largest impact.[5]

CHAPTER 4

Narcissists' Goals
and Motives

T
hink about what motivates you. What are your goals, and what do you hope to be, do, have, and own? Research from the past two decades shows that our narcissistic tendencies can be linked to many of our decisions, from the choices we make in romantic partners to our choices of financial investments—and even our shopping habits. When we listen to our ego, we often opt for a more sophisticated choice because it'll make us look better. We want to feel luxurious, own what's exclusive, and make heads turn, hence the word *bling* for our big diamond rings, stacked necklaces, and brand-name, logo-emblazoned bags. That's often our ego peeking through, hoping to validate a grandiose self image by increasing our vanity and showing off our high-status collection to others. At the same time, the desire to own one of those expensive Mercedes wagons comes from everyday motivational systems.

As soon as creatures of any form started moving, they developed basic goals and motivations. Essentially, the idea in life is to get good things and avoid bad things. A single cell mold can learn to overcome a bitter substance such as quinine, a compound found in tonic water, to get to a food source. The ability to direct, control, or regulate behavior toward desired objects or beliefs and away from harmful or unpleasant objects or beliefs is present everywhere in nature. Plants send taproots to find water and point leaves toward the sun to maximize energy. They also produce fruits to reproduce, which are designed to be attractive to other species who eat them and spread the seeds.

As humans, we share these basic goal systems with our fellow species. As a living thing, we are driven toward nourishment and away from noxious or toxic stimuli. As a sexually dimorphic species, we are motivated both positively and negatively in the complex world of mating. As mammals, we have attachment and caregiving motives, especially through parenting. As a highly social species, we are motivated to secure or increase our place in the community and the dominance hierarchy. Often, social psychologists talk about these as the needs for belongingness or connection and power or status. As modern humans, we have a highly complicated self that we build and defend. We worry about image and self-esteem but also feel lonelier than ever before.

Narcissists' goals and motives are grounded in the same systems as everyone else. That is, no narcissism-related motive or goal is solely exhibited by this small group of people; instead, narcissists' motives and goals are heavily shifted in the direction of the self. With grandiose narcissism, people build and enhance themselves, and with vulnerable narcissism, people protect themselves. In either case, narcissists prioritize self before others.

FOUNDATIONAL NARCISSISTIC MOTIVES: APPROACH AND AVOIDANCE

The narcissistic self is always at risk and can gain status or lose status at any time. The glory of narcissistic victory and the agony of narcissistic defeat are grounded in the same motives that make a mouse run toward cheese or run away from a hawk. We're wired with two foundational motivational systems, approach versus avoidance, which are tuned differently depending on the person. You may be more motivated to chase success or more attuned to avoiding punishment. Just like puppies, some of us are fearful and shy, and others are jaunty and excitable. Importantly, approach orientation and avoidance orientation are not narcissism. Instead, they provide the "push" or "pull" that drives behavior. With narcissism, these approach and avoidance motives are channeled through the self. For instance, narcissists may wonder how to achieve status for themselves or how to gain wealth or power for themselves. It isn't about playing for the love of the game or the good of the community—it is about the self.

For instance, grandiose narcissists focus on looking good, so they constantly hunt for opportunities to shine. Vulnerable narcissists focus on not looking bad, so they scan the environment for potential ego threats. The result in both cases is a life filled with course correction. Narcissists constantly search for short-term opportunities to look good or avoid feeling bad.

These two motives are even easy to spot across different species. Predators, such as hawks or lions, have eyes that face forward and stalk with an intense focus on the goal. When these predators commit to an action, they go for it full on, and even though they may miss many times, they never stop hunting. Their motivation is considered an *approach* tactic.

Prey animals are different. Their eyes sit on the sides of their head, so they have a large field of vision. They are often skittish, mistaking a passing shadow or breaking branch for a potential predator. Their motivation is considered an *avoidance* tactic.

While I was traveling in Botswana, a Kalahari Bushman made a simple statement about hunting oryx that was quite profound to me. He said, "We [people] are predators. We follow the game just like lions." This is correct, of course. Humans wiped out most of the megafauna before turning to husbandry and agriculture. We're also built like predators with our eyes at the front of our head, and we have the ability to focus, plan, and carry out group hunts. At the same time, we are also prey. We're not as small and skittish as a squirrel, but many other species can harm us, including bears, spiders, and especially other people. As humans, we all have to balance our approach goals with our avoidance goals to regulate ourselves, and all of us do that differently.

Grandiose narcissists, in particular, are approach-oriented and sometimes seen as predatory. For example, a grandiose narcissist might ask ten people on a date to get one to say "yes." In the natural world, hiding failure can be difficult. That's why big wave surfers are often humble. In the social world, however, it is easier. The research shows that grandiose narcissistic motivation is related to learning through rewards to their ego.

On the other hand, vulnerable narcissists are particularly avoidance-oriented and often suspicious, fearful, and mistrustful. The world is seen as predatory. The vulnerable narcissist protects the self from that and fights for the recognition that is owed. Most of this fighting is mental and emotional because vulnerable narcissists are often too fearful to confront people directly. In the research, these narcissists report being angry but not particularly aggressive.

APPROACH VERSUS AVOIDANCE: WHAT DRIVES MOTIVATION

The basic drive to approach or to avoid is foundational to how we see ourselves. Nobody is completely approach- or avoidance-oriented all the time. This tension between high risk, high reward and low risk, low suffering occurs constantly. The approach-oriented side wants to go on a vacation to the Caribbean, assuming it will be a wonderful experience, but the avoidance-oriented side wonders if it is risky, worrying that the mosquitoes, toxic seaweed, and customs headaches could cause problems.

These approaches typically fall in the normal range of temperament, and most of us are born with a little bit more hesitance or a little bit more excitability. Genetically, some are more prone to love the idea of a raucous party, and others dream about tranquility and solitude. Beyond that, as you can imagine, early childhood experiences can shape us, and depending on our parents, we may be instilled with an early motivation of duty, success, or adventure. As we experience life, traumatic situations can shift whether we become more anxious or brazen as well. As we age, our priorities and motivations also tend to shift and mellow over time.

As part of our human experience, we tend to develop habits or routines that tip the scales between approach and avoidance in different ways. Drugs that activate the reward system, such as cocaine, make people more approach-oriented. Other drugs, such as alcohol, reduce the avoidance system. People make stupid decisions when they are drunk because their awareness of negative consequences is minimized, which is especially true if they don't have much inhibition to start. Clinically, this is what prescriptions such as Ritalin and Adderall do. These stimulants increase approach orientation or focus in some individuals. On the flip side, antianxiety medications, which are called *anxiolytics* by clinicians, such as Valium or Xanax reduce avoidance motivations.

People differ in their approach and avoidance orientations, which psychologists measure with the behavioral avoidance and inhibition scales that were developed in the mid-1990s to understand how motivations underlie and affect actions. The behavioral approach system, also known as BAS, is the physiological mechanism that regulates appetitive motives, or the approach goal to move toward what is desired. The behavioral inhibition system, also known as BIS, regulates aversive motives, or the avoidance goal to move away from the unpleasant. These motivations can influence decision-making and personality traits.

Approach-oriented individuals are optimistic, energized, and focused on rewards. At the trait level, they are most commonly extraverted, and they have somewhat inflated views of their abilities. People who are focused on winning are often open and overestimate their chances of winning. Avoidance-oriented individuals are more pessimistic. They are anxious and focused on avoiding threats. At the trait level, this lines up with neuroticism, and they tend to have lower self-esteem. People who are focused on not losing often have more accurate views of their abilities yet overestimate their chances of losing.

If you're curious about ways to look at your approach versus avoidance orientation, consider these statements from Carver and White's BIS/BAS scales:

When I want something, I usually go all-out to get it.

When I get something I want, I feel excited and energized.

I worry about making mistakes.

I feel worried when I think I have done poorly at something important.

The first two items relate to approach orientation, and the second two measure avoidance. As you can probably guess, approach orientation is associated with extraversion, and avoidance orientation is associated with neuroticism.

EXTRINSIC VERSUS INTRINSIC GOALS

Beyond approach versus avoidance, researchers who study motivation also break goals into two major types: *extrinsic*, which comes from the external, and *intrinsic*, which arises from the internal. Extrinsic goals deal with public acclaim and power and show the strongest relationship with grandiose narcissism. Intrinsic goals, such as the motivation to increase personal joy, growth, or empathy, are not associated with narcissism. Remember that the main goal of narcissism is to elevate the ego. The extrinsic goals of public acclaim, status, power, and sexual conquest—which I call the three S's: sex, status, and stuff—are tools designed to elevate the narcissistic ego.

"Sex" is all about desirability and success for narcissists. They want to be sexually attractive, tend to initiate short-term sexual relationships, and have "trophy" spouses. Sex relates to social power, not intimacy. Because sex is about the self for narcissists, rejecting sexual requests from others can also be a goal. In this case, sex itself isn't the goal, but the fact that the narcissist is desirable.

"Status" is also related to social position. Narcissists want to be admired and dominate others. They want to be at the top of the social hierarchy, whether as a leader in an organization or as a trendsetter and sophisticated insider. In this case, leadership is about status, influence, and the title, not helping the organization.

Finally, "stuff" means owning highly valuable goods, such as an expensive car, high-end fashion accessories, or trendy clothing. Narcissists aren't hoarders, though. They desire items that enhance their self-image, and they care less about craftsmanship or artistry.

Similarly, vulnerable narcissism deals with extrinsic motivators, though the main goal is to protect the ego rather than enhance it. For instance, vulnerable individuals don't want to be seen as stupid, tend to make excuses for failure, and believe others are jealous of them or out to get them. They live their lives in their heads, where it's easy to make excuses and hide failures. Instead of taking actions toward a leadership position or "trophy" spouse relationship, they may rely on fantasies of power, aggression, and desirability.

SELF-REGULATION: HOW SELF-ESTEEM DRIVES US

To understand narcissistic motives, personality researchers must also think about self-regulation, which involves the control of behavior, emotions, and thoughts in the pursuit of long-term goals, including disruptive emotions and impulses. Just as mechanical control systems self-regulate, humans must as well. Consider a thermostat: If you want to keep your house set to a cozy but practical 68 degrees all winter, you set your thermostat to 68 and forget it. The thermostat then takes over and regulates the temperature of the house, which is simple from an information standpoint. All the thermostat needs to do is check the temperature and make one decision—whether to turn the furnace on or off based on that temperature.

As a second example, cars have a system to self-regulate for fuel. Although this is slightly more complicated, it's also straightforward. The gauge indicates the gas level, and the driver refills the tank before it reaches empty. Modern cars also have warning lights and alerts to remind drivers to fill up the tank whenever the car is turned on, as well as reserve fuel.

This same process exists in social psychological systems (see table 4.1). One of the most important social goals is to regulate our social relationships. Humans are, as Aristotle famously put it, social animals. We need each other to survive. One important goal of the human social system is to belong to a social group. How do we know when we belong? The gas gauge for social belongingness, at least according to one model called the sociometer theory, is self-esteem. High self-esteem signals belongingness to a group, and low self-esteem signals separation or distance.

Table 4.1: Regulation Systems

	TEST	OPERATION
THERMOSTAT	Temperature	Turn furnace on or off
GAS TANK	Fuel level	Fill up tank with gas
SOCIOMETER	Self-esteem	Repair connection
HIEROMETER	Hierarchy	Boost social status

With self-regulation, self-esteem does much of the heavy lifting, whether it comes from the sociometer, which gauges social connection, or the hierometer, which measures hierarchy or social status, as well as competence. Self-esteem can come from many places. For example, someone may feel high self-esteem because they are a kind and hardworking nurse, an attentive or competent cable installer, part of a loving family, part of a great organization, or the winner of a chess tournament. In this sense, feeling good translates into feeling positive about actions and choices that were taken, which reinforces itself.

At the same time, outside forces that try to shape behavior can interfere with regulation. Marketers and politicians actively link self-esteem to a product, person, or belief. When people wear this, they have high self-esteem, or if they don't use this product, they should feel low self-esteem. I ran into this recently when I bought a pair of slip-on shoes for yoga. I received compliments from people and felt good about myself. However, I soon discovered the trap. Although the deep green color was cool at first, the dark blue color became popular next. Keeping up is clearly impossible. Self-regulating based on fashion trends to gain self-esteem is like heating a house and keeping the windows open for the breeze. However, that's how narcissists boost their self-esteem.

NARCISSISTIC SELF-REGULATION: THE PROCESS OF EGO INFLATION

Since narcissistic self-regulation deals with keeping self-esteem elevated and protected, narcissists specifically target extrinsic goals, which are somewhat like spiritual corn syrup. Achieving the goal or status feels great, but it doesn't last. Take sexual conquest versus emotional love as an example. Sexual conquest lasts for the encounter and spurs the desire for greater conquest, but emotional love grows in value as more time is spent with someone. Similarly, fame and attention feel great, but they are short-lived compared with mutual respect among peers. In addition, material possessions are fun to buy and provide a quick dopamine hit, but experiences endure far longer in the memory.

In a narcissist's mind, however, sex, status, and stuff provide energy for an outwardly focused self-regulation machine that keeps going. For example, when a grandiose narcissist receives a promotion at work, she feels high self-esteem, happiness, and pride, and she feels the same about other areas of her life that spark the same emotions, such as a new car and her boyfriend. However, if she feels threatened or doubts herself due to external factors associated with a negative emotion, she'll actively push back. In essence, as personality researchers say, failures and embarrassment bring on an ego threat or self-esteem threat. These "threats" can come from many areas and sometimes seem small, such as a negative comment about the narcissist's clothing or simply someone who looks better than the narcissist, failure at a task at work, or criticism from a friend or romantic partner. To meet their goals or push away threats, narcissists are aggressive, extraverted, charming, and flattering. They must achieve the goal or be extremely defensive.

For a visual representation of narcissistic self-regulation, check the following image. On the left, the basic drives of approach (for grandiose narcissists) and avoidance (for vulnerable narcissists) feed into the narcissistic self. From there, narcissists use ambition and charm to reach their goals of sex, status, and stuff, which sparks self-esteem and pride. If not achieved, the self defends against an ego threat through aggression.

While studying the image, consider this example: Grandiose Chad is energized and goal-seeking by nature, and he thinks he is pretty special. He drives his expensive car to a bar where he meets an attractive woman. He asks her to leave with him, and his goal is reached. As Chad leaves with her, someone calls him a jerk, which causes an ego threat. Chad gut punches the hater and drives off with his new lady friend. Chad is reaffirmed in the idea that he has control and made the right decision. The narcissistic self-regulation is working.

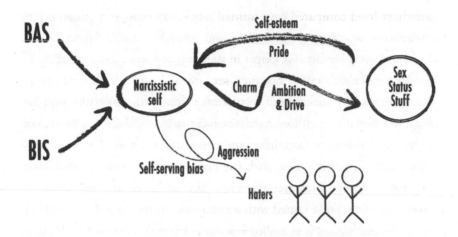

Don't get me wrong—chasing sex, status, and stuff is part of the human condition. I am not saying these goals are bad or wicked. However, chasing sex, status, and stuff in the interest of building one's ego presents a couple of major problems. The first is the *fading goal problem*. Reaching a goal that is relatively stable, such as having a loving family, can provide a long-lasting source of self-esteem and satisfaction. Fleeting goals such as sex, status, and stuff do not create sources of stable self-esteem.

Chasing fame perfectly exemplifies the fleeting nature. Check a *People* magazine from five years ago and try to recall the faces. Though Andy Warhol notoriously said that fame lasts fifteen minutes, it's now measured as "microfame" in microseconds. Status is precarious, and someone is always trying to knock another person off the ladder. Plus, once they reach one level, people tend to always seek more. Wealth can last and grow but is often not satisfying because humans get used to their well-being and comfort level and continually strive for more wealth.

Beauty, of course, is the absolute worst goal to chase for self-esteem. An enormous industry exists around making people look more youthful. More than 1.8 million cosmetic surgeries occurred in 2018, with breast augmentation, liposuction, and nose reshaping at the top of the list. Beyond that, hormone therapies are growing in popularity, and human growth hormone has long been discussed in Hollywood and among other celebrities as a strategy to stay young.

The second big problem with narcissistic self-regulation is the *willing accomplice problem.* If a grandiose narcissist wants to believe she is better than everyone, she has to convince others to praise her, find an attractive romantic partner, and dominate people publicly. It often takes a great deal of buy-in from others to make narcissism work, and narcissists accomplish this with a combination of skills and bluff. Grandiose narcissists, in particular, are extraverted but low in agreeableness, which allows them to build social connections and perform well in shallow social situations, such as cocktail parties, but not care about hurting feelings that interfere with their goals. Low agreeableness seems like it would be a negative trait, but for narcissists, it is a major benefit for their self-regulation. Most people are limited by their close relationships. They don't cheat on their spouse with a better-looking or more successful potential mate because they don't want to hurt their spouse, and they enjoy having an emotionally committed relationship. They don't give up on their favorite team after a few losing seasons because they have a sense of loyalty. They don't take credit away from coworkers or friends. In general, they care about people and don't manipulate them. In contrast, narcissists "fake it till they make it." They self-promote, brag, name-drop, and exaggerate their importance. People believe them, and that bluff becomes a reality.

The truth is that some people tolerate narcissistic tendencies when the person has enough power or looks to pull it off. In older psychoanalytic work, some texts talk about narcissism being associated with singular talents such as artists or scientists, and there certainly is higher narcissism in celebrities and presidents, but people can also be narcissistic without obvious high-status traits. They simply need better storytelling skills.

The third issue is the *reality principle problem.* Under the basic principle of congruence, the psyche works best when perception matches or comes close to reality. When perception and reality are extremely mismatched, people develop delusional disorders such as paranoid schizophrenia. They have complex but incorrect belief systems. On a manageable everyday level, basic self-enhancing ego distortions may lead us to believe that we're slightly more attractive than we are or that our professors are to blame for a bad grade. At the same time, this self-enhancement has negative costs. Feeling good about appearance replaces improving attractiveness. Blaming others for failure prevents studying harder for the next exam. For narcissists, this self-enhancement delusion works well emotionally but doesn't lead to self-improvement. Storytelling continues to build their importance as long as others—and reality—will tolerate it. This manipulation and reality bending bleeds into relationships, leadership, and social media, as I'll discuss in upcoming chapters.

When we understand goals, motivations, orientations, and ego inflation, we can better understand ourselves and how we engage with our partners, coworkers and the wider world. You may realize that your spouse uses external rewards to build self-esteem and behaves somewhat like a narcissist, but I don't want you to be alarmed just yet. Society has grown more materialistic, individualistic, and self-focused, so this behavior isn't surprising. What we're truly concerned about is when this motivation leads to extreme cases and a diagnosable psychiatric disorder, which I'll outline in the next chapter.

NERD HERD: MEASURING SELF-REGULATION

When thinking about systems in social psychology, I always enjoy coming back to the scientific methodology that underlies it and unpacking what we know and don't know—and what we can and can't do. In reality, when compared to the level of precision seen in a field such as systems engineering, psychological systems almost seem metaphorical. Engineers and technical teams can determine energy moving through a circuit or the airflow moving through a skyscraper, but in psychology, there's not a way to measure self-regulation. For instance, there's not a general unit of psychic energy, and there's not a specific self-regulation model that measures what happens.

At the same time, scientists have made some progress in cybernetics, which explores regulatory systems or how humans and animals communicate with each other and control each other. Researchers have been able to make some progress on ideas such as feedback loops and self-organization, and they continue to learn more about concepts such as cognition, adaptation, learning, and connectivity. In psychology in particular, this type of research has paid off in areas such as behavioral psychology, cognitive psychology, and neuropsychology and will continue to improve with better measurement. As a related example in neurobiology, scientists can now image the entire brain of the *Drosophila* fly, including synapses and neural circuits, which may allow them to understand a fly's behavior. Ultimately, this is the goal for humans. Although the hundred-thousand-neuron brain in a fruit fly is much less complex than the hundred-billion-neuron human brain, researchers are finding that some of the basic systems may share common processes with more complex animal brains and humans.

INSIDE SCOOP: RESEARCHING THE SELF-SERVING BIAS

While studying narcissism in graduate school, I was fascinated by the classic social psychological effect of the self-serving bias, or the tendency for people to attribute positive outcomes to their own actions but negative outcomes to other people or external factors. In our studies, we'd invite two students to the research lab to cooperate on a task and then record their reactions when they received feedback about their success or failure on the assignment. During the experiments, we found that narcissistic individuals tended to self-enhance or give themselves credit, and non-narcissists showed more flexibility in self-enhancement. They didn't tend to compare themselves favorably to a partner when successful or put the other person down during failure.

As part of these studies, we induced closeness among the students with the Relationship Closeness Induction Task (RCIT), which prompts partners to spend about ten minutes talking casually while they answer personal questions about themselves based on three lists we provided. Since closeness often comes from self-disclosure, we encouraged this through questions such as "If you could travel anywhere in the world, where would you go and why?" and "What is one emotional experience you've had with a good friend?" Related to narcissism in particular, we wanted to know whether closeness would hinder the self-serving bias. We even used real friends in some of the studies. In both cases, relationships acted as a buffer to self-enhancement, and friends shared responsibility for both their successes and failures—among non-narcissists. As you might expect, narcissists continued to self-enhance and blame others.

If this sounds familiar, you may have read about a similar concept in an extremely popular *New York Times* article published in the "Modern Love" column in 2015, "To Fall in Love with Anyone, Do This."[1] The story lists a series of questions that can be used to prompt closeness and discover more about others. The story was based on research by "love researcher" Art Aron at the State University of New York at Stony Brook, who did research like ours using a similar list of questions and a more complex romantic relationship induction with eye gazing. Amazingly, several participants from his studies got married and were part of the *NYT* article. As we know it now, it's possible to bring strangers closer together in a psychologically meaningful way.

CHAPTER 5

Narcissistic Personality Disorder

The current popular use of *narcissist* in everyday conversation highlights the biggest misconception out there—that narcissism and narcissistic personality disorder (NPD) are the same. To provide context, that's like saying sadness and depression are the same. It's common right now to ask a friend how she's doing and for her to respond that she's feeling depressed. It's understood that she's struggling with sadness, self-esteem, and energy issues, but it doesn't mean she's dealing with major depressive disorder or experiencing a major depressive episode. As the discussion around mental health has expanded and grown, people are now embracing the idea that many of us fluctuate in and out of depressive states, but it doesn't mean we're clinically depressed.

The same idea holds true for narcissism. If you say your lover is a narcissist, you're likely describing someone who is selfish, callous, self-centered, and attention-seeking. We speak colloquially that way. On the other hand, if you say your spouse is a narcissist and you're going through divorce proceedings due to extreme and detrimental behavior, this could indicate a spouse who has a clinical level of narcissism that is relevant to treatment interventions and legal proceedings, or narcissistic personality disorder.

To understand the difference, it's important to see the overview of personality disorders in general and how narcissism became part of the lexicon. In general, personality can be diagnosed as a disorder when there is a specific number of characteristic beliefs or behaviors that are clearly harmful. Overall, personality disorders seem to be extreme forms of normal personality rather than a unique personality configuration or trait. The world isn't made up of wolves and sheep; there are just a lot of humans trying to work together, some wolflike, some sheeplike.

As part of this conversation, I want to make the point that narcissism exists on a continuum, and there's not a definitive line where it's "normal" or "abnormal." I get this question often, so I think there's an important distinction to make. Clinical disorders don't explain whether the behavior is normal or not; instead, a disorder designates whether a behavior is impairing. We experience a range of personalities, and there isn't an "abnormal" personality out there. In other words, the personality isn't the problem—the impairment is. That's why you need a clinician, such as a psychologist or psychiatrist, to diagnose a personality disorder. Based on education and experience, they can make a conclusion about whether the narcissism is causing enough strife to require treatment.

WHY PERSONALITY GOES WRONG

Humans evolved so that "average" and "normal" would be the desirable qualities. People want to be a little taller than average, but not too tall. The most attractive faces are symmetrical and a little different from average, but not too unique. For instance, we want a medium-sized mouth and eyes that aren't too close or too far apart. We want a slightly wider smile than average or eyes that are a little larger, but we don't want lips like a largemouth bass or guppy eyes.

On a broader level, the world is built for "average," such as right-handed desks, the size of airplane seats, and the speed of math courses. Average benefits the most people. When outside of the average zone, someone may either face a disadvantage or benefit slightly. Being small, for instance, makes clothes shopping difficult but airplane flights more comfortable.

This same truth applies to personality. Humans expect people to be "average" and like others who have personalities that are close to "normal." Thanks to the praised idea of individualism, those in the Western world want to be slightly outside of normal—a little above average on extraversion, openness, agreeableness, and conscientiousness and a little below average on neuroticism. The extremes of personality can lead to problems, even for what we see as "positive" personality traits. Extreme extraversion, for example, can mean too much social activity that is not balanced by reflection. Ambition, a part of extraversion, can be beneficial for material success but take a toll on family or personal life. Even extremely low neuroticism can be a problem. Humans get anxious because it protects them from danger. People with extremely low neuroticism can become overly risk-taking, sometimes with the result being an early grave.

As part of this, humans appreciate and understand flexibility in personality, and it's considered normal to be slightly flexible. People are often more extraverted during a social occasion but introverted on a lazy Sunday morning. It's expected to be neurotic in a new or dangerous environment but less so in safe surroundings. At the same time, our personalities are generally stable, and it's not considered normal to mold into every occasion available. Typically, within the range of average personality traits, we dial it up or down to make situations and systems work for everyone involved. In professional or formal settings, we control our language more than when we talk to friends. We save certain jokes for private conversations that we wouldn't say in public. We're respectful and quiet in solemn moments such as funerals but celebratory and gregarious during graduations and birthday parties. Overall, we tend to control or regulate our personalities to the point where we match the moment and aren't too extreme.

The same balance applies to behaviors and actions. Drinking a glass of wine or two is considered appropriate, but excessive drinking that leads to a lack of control is a disorder. Being excited about a new idea is motivational, but being so enamored with a new project that it interrupts sleep and the ability to pay bills can be a disorder. Thinking highly of yourself is considered positive, but seeing yourself as so amazing that others must constantly acknowledge it and downplay their own personalities is negative.

When personalities aren't normal or flexible, personality disorders may develop, which can be described clinically as *extreme* and *inflexible* personality traits. In the case of narcissistic personality disorder (NPD), a person's narcissism has become extreme and inflexible. Imagine a talk show host who has a narcissistic, blowhard style on air. This might work for the on-camera brand as long as he can turn down the narcissism when off-air. When the same narcissism continues into the host's professional or personal life, however, significant problems can ensue. People hate working with self-absorbed people and call them prima donnas, divas, or worse. Coworkers might tolerate the narcissistic host as long as the money is coming in, but they probably don't like him personally, and when the money stops rolling, they will get rid of him as soon as they can.

To be diagnosed with a personality disorder, people with extreme or inflexible personality traits must also experience significant negative consequences in life, or what clinicians call *impairments*. This might include a distorted view of reality that leads a narcissist to make stupid and risky decisions at work, or it could be poor self-control that leads a narcissist to repeatedly make decisions that get attention but lead to failure or depression. Also—and this is quite important to point out with NPD in particular—impairment can be defined as the suffering of others *around* the narcissist. Even if narcissists feel good about themselves, they can be considered to have a personality disorder if they are damaging others' lives due to problems that come from entitlement, the need for admiration, and a disregard for others' feelings. This self-centered, exploitative approach to relationships can include game playing, infidelity, and a lack of empathy, as we will talk about in chapter 7. In short, NPD may be diagnosed when trait narcissism is extreme, inflexible, and impairing.

HOW NPD IS DIAGNOSED

The official diagnosis of personality disorders comes from the *Diagnostic and Statistical Manual of Mental Disorders* (*DSM*) put out by the American Psychiatric Association (APA). This manual has undergone several changes in recent decades, and the current version is the *DSM-5*. The current definition of NPD was carried over into the *DSM-5* from the *DSM-IV*. Despite major research advances, the professional psychologists and psychiatrists who work together to create the manual haven't agreed on new definitions for personality disorders, and although there was a massive effort to make a transition with a new model, it failed. Those models are being tested by researchers, which you can read more about in this chapter's "Inside Scoop."

In this book, I'm focusing on the definition of narcissistic personality disorder that was carried over into the *DSM-5*. I'm not sure if the emerging definitions will be implemented, and frankly, I don't think they will be anytime soon. Moving to a new model of personality disorders is like moving to a new computer system at work: Employees spend years using a system that works fine but has quirks. A new system promises to work well once everyone is trained to use it, but it's tough to implement for the short-term adjustment, so organizations tend to stick with the old, messy system.

When the *DSM* describes disorders such as NPD, the manual first tells a story about the disorder and then gives specific markers of the disorder. The story of NPD starts with the *diagnostic features* described in this statement:

> [T]he essential feature of narcissistic personality disorder is a pervasive pattern of grandiosity, need for admiration, and a lack of empathy that begins by early adulthood and is present in a variety of contexts.[1]

This single sentence captures narcissism well by touching on the key aspects discussed in earlier chapters. Grandiosity and lack of empathy line up with extraversion and low agreeableness, and needing admiration is an example of self-regulation. This description makes NPD sound more grandiose than vulnerable, and that general bias toward grandiosity is consistent throughout the *DSM-IV* (and thus, the *DSM-5*) description of NPD with the exception of some of the narrative portion.

Then the *DSM* provides a longer narrative description of the associated disorders and features of NPD. In this section, the discussion of narcissism contains a good deal of vulnerability. Individuals diagnosed with NPD are said to be highly sensitive to ego threat and emotional injury. In other words, narcissists are fragile, and they can be hurt easily by any information that challenges their inflated self-image. The description also explains that narcissism can be associated with vulnerable features such as social withdrawal.

Within the next section, the *DSM* description of NPD includes the prevalence and age-related features. In general, NPD prevalence matches what might be expected regarding the traits of narcissism. NPD is more common in men than women, and the APA estimates that 50 to 75 percent of those with NPD are male. Importantly, NPD is estimated to be prevalent in less than 1 percent of the general population at any one time. Although this estimate is likely low, researchers can't say for sure without extremely large and thorough sampling. Based on the biggest sample available now from the National Epidemiologic Survey on Alcohol and Related Conditions, which studies the occurrence of more than one psychological disorder or substance use disorder in the same person, NPD prevalence might be around 2 percent. This number is *point prevalence*, or how many people have the disorder at any one point in time, versus *lifetime prevalence*, which looks at how many people have the disorder at *any point* in their lives. The lifetime prevalence of NPD is higher, but given the difficulties in measurement, it is hard to say how much higher.

The *DSM* then describes differential diagnosis, or the process of winnowing out a particular disorder from similar ones. For example, when patients visit a physician with symptoms of a sore throat and fever, that rules out a large number of disorders such as plantar fasciitis or a brain tumor, but it could be a sinus infection, cold, allergies, strep throat, flu, or a combination of those. Physicians use several ways to differentiate between these possible diagnoses. They might ask about body aches, which could indicate the flu, or look at the throat for signs of strep. Then they can run quick tests to make these differential diagnoses more effective, so they may collect a throat swab for strep. Given this information, physicians make the best guess and suggest a treatment. With certain illnesses, such as the flu or strep, early diagnosis and treatment can help.

In the case of NPD, the first differentiation a psychologist might make is between NPD and other possible personality disorders. Without the grandiosity, narcissism looks like antisocial personality disorder, and with a high degree of vulnerability, it looks like borderline personality disorder. This way of dividing the world into specific personality types or disorder types is tricky. Since they share core traits such as antagonism, they "hang together" and are related in some way. In this case, differential diagnosis investigates differences in other areas. One good differentiator between NPD and antisocial personality disorder (or psychopathic personality disorder) is impulsivity, or the need to act on impulsive thoughts and feelings. Narcissism is not typically associated with impulsivity, but antisocial personality disorder is. In the "real world," impulsivity might mean stealing somebody's watch or cheating on a spouse. In extreme cases, people who are antagonistic and highly impulsive often end up in and out of jail. Since they commit impulsive crimes, they get caught, and they don't often build up enough financial resources to protect themselves from some level of societal justice. If someone with NPD had those same antagonistic traits, they'd exhibit less impulsivity, focus more on looking good, and put more thought into committing crimes. To look good publicly, they would need to avoid getting caught, and they would spend more energy focusing on that or operating in gray areas.

Differentiating more vulnerable shades of narcissism from borderline personality disorder is trickier. Some of the midcentury psychodynamic writing puts narcissistic and borderline personality disorder at different levels of organization, with narcissistic personality being somewhat more organized and structured than borderline. At the trait level, more recent research has shown this pattern to hold. Borderline is more strongly associated with impulsivity than vulnerable narcissism and more closely associated with childhood trauma, but the two traits are related similarly when it comes to agreeableness and neuroticism. From a diagnostic perspective, differentiation can get messy, but borderline might be best thought of as an emotion regulation disorder and vulnerable narcissism as an antagonistic disorder.

Another related disorder is the grandiose phase of mania, or hypomanic episodes. The prefix *hypo-* often means "low levels of," and hypomania is a low-level facet of bipolar disorder with a heightened or hyperactive mood, which we will discuss in the next chapter. Manic episodes can create the confidence, energy, and grandiosity of narcissism, but in this case, they're typically not driven by antagonism and attention-seeking. Someone with hypomania may want to achieve a lofty goal like building the tallest structure in the world but not want to put his name on it. Plus, manic episodes tend to be cyclical, either coming and going or moving between the two extremes of what used to be called manic depression but is now classified as a variation of bipolar disorder. Grandiose narcissism or narcissistic personality disorder doesn't cycle, and it directly deals with self-enhancement.

When diagnosing NPD, psychologists and psychiatrists also have to rule out medications or drugs that mimic aspects of narcissism. Cocaine and other stimulants, for instance, might look like narcissism for a short period of time, but once the drugs wear off, the narcissistic behavior should wear off as well. Of course, people may have several disorders that are tough to disentangle. Celebrities often have characteristics that might look like narcissism, drug abuse, or bipolar disorder, and it can be hard to distinguish. That's why good diagnosis is so important.

Finally, and I have to say this cracks me up every time I read it, the *DSM* notes that "many highly successful individuals display personality traits that might be considered narcissistic." The APA makes the point that these traits should only be diagnosed as narcissistic personality disorder if they lead to significant impairment. In the end, if someone has enough status and power and can get away with a large amount of narcissism, it may not be clinically impairing, even if it is extreme. At the same time, I might argue that there is a particular ethical call to treat NPD in high-power individuals because of the damage they can do from their perches of power.

THE CRITERIA FOR NPD DIAGNOSIS

People must meet specific criteria to be diagnosed with NPD. The threshold for the disorder is meeting five of nine, or a majority, of these criteria. They're paraphrased here:

1. *Grandiosity.* This person has a grandiose sense of self and expects to be recognized for it.

2. *Active fantasy life.* Narcissists fantasize about fame, power, and status.

3. *A sense of specialness.* Narcissists see themselves as special and unique, which includes associating with other people who are special and unique.

4. *Admiration.* The *DSM* says that a narcissist "requires excessive admiration." This language is a bit strange because it implies a neediness for admiration rather than an expectation of admiration.

5. *Sense of entitlement.* Narcissism is associated with a pervasive pattern of entitlement to have desires met, even when not appropriate.

6. *Exploitativeness.* Narcissists are willing to exploit others or take advantage of people to meet their own goals.

7. *Lack of empathy.* The *DSM* describes a narcissist as lacking empathy. This is a tricky term because it could mean that narcissists lack the capacity for empathy or that narcissists don't express sufficient empathy. The latest research suggests that the second meaning is closer to reality and that narcissists have the ability to empathize.

8. *Envy.* Narcissists are envious of others or think others are envious of them, which is also worded in an odd way. My guess is that this item was written to capture grandiosity (others are envious) and vulnerability (envious of others) in dealing with social comparison.

9. *Arrogance.* Narcissists exhibit haughty behaviors that are conceited and dismissive.

For a true diagnosis of NPD, someone must show a majority of these criteria in a way that causes significant impairment in love or work. In studies, narcissism is most associated with distress to significant others. In essence, a narcissist's selfish and manipulative behavior often makes friends, family members, and coworkers feel resentful or threatened, and in turn, they dread interacting with the narcissist. They also report feeling devalued and criticized by the narcissist. It's important to note, however, that arrogant and grandiose people who function reasonably and don't hurt others around them shouldn't be diagnosed with a personality disorder. In addition, the signs must be present for an extended period of time in an adult to lead to a diagnosis, versus a short-term personality change that may indicate a major life event has occurred, drug use, or a medical diagnosis such as a stroke, rather than a personality disorder.

Trifurcated Model of Narcissism

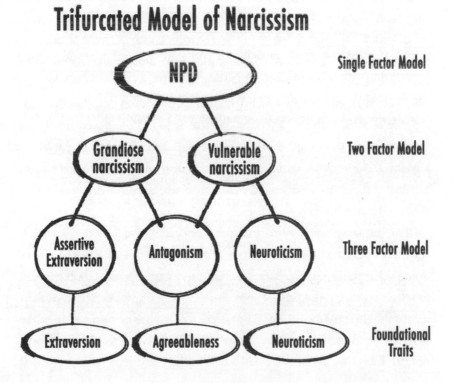

The current debate in the research community revolves around the corners of the Trifurcated Model: how can NPD reflect both extreme grandiose and vulnerable narcissism yet have diagnostic criteria that lean heavily toward grandiose? My colleagues and I have argued that grandiosity, consistent with the criteria, should be more core to NPD than vulnerability, and that any diagnosis of NPD with a large amount of vulnerability should be labeled specifically as NPD with vulnerability. In psychiatric systems, this would be called a *specifier* that identifies the vulnerable form of NPD. For instance, a person with NPD who is primarily grandiose would be labeled simply as NPD, but a person with NPD and a large amount of vulnerability would be labeled as NPD with vulnerability.

This idea poses a challenge in certain cases, though. What about those with NPD who vacillate from grandiosity to vulnerability? The latest research is still investigating this. As you may recall, personality science examines large samples of normal people—often hundreds or thousands—and uses those samples to understand narcissistic personality disorder. Of course, in any of these samples, only a small number of people have NPD, so these studies could miss unique aspects of NPD that need to be studied further. In contrast, psychologists who work with NPD often report seeing patients vacillate from being grandiose to vulnerable and back again. The same person is grandiose when he comes into the office and then becomes vulnerable when he discusses emotionally threatening topics with his therapist. I don't doubt this observation, but it is difficult to observe and measure in research and then make recommendations based on solid science.

For instance, one way to measure personality vacillation is to track someone's personality multiple times during the course of a week or two. Some smartphone apps already exist that can alert users several times a day to reflect on their emotions—happy, anxious, sad, or proud. The apps then record the circumstances around those feelings, such as certain activities like working or socializing and the people who may be triggers for both positive and negative reactions. If used consistently and with science-backed measures, researchers could measure how stable a person's personality and narcissism is, and if it varies, what might cause that change.

The good news is that researchers are doing this kind of work thanks to the widespread use of smartphones and the development of sophisticated data analysis. Even so, it is hard to find specific vacillations in narcissism from grandiose to vulnerable. In fact, grandiose narcissism seems quite stable compared to other traits. This does not mean the debate over vulnerability in grandiose narcissism is resolved. Researchers are always using new technologies to understand personality and behavior, and in a decade, the personality science field will grow much more, which may identify and treat narcissism in new and different ways.

WEIRD, WILD, AND WORRIED: THE THREE PERSONALITY DISORDER CLUSTERS

To better understand how NPD diagnosis works, it's also useful to know how psychologists and psychiatrists organize personality disorders into *clusters*, or higher-order groups. Unlike the Big Five personality traits, personality disorders are currently classified into three clusters. Historically, these clusters are labeled with letters—Cluster A, Cluster B, and Cluster C—that don't stand for anything. As a result, psychology students remember these clusters with nicknames such as the "weird, wild, and worried" or "mad, bad, and sad." (Hint: narcissism falls into the wild/bad Cluster B.)

Cluster A is the odd or eccentric cluster, where personality disorders characterized by weird and unusual behavior or thinking exist. Cluster A includes two disorders that sound extremely similar—schizotypal personality disorder and schizoid personality disorder—as well as paranoid personality disorder. *Schizoid* comes from the word *schism*, which means "split." *Schizotypal personality disorder* includes classic atypical or uncommon thinking that is similar to that seen in schizophrenia. Even though it sounds similar, *schizoid personality disorder* is more about emotional disengagement or detachment. The third personality disorder in this cluster is *paranoid personality disorder*, which reflects pervasive paranoia and perhaps delusions of persecution.

Cluster B disorders are characterized by emotionally erratic, unstable, and dramatic characteristics. Cluster B traits (not necessarily the full-blown disorders) are prominent on reality television shows because they make for such interesting drama—fights, attention-seeking, unstable short-term relationships, and substance use. *Narcissistic personality disorder* is a member of Cluster B, along with *antisocial personality disorder*, which has some antagonism and a large amount of impulsivity, and *histrionic personality disorder*, which includes high drama and attention-seeking. Histrionic personalities are often so dramatic, flirtatious, and attention-seeking that they drive people away. And *borderline personality disorder*, which is characterized by challenges in regulating attachment to others, especially through a fear of rejection, and regulating a sense of self in the face of anxiety. The foundational problems revolve around handling anxiety, which can manifest in everything from cutting behaviors to unstable love-hate relationships.

Cluster C personality disorders are primarily associated with anxiety and worry. *Avoidant personality disorder* is, as the name suggests, a clinical level of avoiding social interaction or social contact with people. *Dependent personality disorder*, also as the name suggests, features an extreme desire to be taken care of or helped by others and is linked to depression. *Obsessive-compulsive personality disorder* deals with a clinically significant degree of impairment caused by maintaining order or following the rules. (This is not the same as *obsessive-compulsive disorder* [OCD], which includes obsessive thoughts coupled with compulsive behaviors such as checking locks or checking your wallet to such an extent that it messes with your life.)

Similar to the models of personality, these three clusters and specific disorders are interrelated. Anxiety and worry, which are the traits of neuroticism, exist in the majority of personality disorders. Antagonism and impulsivity are also common, which are the traits of low agreeableness and low conscientiousness. Theoretically, this makes perfect sense because disorders based on shared personality traits should look similar, but it can also lead to problems with diagnosis. Diagnoses with *comorbidity*, or the existence of two disorders at the same time, occur quite often. For instance, a diagnosis of borderline personality disorder might be accompanied by a narcissistic personality disorder diagnosis. Additionally, about 30 to 40 percent of patients in research samples are diagnosed with a personality disorder that doesn't include a disorder name. They tend to be categorized as PD-NOS, or personality disorder not otherwise specified.

In my opinion, the whole personality disorder system is a bit of a mess. Some people clearly have personality disorders because they have ongoing personality problems that occur long-term and lead to significant impairment. Beyond that, some people also fit cleanly into a box of narcissistic or schizotypal or borderline personality disorder. At the end of the day, however, psychologists and psychiatrists often see ambiguous, subjective fuzz in the system. A patient might be diagnosed as having NPD by one clinician, antisocial personality disorder by a second, and bipolar disorder by a third. In our research, we often see that narcissistic and paranoid personality disorders hang together more than expected from disorders in different clusters. Part of that association is that the people who are paranoid or see the world as "out to get them" can also sound narcissistic. These associations will continue to challenge diagnosis, but future research may make certain aspects clearer.

NARCISSISTIC PERSONALITY DISORDER IN THE FUTURE

Just as medical definitions and diagnoses change over time as knowledge increases, so do personality disorder definitions and diagnoses. For instance, the schizophrenia diagnosis first stepped onto the scene in 1887 when German psychiatrist Emil Kraepelin used the term *dementia praecox*, or early dementia, to describe patients with symptoms such as fragmented thinking. Schizophrenia existed before that but was not recognized as a discrete medical condition. Now the *DSM* includes several categories of schizophrenia, and researchers are still trying to classify new aspects of delusional disorders.

In addition, research can shift the way society views certain disorders, such as autism. Originally seen as a discrete disorder, autism then shifted to a pair of disorders and is now seen as a spectrum. Similarly, personality scientists have made an effort to place schizotypal personality into the broader spectrum of schizophrenia, and this is made explicit in the *DSM-5*.

Furthermore, society faces the issues of economics and medication. If medications existed for narcissism, for instance, which might reduce ego or other narcissistic traits, psychologists and psychiatrists would likely begin diagnosing it on a spectrum. If a treatment exists, doctors want to prescribe what may help, and traditionally in medicine, this can extend outside the lines of what the medication was originally created to treat. Selective serotonin reuptake inhibitors (SSRIs) were intended for depression and anxiety but now are prescribed by nonspecialists to help with general neuroticism. Simply put, if a pill could help people become less of a jerk, doctors would hand them out to everyday jerks in addition to those with diagnosable personality disorders.

It's also possible that the entire structure of personality disorders will be changed to reflect basic personality traits. In that case, narcissistic personality disorder could be diagnosed as a specific class of "disorders of the antagonism" along with psychopathy and antisocial personality disorder. Researchers are testing a trait-based diagnostic system in the European Union and finding that it seems to work.

In the future, however NPD is classified or whatever NPD is called, the same combination of traits and behaviors—grandiosity, lack of empathy, and self-enhancement—will lead to problems if left to run amok. Diagnosis can have important costs and benefits for treatment decisions, insurance coverage, legal consequences, and labeling, and it can also lead to complexity and uncertainty in real life for real individuals who have a real diagnosis.

NERD HERD: PERSONALITY DISORDERS AND THE FIVE-FACTOR MODEL

The tension among the definitions of *normal, abnormal,* and *pathological* gets pulled in different directions at different times. Sigmund Freud and Carl Jung, considered the founding fathers of psychology, studied pathological individuals to learn about normal personality, and both eventually turned to anthropology and related fields. Shortly thereafter, psychiatrists such as Emil Kraepelin needed a clear medical diagnostic system to know who to treat and how to treat them. Thus, psychiatry was built with a medical model where people either did or didn't have a distinct mental illness, and psychology followed.

By the 1980s, however, researchers studying traits such as narcissism began to transition from this medical model to a personality model. At that time, researchers Paul Costa and Robert McCrae published work about personality disorders and the Big Five. Through several studies, they compared personality scales that used the five-factor model with personality disorder scales and found that the five-factor model encompasses both normal and abnormal personality. Moving forward, professionals began integrating traditional personality trait models into psychiatric conceptions of disorder. Pair this with the economic element that it's much less expensive to find and research normal people than clinical samples of people with abnormal traits, and research exploded on the normal trait approach.

INSIDE SCOOP: ARGUMENTS AROUND THE *DSM*

As you may know, psychiatrists are medical doctors (MDs) who study and treat mental illness, and psychologists are PhDs with graduate training in psychology. Psychiatrists have prescription privileges and broader medical training, clinical psychologists with specific medical training have prescription privileges in some jurisdictions, and research psychologists have broader assessment privileges and more research training. Psychologists are really good at diagnosing psychological problems, but psychiatrists are needed to treat the complex medical aspects of these disorders. People may see a psychologist for a diagnosis, a psychiatrist for medical treatment, and perhaps another psychologist or mental health professional for psychotherapy.

As part of the creation of the *DSM*, psychiatrists and psychologists get together as a working group to discuss the latest research on a topic, query the professional members of the American Psychological Association, and put together definitions that make everyone happy. This is really hard to do. To give an example, those who follow Carl Jung's ideas view introversion positively, so using *introversion* as a negative term was seen as slanderous. Instead, the term *detachment* was incorporated into the *DSM*.

Because of these types of internal debates, the *DSM* models that we use now still trace their roots to about three decades ago. Despite huge research advances, there have been no new formulations around personality disorders. There was a massive effort to make a transition, but it failed and now is described as an emerging model. It's not used clinically, as far as I know, but aspects of this new model are always being tested by researchers.

CHAPTER 6

Narcissism's Cousins: The Four Triads

One benefit of using basic traits such as the Big Five (extraversion, openness, agreeableness, neuroticism, and conscientiousness) to describe and define complex traits like narcissism is that you can see what happens when there are small variations in the basic trait recipes or profiles. For example, you can take the trait recipe of grandiose narcissism—mostly assertive extraversion and low agreeableness—and tweak it a bit. Add low conscientiousness or impulsivity or decrease the extraversion and add neuroticism to explore families of traits, also known as *trait cousins*, that are related to each other but also have important differences. Psychologists have developed several sets of cousins to explore traits that are similar to narcissism. Often called a *triad*, these models link one aspect of narcissism, such as the grandiose qualities, to two related traits. First, researchers looked toward the "dark" side, or the negative traits, to form the *Dark Triad*.

The Dark Triads

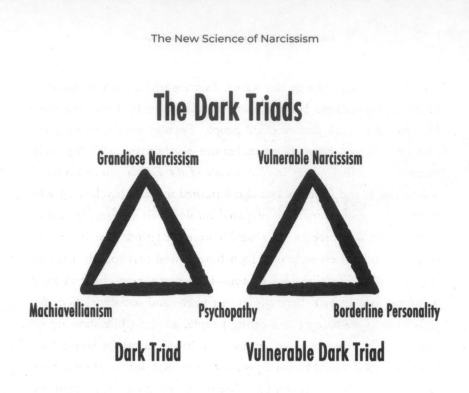

Grandiose Narcissism   Vulnerable Narcissism

Machiavellianism   Psychopathy   Borderline Personality

Dark Triad   Vulnerable Dark Triad

THE DARK TRIAD

The term *Dark Triad* might come across as "bad" or "evil," but in psychology, *dark* tends to describe antagonism. It's not an ideal term, of course, but it stuck, and that's what we've used historically to describe these types of traits. As you'll see later in this chapter, psychologists have been working on a "light" side as well.

Coined in 2002 by psychologist Del Paulhus and his research team in British Columbia, Canada, the Dark Triad contains three traits that share a "dark core" of low agreeableness and a lack of empathy: grandiose narcissism, psychopathy, and Machiavellianism. You'll be able to see how adding a sprinkle of this or a sprinkle of that changes the personality slightly and creates a different "flavor" of the narcissism we've been discussing so far. Grandiose narcissism stands at the top of the triad, and the cousins branch off to the sides.

Psychopathy mixes low agreeableness with low conscientiousness or impulsivity. Imagine someone who is grandiose, cold, callous, and also does whatever he or she wants. Psychopaths are often found in criminal populations because their impulsivity gets them into trouble: they rob, steal, and even kill people. Popular novels, movies, and television shows, however, often feature psychopaths with *high* self-control. Hannibal Lecter in *The Silence of the Lambs*, for example, is a serial killer and cannibal but also a trained forensic psychiatrist who happens to make intricately prepared meals of his victims. In reality, master criminals such as these aren't common. Jeffrey Epstein seemed like a real-world example of a high-functioning psychopath. Instead, it's likely that Epstein—and Lector—is as much a narcissist as he is a psychopath. In fact, Lecter is so intelligent and socially skilled that if he weren't murdering and eating people, all the while showing off his genius by playing cat and mouse with investigators, he would have remained a successful forensic psychiatrist in high leadership positions and at the top of social groups. The more common psychopath has impulses that lead to trouble. In *Game of Thrones*, Joffrey Baratheon is an impulsive and sadistic psychopath who was murdered to keep him out of power. Ramsay Bolton was another sadistic psychopath. Of course, Cersei Lannister is massively narcissistic and psychopathic. She is willing to murder almost anyone to get her way, but she is stable and smart enough to stay in power.

The other cousin in the triad is *Machiavellianism*, named after Niccolo Machiavelli, author of *The Prince*, a guide for leaders in the 1500s that discusses how to wield power successfully. This work often gets a bad rap because it is truly a guide on manipulation, but the manipulation is often done in the service of the greater good. Avoiding war and increasing trade and alliances were crucial for small states in the Middle Ages, and accomplishing these goals meant being incredibly strategic. The character of Littlefinger in *Game of Thrones* is a perfect version of this trait. Machiavellians are often callous and highly manipulative, believing that the importance of their aims justifies even immoral means. In real life, though, Machiavellians of this level are hard to find. Many wannabe

Machiavellians think they are highly manipulative and clever, but they actually look and act like impulsive psychopaths.

A fourth trait associated with this group is *sadism*, and sometimes people add sadism to the Dark Triad to make the Dark Tetrad. Sadism centers around low agreeableness. Unlike narcissists who want to harm people for an ego boost but otherwise wouldn't, sadists take pleasure in harming people and other creatures. In another well-known Paulhus study, for instance, psychology undergraduates were given three pill bugs—Muffin, Ike, and Tootsie—and a modified coffee grinder.[1] They were instructed to drop the bugs into the "bug-crunching machine" and grind them, starting with Muffin. Although a barrier prevented the bugs from reaching the blades, the grinder made a noise to mimic the sound of crunching. The researchers found that the more sadistic students took pleasure in grinding up the bugs. Poor Muffin, Ike, and Tootsie.

The good news is that, despite the suffering in the world, sadism is relatively rare. People generally don't like to see others suffer. Even in an incredibly aggressive sport such as football, when an athlete is harmed, everyone claps if the injured player can walk off the field, including the opposing team. Spectators buy tickets to cheer for greatness and competition but not typically humiliation and suffering, although a few rivalries can get scary.

When sadism mixes with narcissism, however, which combines egotism and the desire to cause pain in others, it creates a dangerous combination called *malignant narcissism*. Social psychologist Erich Fromm first used the term in 1964, calling it "the quintessence of evil."[2] Two decades later, Otto Kernberg introduced it to psychoanalytic literature, but little has been written about it since the 1980s. Interestingly, the characteristics of narcissism were part of our culture long before they had a single name. In a 2010 study by Mila Goldner-Vukov and Laurie Jo Moore at the University of Auckland in New Zealand,[3] they found malignant narcissism in fairy tales dating back to Snow White and Cinderella, particularly in stories with an evil stepmother who tries to psychologically or physically harm her innocent stepdaughter. The stepmother is arrogant, cold, rich, preoccupied with beauty, and has no remorse for her actions. They also looked at the family history of three prominent dictators—Adolf Hitler, Joseph Stalin, and Mao Zedong—and found common themes with antisocial, paranoid, and sadistic behaviors. The good news is that the cases of malignant narcissism are so few and far between that the New Zealand researchers only had a few cases studies to show examples.

Psychologists became fascinated by the Dark Triad because, as Paulhus has phrased it in previous interviews, "dark personalities are more fascinating than shiny, happy people."[4] Similarly, my colleague Josh Miller has described the fascination with psychopathy as similar to a fascination with a lion who can open a bedroom door with a claw. This is a scary image and worthy of study. Others seem to agree. Since the first paper on the Dark Triad, research has increased each year with a large number of papers being published in the past few years, reaching nearly two thousand in 2018. Researchers have concluded, among other things, that Dark Triad traits are attractive to women, linked with insomnia, and potentially related to success.

However, the boom in research—and ensuing coverage in popular media with headlines such as "Why a Little Evil Is Good"—has sparked some backlash.[5] Even a few of my University of Georgia colleagues have spoken up against the literature, publishing a critical appraisal of the Dark Triad in February 2019 and suggesting ways to move forward with more complex, nuanced research rather than methods that oversimplify related personality traits.[6] For instance, it's important to acknowledge the complexity of criminal behavior and the many factors that may contribute to it. Narcissism isn't always related to criminal acts, and not all criminal acts contain narcissism. There are many reasons people may commit a crime, and those that are related to narcissism tend to be selfish. White collar crimes related to narcissism, for example, often stem from a need to enhance the self and continue a lifestyle the narcissist wants to maintain. The complexity of these interactions continues to prompt new conversations about the Dark Triad and other triads, including the three we'll discuss next.

THE VULNERABLE DARK TRIAD

As research started kicking up around the Dark Triad, Josh Miller and I realized there was a mirror to it that would mix dark traits with the emotionally vulnerable side of narcissism. Interestingly, Josh is one of the coauthors of the critical appraisal paper mentioned above, so it makes sense that he had his finger on the pulse of this research and wanted to learn more about other complex interactions. In a study we published in the *Journal of Personality* in 2010, we discussed how there was, in fact, a *Vulnerable Dark Triad* that shares traits associated with neuroticism and antagonism, which includes vulnerable narcissism, borderline personality, and factor 2 psychopathy. Members of the Vulnerable Dark Triad see the world as threatening and hostile, and they have challenges with trust and mood regulation, especially hostility and anxiety.

Borderline personality, the trait associated with borderline personality disorder, is characterized by a large amount of instability in mood and relationships. Borderline individuals can switch between loving someone deeply to not at all, and they have difficulty regulating their negative moods such as loss, sadness, or fear. In essence, they may spiral in anxious and depressive situations, making decisions that lead to worse behaviors rather than finding ways to move to a more positive state. The result is that they can do harmful acts to others and themselves, such as cutting behaviors and even suicide. Borderline characters are well-represented in films, with Glenn Close's role in *Fatal Attraction* being the most famous (and scariest). Beyond that, borderline personality disorder itself is quite messy and complex, as discussed in earlier chapters.

Factor II psychopathy is less well known and represents an extremely impulsive and emotional version of psychopathy. Imagine a twenty-two-year-old male who is hostile and exploitative but not ambitious or ego-driven. This is a marginally employed, legally spotty individual who survives largely by taking advantage of other people. In the movie *Ready Player One*, the aunt's boyfriend, Rick, is a hostile loser who ends up causing harm to everyone around him.

As usual, the vulnerable side tends to draw less attention from researchers, but a few additional studies have been done in recent years. In 2016, a group of psychologists and psychiatrists in Australia concluded that Vulnerable Dark Triad personality traits were associated with religious fundamentalist tendencies.[7] Following that in 2017, University of South Florida researchers investigated dark and vulnerable traits among 500 criminal offenders.[8] They found that vulnerable traits seemed to be particularly relevant for impulsive property crimes, such as theft and robbery, as well as drug offenses. Ultimately, the researchers said, future studies could indicate whether dark traits come together as expected to predict high-risk criminal behaviors. As mentioned above, this research can be tough to untangle from other factors that contribute to criminal acts, including socioeconomic factors and social pressures, but it remains an interesting area for future questions.

THE LIGHT TRIAD

Although researching dark personalities, patterns, thoughts, and feelings can deepen understanding about the darker side of human nature, researchers thought work should be done on the lighter side of human nature, too. In 2019, this idea of a "light," or positive, triad popped up in conversations at the University of Pennsylvania in Philadelphia. My friend and colleague Scott Barry Kaufman, who wrote about this in March 2019, has a more optimistic take on psychology and the human experience and developed the Light Triad to highlight the opposite of narcissism and psychopathy.

Importantly, the Light Triad is not a reverse-scored version of the Dark Triad. Instead, the goal was to step back and create a model of positive traits. The result contains three positive factors or traits. The first, *faith in humanity*, captures the belief that people are generally good and worthy of trust. Someone who has high faith in humanity will enter most situations with the expectation that others are well intentioned and reasonable. The next factor, *humanism*, celebrates the best in humanity. This means appreciating the successes and creations of others, which might be seen in great art or great social achievements such as a reduction in maternal mortality. The third factor, *Kantianism*, is named for the philosopher Immanuel Kant and suggests a preference for integrity and honesty over charade, charm, or manipulativeness.

Kaufman, now at Columbia University, created and posted a 12-item Light Triad Scale online, which is his "first draft measure of a loving and beneficent orientation toward others."[9] In other words, this measures our "everyday saints." In four tests with more than fifteen hundred people, he's found reliability and validity with the scale, and noted that it predicts life satisfaction, growth orientation, and self-transcendence among those who score high. They also tend to show humility, be intellectually curious, demonstrate tolerance of other perspectives, and show a low need for power over others.

Since the scale is brand-new, little research backs it up, but it is promising because it captures an active form of lightness. Researchers have debated for decades what the opposite of narcissism might be, particularly when it comes to humility or submission. In general, humility is seen as a positive trait in successful people, and submissiveness is seen as a negative in Western societies that praise individualism and freedom or a positive in relation to service-oriented behavior. The Light Triad factors, especially humanism, match up with the humility that celebrates human achievement and success without bitterness and jealousy. Plus, the Kantianism trait highlights authenticity and integrity, and faith in humanity relies on trust. In a sense, the active practice of these lighter traits could potentially combat narcissism. Faith in humanity combats mistrust, humanism combats misanthropy and exploitative behavior, and Kantianism combats an inflated self-image to replace it with a more secure and authentic one. The Light Triad figure shows some of the qualities that relate to the three factors and how researchers are trying to measure this new concept.

The Light Triad

Humanism
"I tend to treat other people as valuable."

Faith in Humanity
"I tend to see the best in people."

Kantianism
"I prefer honesty over charm."

The Energized Triad

Grandiose Narcissism

Hypomania   Boldness

THE ENERGIZED TRIAD

Even newer than the Light Triad, a fourth triad of traits that often pop up together in discussions of grandiose narcissism, especially in the world of leadership, is what I'm calling the Energized Triad. These are traits that share the core of agentic extraversion, which is the aspect of extraversion that includes reward-seeking, ambition, and drive. It is a bit like personality jet fuel.

Grandiose narcissism mixes this core energy with antagonism, but if antagonism is removed and self-esteem is added, it results in *boldness*, or what academics call fearless dominance. Boldness sounds healthier than grandiose narcissism, and it seems to be at the individual level. At the cultural level, boldness leads to change, and that can be good or bad depending on the perspective. In the scientific field, society often admires the boldness of past researchers, such as famous scientist Jonas Salk who injected himself with his own vaccines, but in everyday life, science rewards plodding caution. Boldness is included in some models of psychopathy, but it remains a controversial position.

On the other corner of the triad, *hypomania* is a personality trait associated with a low (*hypo*) level of mania. As mentioned in a previous chapter, one way to understand this is somebody who doesn't have full-blown mania or a manic disorder but a relatively low level of persistent mania over time. Just like narcissism can be both a trait and an aspect of narcissistic personality disorder, hypomania can as well. Hypomania and grandiose narcissism share that core of agentic extraversion and drive, sometimes including elevated frustration and hostility when hypomanic individuals struggle to make the world work as quickly as they do. The Marvel character Iron Man, the alter ego of Tony Stark, is a good example of grandiose narcissism with hypomania.

Hypomanic extraversion and drive can look like grandiosity because, in a way, it is a form of grandiosity. Entrepreneurs may say their new idea will revolutionize the world, be a game-changer, or at least make them rich. Even if it rarely works out, they convince themselves that their project or idea will have a widespread effect. The difference between this and grandiosity is that hypomania isn't concerned with taking others down or beating them. Instead, the drive is related to the idea, not the person. Even if progress toward the goal means taking down others, the motivation comes from the project rather than a sense of status or superiority.

Overall, this energy can be a positive, and society is often drawn to energetic and exciting individuals. The biggest risk and challenge can happen when this type of energy is attached to destructive traits such as antagonism. In a military analogy, antagonism is the warhead and energy is the rocket fuel. This triad is so new that we don't have any research to date to back it up, but I'm interested in exploring it in the future.

NERD HERD: CREATING NEW SCALES

There is a constant balance in personality measures between "If it ain't broke, don't fix it" and creating a scale built on the latest psychometric properties. The longer a scale is used, the more researchers understand its properties, validity, and reliability. For example, researchers will test the subfactors of a scale in hundreds of different samples over the years. During that process, the scale will improve, with some items dropped and some wording tweaked. Based on the revisions, academics can predict correlations between scales remarkably well.

Sometimes, though, a psychological trait might not have a measure— or not a very good one. In that case, researchers might build a scale and then test it for incremental validity to see if it works incrementally better than the available tools. Experts in the field toss it back and forth, questioning if the concept is actually new or built on a previous scale that still works well.

As an example, consider the case of the Grit Scale, created by psychologist Angela Duckworth, who wrote about it in her bestselling book *Grit: The Power of Passion and Perseverance*. Her TED Talk on grit is one of the most viewed. The Grit Scale captures an important trait in what determines success versus adversity, especially for long-term goals. However, as several researchers reported in a 2017 meta-analysis, grit turns out to be a variant of the Big Five trait of conscientiousness—but with a cooler name. That doesn't mean there is anything wrong with the Grit Scale, and in fact, it means the scale was well built, but it is redundant in some ways. My entitlement scale is similar in that it is well explained by low agreeableness.

INSIDE SCOOP: DEVELOPING THE ENERGIZED TRIAD

The Energized Triad is so new that we have little research on it, but I can provide some insight because a student at the University of Georgia, Lane

Siedor, sparked the idea behind it. As part of her research, Siedor became interested in hypomanic leadership, which is also extremely understudied, but it fits with the traits of fearless dominance and boldness.

In a study published in *Current Psychology* in 2016, Siedor looked at the relationship between narcissism and hypomania, specifically the grandiose and vulnerable sides of narcissism and the three dimensions of hypomania—social vitality, mood volatility, and excitement—as they relate to impulsivity and experiences.[10] As anticipated, grandiose narcissism and hypomania shared similar components of social vitality, and to some extent, excitement. Vulnerable narcissism was more related to the mood volatility.

That began the conversation around energy and links among the Energized Triad. Future research could shift toward either the positive, in the case of revolutionary entrepreneurs, or the negative, in the case of antagonistic leaders, whom we discuss in chapter 8.

II

OBSERVING NARCISSISM IN THE WORLD AROUND YOU

CHAPTER 7

Relationships and Narcissism

A h, love. Many people wait for their soul mate to show up at a bar and pick them up, using the perfect conversation starter and saying everything they want to hear. Well, someone just might do that—if that person is a narcissist. If you're like me, you may find this one of the most fascinating aspects of narcissism. In fact, I was so intrigued by the ideas and questions about narcissism in romantic relationships that I wrote my dissertation on it, and eventually, I also wrote the book *When You Love a Man Who Loves Himself*, which explains why narcissistic men seem like the ultimate catch—at first.

As I studied narcissism and relationships in graduate school, I came across different versions of the story of Narcissus, which ended up in many of my papers. You may be familiar with the Greek or Roman myths, which center around the idea of a beautiful young man who wanders the world looking for the perfect partner. Many fall in love with him, but he rejects them. A wood nymph named Echo falls for him, but he pushes her away and tells her not to disturb him. In despair, she roams the woods for the rest of her life and fades away until all that remains is her echoing sound.

Nemesis, the goddess of revenge, punishes Narcissus by leading him to a pool, where he ends up falling in love with his own reflection and ultimately dies alone. He loses himself by forsaking the love of others, and his own self-love becomes his demise. This old tale can be interpreted in many ways, but ultimately, we see the clear illustration of how an impairing amount of narcissism can affect relationships, as well as the narcissist.

Over time, research on narcissism in relationships has flourished, and the most recent research has found that narcissists are pretty great dates at first. The traits that make people attractive to date are different from the traits that make people caring and committed partners. In general, humans often look for confidence and an outgoing personality, which can be elements of narcissism. Nobody lines up to get into a relationship with a narcissist, and nobody includes "in search of a self-absorbed jerk" on dating apps. In most cases, we don't like self-centered people once we get to know them. At the beginning, though, many of us are attracted to narcissistic qualities in partners until they have problems with commitment and mutual respect.

This idea applies to more than romantic relationships, of course. We gravitate toward outgoing and confident friends, coworkers, and family members as well. As a new relationship develops, though, it's important to look for the signs of narcissism and to understand how narcissism works in relationships, what's in it for the narcissist, and the long-term consequences of narcissism. The process of narcissistic self-enhancement or self-regulation, using other people to maintain the narcissist's positive self-image, make relationships work to the narcissist's advantage.

A THIRTY-THOUSAND-FOOT VIEW OF RELATIONSHIPS

It's nice to have a high-level view of narcissism to understand relationships, and for this, the Trifurcated Model comes in handy. At its core, a high level of antagonism exists that can reveal itself in different ways, including as dominance, superiority, and arrogance. This might involve bragging, showing off, or entitlement. Outwardly, grandiose narcissists demand respect and special treatment. Internally, vulnerable narcissists may sit and stew about what they deserve. Both types may use bullying, manipulativeness, and mistrust to reach their goals.

In essence, all relationships with narcissists involve some aspect of the core ingredients of narcissism, though the traits may present in different ways. Grandiose people may use extraversion to carry this dark aspect of narcissism in a way that seems positive, particularly through networking, gregariousness, interpersonal charm, and the ability to build broad but shallow social networks. Vulnerable people tend to rely on neuroticism, which comes across as neediness, reactivity, or fragility.

Looking at narcissism in these two pieces (grandiose and vulnerable) can help us understand the conflicts that always come up in relationships with narcissists. Grandiose dynamics tend to have a mix of good and bad relationship behaviors, and vulnerable dynamics lean toward bad and sad. The following figure shows how these qualities merge and diverge. Grandiose narcissism contains positive aspects that are helpful for starting relationships, such as social boldness, confidence, and large social networks, but it also includes negative aspects that push away relationships, such as entitlement, manipulativeness, and arrogance.

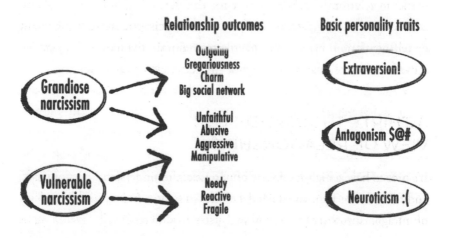

As an example, in the movie *Crazy Rich Asians*, the character Bernard Tai is a classic grandiose narcissist. Played by Jimmy O. Yang, who is best known for his role as Jian-Yang in the HBO series *Silicon Valley*, he is highly extraverted and has a broad social network with multiple shallow relationships. He's the party boy who plans an over-the-top bachelor party that makes him the center of attention and annoys the groom-to-be. Bernard is highly antagonistic, obnoxious, and rich. He tells the groom that the bride doesn't belong in their wealthy world, and he thinks his friends should only associate with and date others of equal social status.

As an everyday juxtaposition, helicopter parents who always hover around their kids and demand attention could be classic vulnerable narcissists. Although the line between a supportive parent and a needy parent can blur, you know the ones who live vicariously through their children, demand special exceptions, and require affirmation as the "best" parent that can be. They express antagonism but in a subtle form with a sense of entitlement and suspicion of others, alongside insecurity and fragility. They think more about fantasy and rage than action.

HOW DO NARCISSISTS BENEFIT FROM RELATIONSHIPS?

In typical everyday relationships, all humans look for status, esteem, and positivity. That's normal. With narcissism, however, the focus is on enhancement, and this is where the "sex, status, and stuff" becomes relevant. A narcissist wants a relationship with someone who can boost self-esteem through high status, physical attraction, or money. Essentially, the narcissist's partner is a tool for inflating the narcissist's ego. For instance, dating someone who is famous or successful makes the narcissist look good by association. In addition, sleeping with someone attractive, or simply sleeping with as many people as possible, makes the narcissist feel powerful and appealing. Being in a relationship with someone who has money makes the narcissist look wealthy and able to afford jewelry or an invitation to an exclusive party.

As the relationship progresses, though, narcissists place less focus on commitment, compassion, or connection. This doesn't mean that people who are narcissistic don't want commitment or that they don't see that connection is missing, but it's not as much of a priority. In reality, narcissists want to be loved, but they're not as interested in loving back or reciprocal emotional support. To get what they want out of relationships, narcissists use four strategies to meet their needs, as illustrated in table 7.1.

Table 7.1: Relationship Strategies

SELF-REGULATION	EXAMPLES
Association	Trophy spouse Celebrity friends
Admiration	Posse Admiring/adoring spouse
Domination	Bullying/aggression Manipulativeness Violence
Consolation	Comfort-seeking Reassurance of worth

The first strategy that is commonly used in relationships, especially among grandiose narcissists, is *association*. The idea is to build esteem or social status by being in a relationship, whether with a romantic partner, friend, or coworker, that benefits them. Even a distant relationship can serve a purpose, such as being friends with a friend who knows Beyoncé. In common culture, the term *trophy wife* or *trophy spouse* is often used to describe someone who is used in a relationship as a way to boost self-esteem rather than build a meaningful partnership.

My own dissertation looked at this, testing the idea that narcissistic individuals are more likely to use association to get status in relationships, and they like partners who get them that status. The idea was to link up personality, relationships, and self-regulation to show how they work together in narcissists' romantic pursuits. Attraction was a good first step, and my model suggested that narcissists are attracted to people who admire them and less attracted to those who want emotional intimacy. Five subsequent studies supported this idea from my dissertation, which was published in the *Journal of Personality and Social Psychology* back in 1999.[1] My dissertation concluded that, overall, narcissists prefer more self-oriented qualities in an "ideal partner," and their romantic attraction comes from their strategy of enhancing self-esteem.

Since then, studies of dating relationships have shown a small correlation between grandiose narcissism and their partner choices as well—that is, people who are narcissistic tend to have partners who are also a little narcissistic. If two people are shallow, materialistic, and attention-seeking, they're both looking to meet those needs. Together, this works well and can be effective. The problem occurs, of course, when one partner isn't narcissistic and seeks commitment in addition to attractiveness and excitement in a new relationship. The mismatch in interests sparks issues.

The second strategy for finding status or esteem in relationships is *admiration*. Again, most humans seek admiration, but it's particularly true for narcissists, and it can happen in a variety of ways. Take a trip to Washington, DC, and watch a congressman walk down the street followed by a pack of young adults. They look like ducklings. He's receiving a great deal of attention because he has power. At the same time, his attention needs and status needs are being met, and his followers' esteem needs are being met because they're associated with a congressman, even if momentarily. Outside of the posses that surround politicians and celebrities, it's nice to be admired in close relationships, particularly by an adoring partner and especially if you're narcissistic. This is most relevant if the partner is high in status. Narcissistic individuals don't want low-status "losers" to admire them. Instead, it's important for narcissists to feel they're receiving value.

Another strategy for esteem, albeit more negative, is *domination*. This can come across as bullying or even abuse and can translate into physical, emotional, or mental domination. In the research world, narcissistic abuse in relationships comes from the core feature of antagonism, regardless of grandiosity or vulnerability. That antagonism predicts aggression when people are threatened. In fact, it predicts aggression even when they're not, but threat is a big trigger, including being rejected, being told they're not good enough, or being told they can't do what they want. In a 2018 meta-analysis, Courtland Hyatt at the University of Georgia found that narcissism and similar dark traits, such as antagonism and psychopathy, predicted aggression.[2] The core trait of antagonism seems to be the key—at least in a lab setting. What we find in these studies is that narcissists use control tactics to manipulate another person. *Game of Thrones* is filled with examples of psychopathic individuals in relationships, where the level of dominance and deep control is an extreme form of narcissism.

In several studies about sexual assault published in 2013, Brad Bushman and colleagues at Ohio State University found that narcissistic reactance is linked to sexual coercion.[3] Notably, they saw that narcissism correlated with rape-supportive beliefs and a lack of empathy for rape victims. They also found that narcissists enjoyed (more than other men) film depictions of consensual, affectionate activity followed by rape and were more punitive of a female colleague who refused to read a sexually arousing passage aloud to them. Studies in subsequent years at other colleges around the country concluded that narcissistic traits such as entitlement and a willingness to exploit others were associated with sexual aggression, and college men who had higher scores on narcissism scales were more likely to be sexually aggressive, especially when alcohol and drugs were involved.

The final strategy to extract esteem, which isn't considered as much with narcissism, is *consolation*. Some narcissistic people in relationships, particularly vulnerable ones, often need their partners to console them, make them feel like they're not rejected, and reassure them that they're worthy of affection. Pennsylvania State University researchers Kelly Dickinson and Aaron Pincus have found that vulnerable narcissists report high interpersonal distress and greater domineering, vindictive, and cold relationship issues.[4] Their attachment styles reflect negative self-representations based on fear and abandonment. Similarly, Israeli psychologists Avi Besser and Beatriz Priel at Ben-Gurion University noted in a 2010 study that vulnerable narcissists are sensitive to negative interpersonal interactions that involve rejection or shaming.[5]

THE ATTRACTIVENESS OF NARCISSISM AND PHYSICAL APPEARANCE

A foundational question about narcissism, going back to the Greek myth of Narcissus, is whether narcissists are attractive. Tied to this are the questions of whether narcissists believe they're attractive when they're not and whether they make up for unattractiveness by being boastful. Researchers have investigated these questions since the 1990s, when the first studies at Michigan State University found that narcissists had more favorable body images.[6] Another study, at the University of North Texas, found they overestimated their own intelligence as well.[7] Yet another study, by University of California researchers, concluded that narcissists overestimated their performance, and when they watched it on videotape, their self-admiration increased even more.[8] Grandiose people, in particular, are more likely to rate their attractiveness higher on a scale by a point or two. In fact, the general population does this. When I ask my undergraduate psychology students to rate themselves on a 10-point scale, the class average is around 7. In reality, this isn't statistically likely. While most people overestimate, narcissists do so even more.

When researchers look at the specifics, though, an interesting story emerges. When pairing the ratings from narcissists with the ratings by peers and experts, some studies show that pictures of narcissists are rated slightly higher. In a 2010 meta-analysis by Nicolas Holtzman and Michael Strube at Washington University, narcissism and attractiveness were found to be related.[9] This sparked interest, and psychologists began to wonder why and how people who are narcissistic would be more attractive. Evolutionarily, are those who tend to be more exploitative and manipulative born with more attractive features that allow them to get away with it? That didn't seem likely.

Personality scientists developed another explanation related to self-regulation, which posed that narcissists put more effort into their looks since they care about appearance, and that seems to accurately reflect what's happening. Holtzman did another study—one of my favorites—in 2012 on narcissism and attractiveness that directed participants to take a photo of themselves in a neutral posture, dressed just as they were as they came into the lab.[10] Then he instructed them to take photos with their hair pulled back, makeup removed if women, facial hair shaved if men, and gave them neutral smocks to wear. As you can imagine, the first rating indicates how the person appears during everyday interactions, and the second rating indicates the person's basic physical appearance as stripped away as possible in a lab setting. Obviously, aspects such as plastic surgery can't be removed, but for the most part, this does the trick for a study. Then researchers calculated a score called "effective adornment" for the first image, which measures the difference between the ratings. Those who score a 5 with basic physical appearance but a 7 with makeup, facial hair, and attractive clothing, for example, are effectively adorning themselves.

Interestingly, narcissism and the Dark Triad predicted this effective adornment. These study participants put more effort into appearing attractive, and not only do they expend more effort when grooming and dressing, they also seem to be quite effective at it. This conclusion comes with a caveat, of course. I don't want to give the false impression that those who attend to their appearance are narcissistic or that doing so is bad. Instead, what I'm saying is that people who spend time on their appearance and look confident are better liked, and people who are narcissistic do this to be liked. It's a strategy that works for people in general, so those who are narcissistic most likely adapted the strategy effectively to meet their need for attention.

THE ATTRACTIVENESS OF NARCISSISM AND THIN SLICES

Beyond physical appearance, personality scientists have been interested in narcissists' attractiveness during initial interactions. To study this, my colleagues use a technique called "thin slices," where they film participants for brief thirty-second or sixty-second clips to analyze how people introduce themselves and talk about themselves. Other studies have filmed people making introductions in the real world, and they showed similar results. What they find, particularly with grandiose narcissists, is that other people like them during first meetings. For the most part, narcissists seem attractive, and this matches their appearance. Plus, they don't immediately display a large amount of arrogance, and they certainly don't wear hoodies that say, "I'm a narcissistic jerk, and I'm going to sleep with your sister." They don't come across that way.

One of my favorite studies on this, by Mitja Back and colleagues in Germany, indicates that a number of factors are linked to narcissists' initial attractiveness in these thin slices.[11] For one, their appearance is flashy and intriguing—think of colorful dresses and charming facial expressions. They come across as engaged and likable, not grumpy. Their body movements are also more self-assured, so their posture is straighter, and they have more dominant body language, so they exhibit more expansive body gestures. It makes sense that someone who is well-groomed, poised, and energetic is attractive. Nonromantic relationships work the same way, and the "thin slices" research shows this as well. Although friendships and coworker relationships are often less extreme and less saturated with emotion than romantic relationships, narcissists are still appealing because they're likable, extraverted, and confident.

What doesn't show initially is the antagonism and neuroticism, which won't make an appearance until the relationship progresses. Over time, the façade of likability drops, and narcissists become dislikable. In a 2015 study, people took the narcissistic personality inventory and then met in groups during a period of several weeks.[12] The impressions of the narcissists shifted from positive in the first meeting to negative rather quickly. Narcissists are built for shallow, lukewarm, and extraverted relationships. They can leave one relationship or friendship group and move to the next easily, but they often leave others emotionally drained. With family, the challenges are much tougher. It is hard to leave family and move on, and narcissistic family members often can charm and manipulate others outside (and even inside) the family, which can lead to exhaustion and strained relationships. Table 7.2 shows several narcissistic relationship strategies with examples of each.

Table 7.2: Relationship Strategies of Narcissists

STRATEGY	EXAMPLES
Effective adornment	Hair and makeup
Flashy and neat dress	Stylish Colorful
Charming facial expression	Self-assured Upbeat
Self-assured body movement	Straight posture Dominant behaviors

THE ATTRACTIVENESS OF NARCISSISM AND HOMOPHILY

When it comes to the initial attraction stage in a relationship, I'm often asked if anyone has a predisposition for falling in love with a narcissist. Some have talked about empathic people, or those who are highly aware of others' emotions and even feel them, and whether they are drawn to narcissists. Others tend to say that enablers end up with narcissistic spouses. In both cases, studies haven't found evidence that this is true. It certainly happens sometimes, but there doesn't seem to be a dominant pattern that we have been able to detect in research.

The other question that comes up when talking about narcissism and relationships is the idea of "like attracting like." As the saying goes, "Birds of a feather flock together," and researchers have wondered whether this "homophily" applies to narcissists attracting others like them. With grandiose narcissists, as several of our studies showed, there's a small correlation between partners on their narcissism levels.[13] This does not mean that if you are in a relationship with a narcissist that you are one, just that there is a small chance of matching.

For example, in a 2015 study, Michael Grosz and colleagues in Germany and the Netherlands found that couples preferred romantic partners with a similar level of narcissism.[14] Social psychology research on attraction may explain why. The similarity-attraction hypothesis suggests that people like others who share similar political, religious, and value beliefs, which makes relationships easier. People with the same beliefs tend to get along and have discussions without conflict. In the case of narcissism, similar attitudes about materialism, public displays of worth, and showing off could be mutually admired. Extraversion and confidence likely bring narcissistic people together as well.

Even research on nonhuman primates such as macaque monkeys shows that those who tend to be similar, especially socially, pair up and form relationships over time. With grandiose narcissists in particular, this basic sociability likely lends a hand in forming pairs. That said, homophily remains a major question for future research as personality scientists dig deeper into these theories, especially since it isn't a strong signal in every relationship. As you can imagine, this type of attraction isn't always the case, and I certainly don't want those who are in relationships with narcissists to believe that they are also narcissists, or on the other hand with empaths, that they "deserve it" in some way because they are too nice or caring. That's like blaming a deer for being eaten by a cougar: you can't say the deer "should have known" or should have been faster. With narcissists, we can't always see the red flags of behavior until much later in a relationship.

THE UNATTRACTIVENESS OF NARCISSISM

Now it's time to dig into the downsides of narcissism in relationships, which are numerous and have been documented thoroughly. Based on the Trifurcated Model, which addresses both grandiose and vulnerable narcissism, these downsides can differ dramatically and lead to different problems that appear during different moments in a relationship. As expected, the downsides deal with changes in extraversion, antagonism, and neuroticism as a narcissist moves through a relationship.

Agentic extraversion, which is generally seen as a positive trait to have at the beginning of a relationship, tends to be short-lived. Narcissists love the honeymoon period that's filled with excitement, passion, and confidence, but we all know it doesn't last forever. Part of that inevitable boredom and routine comes from self-expansion, which occurs as people get to know others and incorporate aspects of those people into their lives. For example, if someone starts a relationship with an attorney, the beginning of the relationship is likely filled with interesting stories about the law and court cases, and that learning leads to excitement. Over time, however, that feeling wears off. Even though it may still be interesting to talk about the day-to-day work, that excitement is replaced with familiarity and comfortable conversation.

To explain this concept to my undergraduate psychology students, I use the example of the *Twilight* series because it captures the idea of being attracted to someone who is interesting and unique. The protagonist meets a vampire who is cool, glows in the sun, and sparkles like a diamond. This sounds exciting. After some time, though, it might suck. You can't take your vampire boyfriend out to eat with friends without drawing attention, you can't go to the beach in the sun with the vampire—only hang out at dark clubs and in the woods—and the vampire is somewhat "emo." The relationship that started as an exciting adventure transitions into a predictable routine. The same happens in any relationship, but with narcissists, the routine can be filled with manipulation and abuse.

In addition, the antagonism that brings on callousness, low agreeableness, and entitlement causes problems for long-term relationships with narcissists. Those who feel they deserve special treatment may feel they're not receiving enough attention or praise, especially over time. Pair this with the fact that everyday married people tend to overestimate how much they do and underestimate how much their partner does. In normal relationships, spouses see themselves take out the trash and do the dishes, but they likely don't pay as much attention when their partner does, which can interfere with a sense of fairness in the relationship. This regular phenomenon is exacerbated in relationships with narcissists, who feel constantly mistreated, underappreciated, and unacknowledged.

Beyond that, antagonism also seems to be responsible for narcissistic aggression, as we learned from Courtland Hyatt's meta-analysis mentioned above. In many lab studies, aggression is measured with tools such as noise blasts and electric shocks. In a typical setup, a participant is told they're competing with another participant in another room, who isn't actually there (a "confederate" of the experimenter, as they are called). They're instructed to administer shocks to the confederate based on the study's criteria, and they receive shocks in return. The study team measures the intensity of the shocks as a physical measure of aggression.

These studies have shown that narcissists are more willing to shock others or give them loud noise blasts after they're aggressed against.

This research, however, is not without its faults, especially when it comes to how aggression is measured in a lab setting. People have been slippery about how to do it, myself included, so it's important to look at real-world narcissism and aggression. Fortunately, several recent studies, including one in Italy in 2018, one in the US in 2018, and one in the UK in 2018, have measured narcissism and personality scales in prison settings.[15] Both studies found that narcissism predicts physical aggression, both criminally and inside prison systems. It doesn't mean every narcissistic person commits crimes or causes violence—in fact, most people never commit a violent crime—but those who do tend to exhibit higher levels of narcissism. This can be particularly harmful in relationships.

The final downside to narcissism in relationships is neuroticism, which comes out as neediness and relational insecurity. Studies show that vulnerable narcissism, in particular, is associated with insecure attachment styles, and vulnerable narcissists tend to need a partner who reassures them, makes them feel accepted, or ensures that they are connected in the relationship. This experience of being with a partner who is needy is not pleasant, especially as it develops into a long-term relationship. In the short-term, providing this comfort can make partners feel good about themselves because they're helping someone, stabilizing that person, and reinforcing their own idea that they matter. In the long-term, however, this pressure becomes exhausting because the partner exists to establish someone else's self-esteem, and this builds as both partners realize they don't like being in a relationship with the other person anymore. Plus, this neuroticism lends itself to depression, aggression, and hostility. It's often emotional, reactive, and impulsive, which can lead to snappy remarks and quick arguments.

As part of the downsides, I'm often asked about "love bombing" and whether narcissists have a tendency to overload you with affection and then ghost you once they're bored. Although research shows that narcissists tend to be more positive and attractive during the initial phase of a relationship, researchers haven't found any good evidence to back up the idea of love bombs in particular. There's a possibility that this behavior could be related to vulnerable narcissism and the tendency to seek love and attention through a sense of neediness and entitlement. Since there are few studies around this currently, however, we can't say for sure.

Similarly, researchers haven't yet studied the links between narcissism and "gaslighting," or the act of manipulating someone into questioning their sanity and memory by sowing seeds of doubt about a memory or feeling. An example could be your significant other calling you flirtatious and disloyal, when in fact, they're the one who is cheating. Since this form of control can be common among narcissistic abusers and cult leaders, for instance, the research may show that narcissism is indeed related. For now, the manipulation tactic has been discussed more in the philosophical literature rather than psychology, but I know of several students who are diving into this concept now, which should bring about some interesting results and conversations in the next few years.

NARCISSISTIC RELATIONSHIP PATTERNS

Overall, relationships with narcissists follow different patterns because of the mixture of likability, antagonism, and vulnerability that different people express. A 2014 study of narcissistic friendships looked at a Polish academy, where teams worked together on projects for extended periods of time, much like the team-based models used in some US business schools.[16] The group members were instructed to rate whether they liked or disliked their peers, and not surprisingly, both types of narcissists were disliked by other group members. Grandiose narcissists received a larger number of "dislikes" from their peers, and vulnerable narcissists received fewer "likes" from their peers. The study authors concluded that both forms of narcissism were predictors of unpopularity in groups.

The best way I've found to describe this transition in likability in relationships is what I call the "chocolate cake model." Based on the research at the time, I included an early version of this model in my 2005 book *When You Love a Man Who Loves Himself*, which focuses on grandiose narcissists and relationships. Under the chocolate cake model, if presented with two choices—say, a piece of chocolate cake or a healthy salad with chicken—most people will choose the attractive chocolate cake, and they'll do this for logical reasons. The chocolate cake looks better, tastes better, and feels better in the moment. The problem is this benefit only lasts in the short-term when enjoyed.

An hour later, however, the chocolate cake doesn't feel quite as good. For some, their stomach may hurt. For others, eating the cake doesn't equate with being healthy. For most, the sugar boost leads to a sugar crash. Although the choice to eat chocolate was rational, it's only rational in the short-term. This is true for many other choices that first seem appealing and then fall apart later, such as drugs, sex, and other addictions.

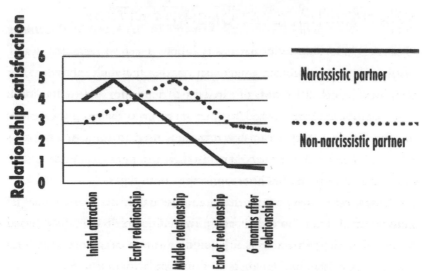

Chocolate Cake Model

— 129 —

On the other hand, choosing to eat the healthy option likely provides a long-term benefit. At first, it may not taste as great, especially when thinking about the decadent, guilty-pleasure option. But an hour later, people feel fine and maybe even healthy. Even the next day, some might believe, "I'm a good person. I eat healthy food. I take care of myself. I didn't get the sugar rush from the chocolate cake, but the next day, I'm always happy." With this model, it's easier to see that dating people who are narcissistic, especially grandiose ones, fulfills the short-term excitement but leads to long-term disappointment.

Studies have confirmed the chocolate cake idea, to some extent. In 2002, we asked people to graph their relationships over time with narcissistic and non-narcissistic partners.[17] We found that narcissistic relationships usually start with a big rush of satisfaction and then end with a full-on collapse. With non-narcissists, the initial rush doesn't exist, but satisfaction grows over time—and doesn't end in a crash.

Since then, psychologists' understanding of narcissism has changed to include the Trifurcated Model and vulnerable narcissism as well, which has in turn changed views about narcissistic relationship patterns. To incorporate this, researchers broke down narcissistic characteristics in relationships into the more agentic extraverted side, called *admiration*, and the more antagonistic side, called *rivalry*. In 2014, a team of German psychologists looked at this juxtaposition between short-term dating and long-term relationships, surmising that narcissists switch motives along the way.[18] At first, they thought, narcissists search for admiration from a new significant other. Once that person is "captured" and the goal is attained, however, they need a new one. Now they continue to build self-worth through rivalry, or they put down their partner to feel better about themselves. Similar studies have found the same.

What these studies reveal is that the more agentic extraverted piece in relationships is attractive at the beginning and then falls over time, but it doesn't become unattractive at any point. It's never negatively related to relationship satisfaction. It simply moves from being positive to neutral.

The antagonism, on the other hand, starts off as slightly negative and gets worse over time. An additional possibility is to measure the change in neuroticism as well. Nobody has studied this formally, as far as I know, but researchers might predict that more neuroticism and more vulnerable narcissism wouldn't be attractive to begin with, which would lead to an unsatisfying relationship quickly.

The final piece of the puzzle, which hasn't yet been tested since I proposed it a decade ago, is the extent that narcissistic relationships may have a negative aftereffect. Specifically, they may lead to confusion and a drop in confidence in the non-narcissist partner. Grandiose narcissists are more likely to be extraverted and more likely to cheat, and although this may not necessarily make them antagonistic toward a partner or spouse, it makes them unfaithful and untrustworthy. Even when the partner believes the narcissist is smart, engaging, and attractive, and that the relationship is decent, in the end, the relationship may prove troubling. After these relationships are over, non-narcissistic partners may question the relationship and themselves, wondering what they did, how they went wrong, and what they could have done differently. They may even believe they weren't attractive or engaging enough to keep their partner's attention. Of course, this isn't the case. Narcissists who express high interest in sexual novelty-seeking are, by definition, high in sexual novelty-seeking, which means no person or relationship can satisfy them.

Long-term ripple effects may occur as well. Abusive or violent relationships in particular may lead to post-traumatic stress disorder. When people in these relationships get out of them, they're typically relieved, but they also wonder how they "allowed" the relationship to happen in the first place or why they were "so stupid" to stay in it. With more grandiose narcissists, even if someone understands how or why they were attracted, the remaining questions may center around why they couldn't keep it going. This is where the most long-term damage can be done, and it's a big area that psychologists need to study next.

These patterns apply to relationships outside the romantic realm as well. Grandiose relationships tend to rise and fall until they flatline, and vulnerable relationships tend to grow worse until they fail. What hasn't been studied outside of romantic relationships, however, is the core issue of "dealing with it." Many people deal with narcissistic friends, relatives, bosses, coworkers, and others, and they don't address this, simply stating that their personality is the "way they are."

Referencing the Bernard Tai character in the movie *Crazy Rich Asians* again, this grandiose narcissist is self-centered and annoying but also entertaining. For the bachelor party scene, he carts everyone by helicopter to a giant tanker, where he set up an extravagant celebration. He's shooting machine guns and focusing entirely on himself, not the groom or anyone else—yet, to the viewer, it's a great party. The other characters put up with him and accept him as a friend, but they don't expect much from him in terms of closeness or putting their needs over his. Relationships like these likely occur, in my opinion, because human relationships don't solely rely on personality. We choose our friends to some extent, but often, our friendships come from the circumstances and groups we're around, such as college classmates or coworkers who are nearby on a daily basis. In the end, we all may end up with narcissistic friends or partners at some point, and sometimes we cut ties with those people, but other times, we simply cope.

NERD HERD: DARK INTELLIGENCE AND RELATIONSHIPS

One idea often bandied about when it comes to relationships is that dark traits are associated with intelligence. Think of it as the evil genius stereotype. People like to talk about this—and read about it in popular media—because the headlines are catchy. Consider the viral stories you've likely seen in recent years that claim people who curse are more intelligent.

However, few researchers have tested this idea by comparing dark traits with IQ. Even a 2013 meta-analysis by several US psychologists found little relation between the two.[19] In particular, researchers looked at general mental ability and the Dark Triad to determine if those with socially exploitative qualities tend to be more intelligent. Overall, mental ability had no consistent relation with any dark trait. The conclusion didn't support either the evil genius hypothesis or the compensatory hypothesis that less intelligent people compensate for their disadvantages by adopting manipulative behaviors.

INSIDE SCOOP: THE NARCISSISTIC EMPLOYEE

Narcissistic employees often come up as a huge issue because they can be likable and successful at certain aspects of their job. I often hear about this as the "rainmakers" who are kept onboard at a high level, simply because they get the work done. The cost of narcissistic employees, however, is counterproductive work behavior. Cue Steve Jobs. In numerous accounts, former employees praised his brilliance but dreaded his management style, saying he acted without thinking and with bad judgement, didn't give credit where credit was due, and immediately attacked new ideas—sometimes stealing them later as his own.

Organizational researchers have looked at this more closely than personality scientists have in recent years, and the results are interesting. A 2014 study indicates that narcissists struggle with interpersonal workplace relationships and act impulsively, which can cause those counterproductive work behaviors.[20] At the same time, the study authors say, narcissists may be useful in four areas: international management, social issues in management/corporate social responsibility, entrepreneurship, and negotiation, as long as it plays to their goals and self-esteem.

Leadership and Narcissism

CHAPTER 8

Leadership and Narcissism

When it comes to narcissism and leadership, we're all likely thinking the same thing: what's the latest news on Donald Trump? Throughout his time as president, psychologists and mental health experts have continued to disagree on whether the top leader of the United States could (and should) be diagnosed formally with narcissistic personality disorder. At the same time, they all seem to agree that he exhibits narcissistic traits and behaviors.

During Trump's first year in office, several Democrats asked psychiatrists at Yale University to create a panel to assess his mental health. Then nineteen legislators—all Democrats—cosponsored a bill to establish the Oversight Commission on Presidential Capacity Act. Under the Twenty-Fifth Amendment, the bill would give the legislative branch the ability to declare a president "unable to discharge the powers and duties of his office" and allow Congress to conduct a medical exam to determine whether he is temporarily or permanently impaired by a physical illness, mental illness, or substance abuse problem that prevents him from executing the duties associated with presidency. Created in April 2017, the bill was introduced to the House floor less than a month later and then referred to the Subcommittee on the Constitution and Civil Justice. It's still there, even though many more Democrats have signed their names to the bill, bringing the total to sixty-seven.

Clinically, some experts have offered formal diagnoses of narcissistic personality disorder, and others have commented on Trump's behavior and speech regarding impulsivity and paranoia. In *The Dangerous Case of Donald Trump*, a book released in 2017, twenty-seven psychiatrists and other mental health experts discuss his mental status and assert that he presents a danger to the nation and to Americans' mental health.[1] I wrote about this book and the Twenty-Fifth Amendment bill in a post for the website Medium, and my views remain the same.[2] I have little doubt that Trump is narcissistic, and although I believe his narcissism has both harmed and helped him, I don't believe it represents a clinical level of impairment. For instance, he has not overreacted to threats or promoted himself over others to the extent that I thought was possible. He has not been caught having affairs or stealing funds from the government. He was impeached exactly as the narcissism research predicted, and although that could be seen as a clinical manifestation of narcissism, it was partisan like Bill Clinton's impeachment, so it's hard to say. I have plenty of colleagues that disagree with me and see Trump as mentally ill, and I might be biased in that I expect leaders to be narcissistic.

Trump's narcissism was one of the inspirations for my dissertation on narcissism and romantic attraction (hint: trophy spouses) more than twenty years ago, but he is not unique in this personality trait as a leader. Narcissistic leaders have been around throughout history, including plenty of other US presidents, and narcissism can lead to both great benefits and costs during leadership. It is truly a double-edged sword.

Narcissism and leadership go together like picnics and ants. Leadership is a goal for narcissists because it means status, power, and attention. It means wealth, and it even means sex. Especially for men, leadership is a great way to gain the affection of—or simply to exploit—others for sex. Trump is now infamous for his comments on fame and female genitalia, but he is not alone. Bill Clinton derailed his presidency over his relationship with intern Monica Lewinsky, and former Democratic congressman Anthony Weiner lost his career twice, as well as being sentenced to jail time, for sexting minors. President John F. Kennedy was notorious for his affairs (and his boldness when commanding the PT-109 torpedo boat in the Pacific theater during World War II), and the even more narcissistic President Lyndon Johnson claimed that he had stumbled into more sex than JFK had gotten on purpose.

Since leadership is a complex process, and there are schools dedicated to its study, a short chapter on narcissism and leadership must chop it down to make sense of it. First, leadership is defined here as the ability to motivate and direct a group toward a goal, which can apply to an elementary school line leader or chief executive officer. Leadership, like love, is simple as a concept but complex in execution. Personality traits like narcissism play a big role in who we select as leaders and how those leaders perform.

To better study this in research, personality scientists look at leadership *emergence*, or the rise to leadership, and *effectiveness*, which occurs once someone is in power. Importantly, emergent leaders are not necessarily effective, and effective leaders do not always emerge. Beyond that, questions arise about leaders and the way they direct or transform organizations. Some leadership jobs are meant to keep the organizational ship sailing in the same direction, and others are about making big course corrections or swapping out engines midsail. Narcissistic leaders are better suited for the big changes.

NARCISSISTIC LEADERS AND EMERGENT LEADERSHIP

Emergent leadership happens when someone ascends into the position of leader in a group. This process can happen at all sorts of levels. In psychology research, study teams often group students together to "work on a project," and then at the end, ask who the leader is. Someone inevitably emerges as a leader. In fact, across animal studies, leadership emergence happens quickly, typically within minutes. Those who want it and are bold, whether monkeys, dogs, or humans, emerge quickly through displays of confidence and dominance.

This emergent leadership occurs in more civilized groups as well. In the military service academies, such as West Point or the Air Force, cadets are judged as leaders throughout the year as they work in their squad. Those data points can be used to consider emergent leadership, even though they happen over a semester or year in the academy.

At the broader career level, people rise to the level of CEO or become a political figure, congressional representative, or president. In those cases, emergent leadership happens over decades or a lifetime, but there's a constant process of upward progression through the system.

A multitude of qualities can contribute to someone emerging as a leader, of course, such as intelligence, height, and expertise, and a variety of factors motivate people to pursue leadership, including competence, status, power hunger, or a desire for change. Plenty of great leaders hope to change the world for the better, and they work hard to first rise to the position and then tackle the challenges of the role. Narcissists, on the other hand, are in it for the ego. They want the status boost, and any system that allows for status and power will be appealing to someone with narcissistic tendencies. Just like rock 'n' roll, they're not in it for the music, they're in it for the lifestyle.

The easiest way to observe or compare the profile of an emergent leader is to look at the five-factor model. With narcissism in particular, that means looking at three of those factors—extraversion, neuroticism, and antagonism. As it lines up with previous chapters, extraversion is related to grandiosity, neuroticism lines up with vulnerability, and antagonism matches with both.

Several studies that have investigated the Big Five traits and leadership suggest that vulnerable traits don't tend to do well. In several great meta-analyses, psychologist Tim Judge and colleagues observed that neuroticism isn't great for leadership.[3] People with high levels of neuroticism likely won't emerge as leaders nor be effective. In a high-threat environment, a neurotic leader may do well at detecting threats, but in general, those who are anxious or depressed won't deal well with the pressure of being in a leadership position. This means vulnerable narcissism won't predict leadership performance in a positive way. Although it might predict leadership in a negative way, the studies don't exist because the interest isn't there in the research community. Instead, the research has focused on major public figures such as Trump, Steve Jobs, General George Patton, and the classic Rockefellers.

Next on the list, researchers looked at agreeableness and found that effective leadership is based on agreeableness to some extent. However, those who rise to leadership aren't considered more agreeable than anyone else.

Extraversion turns out to be the trait that is positively associated with leadership and narcissism. Extraversion is associated with both leadership effectiveness and performance but primarily with emergence. High extraversion is the personality fuel for leadership emergence.

On the flip side, introversion doesn't tend to predict leadership emergence either, which makes sense since introverts aren't naturally drawn to these gregarious positions. This isn't always the case, of course, and it depends on how you define introversion. Susan Cain's 2012 book *Quiet*, for instance, speaks to the Western culture that misunderstands and undervalues the traits and capabilities of introverts.[4] In this case, her definition includes "openness to experience," which could provide an important link between introversion and an interest in leadership. Quiet creatives who exhibit openness, for instance, may be able to engage others through inspirational motivation. With traditional definitions of introversion in psychology labs, however, introversion predicts low levels of leadership emergence. Introverts simply aren't as interested or driven to obtain leadership positions.

Leaders who exhibit both types of narcissism may not do well either. Bob Hogan, a well-known personality psychologist and industrial psychologist, has said that this is the worst combination he sees when working with high-level executives. People who are highly narcissistic but also neurotic and vulnerable take slights easily and are immune to criticism. They go off the handle. They throw things. People who are power hungry but also have thin skins are a problem.

On the other hand, grandiose narcissists tend to do reasonably well. The combination of high extraversion and flat agreeableness matches with the personality traits for emergent leadership. This doesn't mean that anyone who wants to be a leader is going to be narcissistic. Rather, high extraversion shown by narcissists often obscures the low agreeableness, and the result can be leaders who are more callous or self-serving than you might want.

This same pattern occurs in formal assessment centers and leaderless group paradigms. Study teams give four executives or business students a working portfolio, for example, where they discuss a case for an hour. Then they watch who emerges as a leader. Even in assessment centers designed to select the best potential leaders, at least in our research, narcissists are more likely to step up as leaders.

As a result, narcissistic leaders emerge in all types of systems, including churches. In a 2014 study in Canada, grandiose narcissism was associated with larger congregations—and becoming heads of big churches.[5] Similarly in India, "god men," or proclaimed holy men, amass a large amount of control. Some of these people may indeed be holy men, and some may not, but the challenge is that the only people willing to claim that they are holy men are those who are incredibly narcissistic or those who are actually holy, and it can be tough for followers to gauge.

EMERGENT LEADERSHIP: DOMINANCE VERSUS PRESTIGE

Additional factors that spur leaders to emerge are dominance, prestige, and pride within a role. This always prompts me to think about General George Patton and his style of leadership. When I began working at the University of Georgia, I was enthralled by the stories that my colleague, an emeritus professor and social psychologist named Sid Rosen, told me about his days in the Tank Corps during World War II before he joined academia. Rosen was involved in the invasion of Italy and fought with Patton and General Omar Bradley, who succeeded Patton. When he told me that it was terrible to fight under Patton, I was surprised because the general seemed confident and sure of himself. He stood up alone against a German plane and had old pistols. He looked like a leader.

What I learned, though, was that serving under Patton meant dealing with a narcissistic general who put his needs before others. As Sid said, the US tanks were no match for the German tanks, so the corps would up-armor their tanks to fight. They'd add sandbags, barbed wire, and anything else they could find to make them sturdier. However, Patton told them to remove the up-armor because it made them look weak. From Sid's perspective, he was going to die so Patton could lead a good-looking crew.

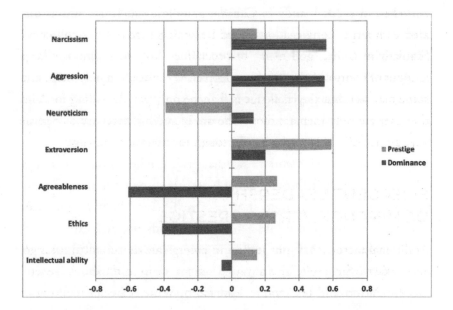

Bradley, however, was a different type of general. He focused on the troops. At least according to Sid, he cared about logistics, getting food to them, and making sure they survived. People don't hear about Bradley to the extent they hear about Patton, likely because Bradley wasn't quite as much of an egomaniac. At the same time, Bradley had a more successful career. Patton was eventually derailed and run out of his job. Both men made it to the top of the military, which is an incredibly competitive hierarchy, but they did it in two different ways. Patton followed the narcissistic way of dominance, which uses aggression, arrogance, and confidence, forcing his way to the top of the system.

On the other hand, Bradley followed the path of prestige, which lifts the leader to the top of the pack. People high in prestige are not more narcissistic than the average. They're not low in narcissism, but they don't express more than the average person either. At the same time, they're less aggressive and more extraverted, though not nearly to the extent of the dominance-oriented leaders. In general, they're more agreeable, ethical, and emotionally stable, and they're seen as wise and competent. Because of this, people want them in leadership roles. This is the classic model for "servant leaders" such as Martin Luther King Jr., Mahatma Gandhi, and Mother Teresa who make a major impact by being lifted up and allowing others to be lifted as well.

Another way to dial in the difference between narcissistic and agreeable leadership styles is through the expression of an emotion like pride. Jessica Tracy, a psychology researcher at the University of British Columbia, researches the misunderstood emotion of pride and how it shapes our culture. Her work shows that pride can be expressed through dominance, which focuses on being better than someone else, or prestige, which looks for an internal surge of well-being.[6] With dominance, think of someone who dunks a basketball, puffs up, and exuberantly says, "In your face!" With authentic pride, the basketball dunker is more likely to celebrate by jumping with joy, doing a dance, or pumping their fist like Tiger Woods. Gestures like these are less aggressive or intimidating. With narcissism, pride is related to antagonism and hubris, or the dominance, mistrust, and disagreeableness associated with narcissistic traits.

Ultimately, narcissism and leadership create a complex challenge. Groups need people who want to lead, are confident in leading, and care about followers. However, those who want to lead may come from a pool overrepresented by grandiose narcissists. As I see it, we're fishing for tuna by using shark bait, and we wonder why we keep getting sharks. In the end, the key to getting the right people into leadership positions is creating systems that look at qualities beyond these emergent leadership qualities.

NARCISSISTIC LEADERS AND LEADERSHIP EFFECTIVENESS

Once narcissists emerge to a leadership position, do they make effective leaders? It depends. Looking at the Trifurcated Model, grandiose narcissism seems to work because of the high extraversion, but vulnerable narcissism isn't that effective. Even when examining grandiose narcissism, though, the question is more complicated than it may first appear. Those who work for narcissistic bosses may see them as absolute tyrants, and they may be horrible to work for, but they often can play an effective and important role in organizations, especially during organizational change.

In fact, studies show that some followers do well with a narcissistic leader. A friend of mine who is a consultant has a leadership style of "feed the eagle, starve the pigeons," and he'd look for more narcissistic leaders. With high confidence and high self-esteem, this type of worker thrives in incentive-based organizations where he can work hard, close sales, and boost performance. On the other hand, those with low self-esteem, who are insecure and more likely to experience impostor syndrome, or a lack of confidence in a role so much that they feel like an impersonator, do poorly with narcissistic leaders. They feel bullied, harassed, and vulnerable. To be effective, narcissistic leaders need tough, resilient followers who allow—and even thrive—under their leadership style.

Context matters a great deal for narcissistic leadership effectiveness as well. When times are good, and when things are stable and working the way they should, there is no demand for narcissistic leadership. People in those situations want a good king, a competent manager, or a jovial boss who keeps the ship sailing. However, when things become chaotic and unstable, when people feel that the economy or their life doesn't make sense, or when things feel out of control, people gravitate toward narcissistic leaders who make promises of stability, confidence, and direction, whether or not they can actually provide it. The problem with this, of course, is that this is exactly the situation that leads to either detrimental leaders such as Adolf Hitler, who rose to power in the economic instability of Germany following World War I, or extreme spiritual leaders, like Jim Jones, who promise to fill the spiritual void but derive power from cultish behavior.

Perspective changes this evaluation, too. For narcissistic leaders, these moments of turbulence provide perfect opportunities to rise in fame, wealth, or sexual access. To the cult leader, religious leader, political figure, or CEO, they're as effective as they said they would be, and it serves their interests and goals well. Their followers, though, may tell a different story. Those who believe the leader acts in their best interest and fulfills promises are more likely to be happy, but those who see the leader as self-interested, exploitative, and manipulative won't. In this case, they watch the leader extract benefits from the organization and leave the people to suffer.

Because this discontent brews, narcissistic leadership is often short-lived, and these leaders are derailed over time. Consider the story of Gary Hart's 1988 run for office, when he was accused of an affair and denied it. Rather than stick to himself during the campaign, he was discovered with a woman who wasn't his wife on a boat in Florida called *Monkey Business*. Of course, the photo made national news and destroyed his campaign. A more current example is the #MeToo movement, which is successfully putting a stop to careers of narcissistic, perhaps even psychopathic, high-status figures in media, entertainment, and politics. As more people step up to make statements and share their stories, more cases are uncovered. As I am writing this, extreme cases of sexual abuse by high-status, seemingly narcissistic men are being uncovered—albeit much more slowly than if they were low-powered men.

In addition to sexual risks, narcissistic leaders are known for taking major public risks in corporate asset purchases, bold leadership strategies, and daring product launches. When these risks work out, the leader is seen as a genius, but when they don't, the leader is dropped, and the process happens again at the next company. In the corporate finance heyday of the 1980s and 1990s, leaders such as "Chainsaw" Al Dunlop and "Neutron" Jack Welch were praised for destroying companies, cutting out the fat, and building them into leaner operations. Depending on where someone stands, the changes can improve business in the short-term but harm employees in the long-term.

In an attempt to choose an effective leader, people may try to intervene preemptively by selecting non-narcissistic leaders, which is more difficult to do than it may sound. In corporations, leaders are typically hired by boards and search firms, which draw in high-profile, high-visibility outside candidates who likely lean toward narcissism. In democracies, leaders are elected by the people or an electoral college, which often turns into a popularity contest that leans toward narcissistic individuals as well. In the US alone, the winners tend to capitalize on the new technology of the time, with Franklin Delano Roosevelt on the radio, John F. Kennedy on television, Barack Obama on Facebook, and Donald Trump on Twitter. The 2020 presidential candidates will move to the next platform, where the best narcissistic actors and manipulators draw the largest and most polarized followings on social media.

Several other leadership selection methods exist as well. In the competence-based model, those who succeed are bumped to the top. This works well as a reward-based system that reduces the likelihood of narcissism, but at the same time, good workers may not be good leaders. In spiritual-based groups, such as Buddhist tradition, leaders are discovered at a young age and raised into their role, which can indoctrinate them into their identity and reduce the chance of encountering a narcissistic self-proclaimed holy man. Of course, this fate-based designation can't work for many systems or leadership positions.

Due to this complex relationship with effectiveness, narcissistic leaders face a double-edged sword, or a trade-off between agency and communion (see table 8.1). Their assertive extraversion, seen as a positive, often battles the reactive antagonism, which is seen as a negative. For instance, narcissistic leaders are great at networking and speaking with news media, and they're willing to take big public risks. At the same time, they're more likely to be corrupt, or tolerate corruption, and exploit others for their own gain.

Table 8.1: Benefits and Costs: The Double-Edged Sword of Narcissistic Leaders

BENEFITS	COSTS
Charisma	Overconfidence
Confidence	Destructive risk-taking
Risk-taking	Failure to learn from mistakes
Entrepreneurship	Poor ethics
Public performance	Self-serving decision-making

To better understand the positive and negative aspects of narcissism and leadership, particularly among presidents, Ashley Watts and colleagues at Emory University examined personality and biological data for the forty-two US presidents leading up to George W. Bush. [7] Drawing from a larger project of US presidents, where pre-office personality was rated by biographers based on the Big Five traits, Watts converted the ratings to narcissism scores and plotted them on a chart. In the top five, Lyndon Johnson, Teddy Roosevelt, Andrew Jackson, Franklin Roosevelt, and John F. Kennedy placed highest for grandiose narcissism, followed by Richard Nixon and Bill Clinton.

The most narcissistic presidents were often seen as the greatest, although certainly not always, which was based on accomplishments. Those achievements might be considered good or bad depending on political perspective. It's also important to note that many narcissistic leaders had complex records, with Lyndon Johnson passing the Civil Rights Act and pushing America further into Vietnam; Nixon passing the Clean Air Act and starting the war on drugs; and John F. Kennedy leading with a strong voice but being revealed as a womanizer. The even more interesting aspect of the data was the clear trade-off between agency and communion in narcissistic presidents. The grandiose leaders had high levels of bright traits such as public persuasiveness and crisis management, but they also exhibited dark traits such as cheating, abuse of power, and generally poor ethics (see table 8.2). If you are looking for good people to be leaders, avoid narcissism, but if you want effective leaders, sometimes you are going to get a good dose of narcissism.

U.S. Presidents and Grandiose Narcissism

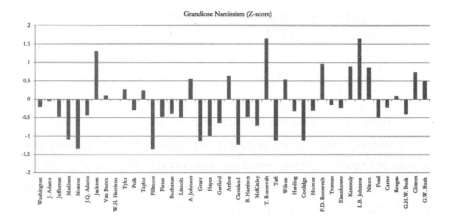

Grandiose Narcissism (Z-score)

Table 8.2: Bright and Dark Sides of US Presidents High in Grandiose Narcissism

BRIGHT	DARK
Popular vote numbers	Abuse of power
Crisis management	Cheating (spouses, taxes, etc.)
Publicly persuasive	Putting political success before policy
Risk-taking	Power-oriented
Rated as "great"	Unethical (self and others surrounding)

To put this in perspective, when George Washington gave up the presidency of the United States, it was such a remarkable act that Washington was compared to Roman leader Lucius Quinctius Cincinnatus, who was the most recent prior example of a leader to take rule when needed in war and then step aside. Washington was even carved in marble as Cincinnatus, showing the bond between these two generals who relinquished power. Selfless leaders are remarkably rare in history.

NARCISSISM AND ORGANIZATIONAL CHANGE: THE GREAT CLASH

When a strong leader with grandiose narcissistic tendencies hits an organization, the impact can feel like a wrecking ball. However, the system doesn't just sit there and take it. The system reacts, and over time, equilibrium is reached. In psychology, the Energy Clash Model illustrates what happens when a narcissistic leader enters an organization, which moves through three steps.

At first, the organization goes through a state of *perturbation*, where the system is destabilized, and no one quite knows what the leader will do. As the narcissist begins to make bold changes and announce new directions, people get nervous. Initially, they support the narcissistic leader. Once the leader begins to build a new team and make changes, however, parts of the system line up in opposition, which begins the *conflict* stage. The people who are hurt by change either move out of the way or band together for bureaucratic warfare. That conflict leads to the *resolution* stage, where the narcissistic leader sets a vision that is either integrated or rejected. For example, a new aggressive CEO was brought into The Home Depot to streamline operations, ditch the old people, and change the management structure. It saved costs in the short-term and changed the culture of the business in a way that customers didn't like, but in the end, the new CEO won the battle. In a case of rejection, Jack Griffin served as CEO of Time Inc. for just five months before being expelled for being aggressive in his management style.

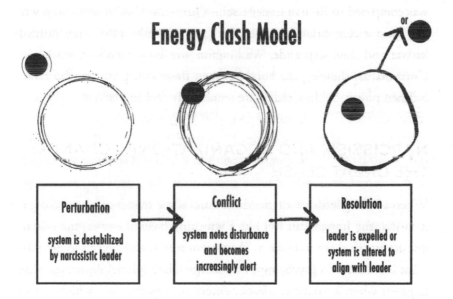

The Energy Clash Model, of course, applies perfectly to the presidency of Donald Trump. When he came into power, the honeymoon period was shorter than typical and quickly moved to a state of perturbation. People didn't know what to expect from someone who hadn't held a political job before, and what we've seen is years of ensuing conflict between two groups who either want to keep him in power and move an agenda or boot him from the office through impeachment. Either way, the conflict is resolved in some form in the end, and the same pattern will continue in the future with other leaders as well.

NERD HERD: NARCISSISTS IN ORGANIZATIONS

As organizational structures change, so does our understanding of how narcissists may operate within them. Rather than a classic organizational chart with a specific hierarchy that describes every member's role and reporting responsibility, flat organizations are becoming more popular that have few levels of management and an informal network of informational flow. Narcissistic leadership thrives in a hierarchy, so when organizational power becomes hidden in a network rather than formalized in a hierarchy, researchers aren't quite sure how narcissism will work.

At the same time, all structures must have some people who make decisions, know tasks and projects, and keep others accountable. Based on the current research, my guess is that narcissists may gain some centrality in organizational networks, yet they will eventually be pushed aside or isolated due to company culture. Classic Machiavellians might be able to navigate a web of social power, so it likely depends on the network and those who are employed. Studies show that even organizations themselves can be narcissistic, with the culture focused on power, success, and devotion, which can create an imbalance in workers' lives to achieve corporate demands at the expense of employees.

INSIDE SCOOP: DIAGNOSING PRESIDENTS AND PUBLIC FIGURES

The debate over Trump's mental health brings up important questions that have been asked before: Can psychologists and psychiatrists offer their professional opinions about public figures from afar? Can they diagnose someone they haven't directly examined? These questions drew particular attention during the 1964 presidential election with Barry Goldwater. At that time, a group of psychiatrists claimed that he was mentally unwell, and he later sued them. Now the APA's "Goldwater Rule" prohibits psychiatrists from offering diagnostic opinions when they've never met the person, but it doesn't include *psychologists*. This is why some psychiatrists talk about Trump's instability without making a specific diagnosis. It doesn't mean they don't have a diagnosis in mind, but they are constrained more than other citizens in their political speech.

Since the 2016 campaign, several researchers have called this rule into question. In fact, my colleague Josh Miller and others published about this in 2017 and updated the manuscript in 2018, saying the rule is outdated and based on unreliable scientific assumptions.[8] They took it a step further by saying that, in some cases, psychologists with particular expertise may have a "duty to inform" about mental health concerns and should be able to offer informed opinions under certain circumstances. Plus, as their paper points out, there is pretty good evidence that diagnosis from afar is reasonable with a public figure who has a long track record of behavior. Eliminating the views of medically trained individuals from public debate seems counterproductive. I tend to agree with them—psychiatrists should be able to criticize politicians like the rest of us.

CHAPTER 9

Social Media and Narcissism

opey didn't realize he launched a worldwide fad when he took a picture of his busted lip and posted it online in 2002. The twenty-one-year-old science student, based north of Sydney, Australia, was drunk at a friend's birthday party when he tripped and landed face-first on some steps. The picture wasn't pretty, but he wanted to show people. And he was seeking advice about whether licking his lips would make the stitches dissolve too soon.

"Sorry about the focus," he wrote when he posted the pic. "It was a selfie."

Once we all caught on to the term a decade later, the *Oxford English Dictionary* named *selfie* its word of the year in 2013, citing Hopey's post as the first known use of the term.

Thanks to Hopey and the Australian English tendency to shorten words and end them with *-ie*, we now have a new narcissist playground fit for millennials and Kardashians alike.

"The use of the diminutive *-ie* suffix is notable as it helps to turn an essentially narcissistic enterprise into something rather more endearing," said Judy Pearsall, the dictionary's editorial director.[1]

NARCISSISM AND SELFIES

Self-portraits are not a new invention. They have been a staple of painters in the same way that autobiographies have long been a popular genre of writing. Early cameras were even designed to make self-portraits possible, with long cords connected to a button to snap the picture. It wasn't that long ago when it became possible to set up a camera, hit the timer, and then run and hold a smile until it clicked. Technology steadily advanced to make modern selfies possible. First, cameras moved from film to digital. Film was expensive and time-consuming. Even with the invention of one-hour photo services, it took time, effort, and cash to take pictures. With digital photos, the cost per picture essentially dropped to zero, and selfies were then only constrained by storage space.

Second, cameras shifted from only front-facing to dual-lens. With traditional digital and film cameras, the photographer looked through the viewfinder to compose, focus, and adjust the lighting in the shot. Even as digital self-portraits became popular, a selfie involved sticking out an arm to capture self-images and then swiping through the images to find the perfect pose and facial expression. Reverse screens changed this, and it became possible to take selfies quickly and easily, even when in a crowded space or classroom where the professor can't see.

The third change, and probably the most important, was the development of social media that allowed people to easily share selfies with others. Before then, sharing happened with photo albums and tangible copies of photos, and friends or family often got trapped into looking at pages of vacation pictures. Later, it became possible to email photos, which was limited by server space and small mailing lists. When social media made its debut, however, it became possible to take a selfie, and with a few clicks, make it look presentable for friends and followers. Now celebrities like Kim Kardashian and Kanye West have more than 100 million people who can see their selfies daily. Let's put that into perspective: Vincent van Gogh, perhaps the most famous artist of self-portraits, is viewed about two million times a year at the Van Gogh Museum in Amsterdam. Compare that to Kardashian's selfies, which are fifty times more popular than van Gogh's portraits in a single year.

As expected, grandiose narcissists are drawn to the selfie format. It's a great way to show off and build the self-esteem they seek. Based on research from the past decade, narcissists take more selfies than others. Although almost everyone takes selfies, narcissists' selfies are a little different. Narcissists are more likely to take photos of only themselves, not so much the "usfies" or "groupfies" with others in them, and they're more likely to appreciate others' selfies. A 2016 study in Korea indicates that those with higher narcissism scores are more likely to see selfie-posting behavior favorably, get involved with selfie-related feedback on social networking sites, and be observant of other people's selfies.[2]

Narcissists are also more likely to include more than their faces—think gym selfies with abs. In a 2016 study of selfies and Instagram, my student Jessica McCain found that grandiose narcissism is associated with taking and posting more selfies, as well as self-reported self-presentation motives.[3] Essentially, grandiose narcissists feel particularly happy sending out pictures of themselves. Vulnerable narcissists often have mixed feelings about selfies. The potential for positive feedback is there, but they are nervous about the threat of negative feedback, and not without reason. A 2017 study by Cornell University researchers found that people are beginning to view selfies in a different light overall.[4] Even though we love taking them, we often judge others who post them, especially when the posts seem inauthentic and phonily intimate. In fact, the study noted that participants rated posts with selfies as more narcissistic, inappropriate, and less socially attractive. Because of this, vulnerable narcissists often spend more time working on their selfies and the words that go with them.

In the end, narcissists agree that they take selfies to promote themselves. At the same time, narcissistic selfies aren't *only* about self-promotion. The distraction, humor, and closeness are perks, just not to the same extent as for others. People who aren't particularly narcissistic like the self-promotional aspect of selfies, too, just not as much. As technology continues to develop, narcissists will likely find new ways to benefit from the selfie route. New smartphones, for instance, with new filters and high-resolution, front-focused cameras, have evolved for the narcissist's modern habitat.

OUR MODERN STOMPING GROUNDS

Social media has become the narcissists' savanna. The shallow and broad relationships of social media are perfect for narcissists' skills. The different platforms play to their strengths, especially extraversion, and limit their weaknesses, including the inability and lack of desire to have deep emotional relationships. Social media sites are also structured to give more positive than negative feedback. There are likes and hearts and claps. This, of course, is intentional; these networks are designed to encourage people to share information. Narcissists are sure to get rewarded for what they do. Social media allows people to curate their public image, too. Narcissists want to look good, especially when it comes to appearance and success, and social media gives them that opportunity. All narcissists need to do on social media is to do what they do best—expand their audience of friends and followers and promote themselves.

After a dozen years of research on narcissism and social media, here is what we find: narcissists have larger social media networks than others. This means social media streams exhibit more narcissism, and this gives a distorted view of reality, just as reality television does. One important reason narcissists have larger social media networks is that they work at it. They request connections on sites that work that way, such as Facebook and LinkedIn, and they gain followers on other sites such as Twitter and Instagram. Narcissists also seem to use social networks more than others, although research indicates that this association is small.

This may not be much of a surprise. Narcissism has been discussed alongside social media since the days of Myspace. Back then, people were interested in the profile pictures—usually selfies—that users took. Now known as the "Myspace pro pic," they were shot by holding a camera and trying to take the picture without seeing through the viewer, often distorting the image from odd angles and showing bathroom mirrors with pouty faces. Because Myspace was started as an alternative social media site where creativity and music were key, it was acceptable for pictures to have an odd, almost artistic quality to them. As its clean-cut competitor, Facebook—an electronic version of what were literally called "face books" in some prep schools, colleges, and universities—changed the way we took those selfies.

In both cases, narcissism thrived. Think about social media as an environmental niche, like the savanna, tropical seas, or alpine terrain. In any ecosystem, some animals thrive and some struggle or even die out. Lions thrive in a savanna where they have prey, blend in with the dry grass, and establish large territories. In a new savanna filled with game, lions quickly move in and establish territories. But if you stick a lion in a jungle, where it has fewer prey and no camouflage, it would do poorly. In fact, it would avoid the jungle if it could.

Similarly, narcissists use networks to promote themselves. They tend to have more attractive photos of themselves, more selfies, and more self-enhancing content. Narcissists' social media use is not just about self-promotion and self-enhancement—and for people who aren't narcissistic, self-promotion is still important at times—but self-promotion is central to understanding narcissism and social media.

AN AUDIENCE IN YOUR POCKET

Social media can be used to connect in many ways. People use social media to learn about big-picture events, like the national news, and household skills, like how to fix a broken doorknob. People also use social media for entertainment, thus the massive popularity of cat memes and postanesthesia videos. Social media allows us to connect with friends and family. Narcissists stand out, however, in their desire to use social media to promote and enhance themselves.

This process is simple and an online version of what's been discussed in earlier chapters. Narcissists want to feel good, have high self-esteem, and be seen as high in status, success, and attraction. This falls into those classic S categories of status, sex, and stuff. A popular version of this is the first-class airline selfie with the person sitting in first class on an international flight with a glass of champagne. This is the self-enhancement trifecta. First class equals status; an attractive photo equals sexual value; and flying first class, which is really, really expensive, equals stuff.

The process of self-enhancement, though, benefits a great deal from social media. In this example, you are on the plane and may ask a flight attendant to take the photo. You feel pretty good just being there. Then you share the picture on various social media accounts. Maybe you use Instagram (#livingthedream) or Facebook. You might be a little sophisticated in your self-enhancement and realize that openly bragging might make you look obnoxious, so you try a classic humblebrag by writing a caption that is more socially acceptable. In this case, #greatdayforflying and #blessed seem right. You show a little gratitude and people like you even more.

Simply sharing the picture on social media gives you a boost of self-esteem, but then the positive feedback starts rolling in. You have 450 followers on Instagram, and they have three choices: they can hit the heart button to show their love, they can write a brief comment ("Sweet ride!"), or they can ignore you. With this feedback setup, the social norms, and your curation of followers (since you block the ones who give you negative feedback), you get exactly what you expect—twenty-seven hearts and three positive comments. This feedback gives you even more of an ego boost. It is now ten minutes before takeoff, you've finished your champagne, and you are truly living the dream. In the Trifurcated Model, vulnerable narcissists see some perceived risk in sharing that international flight selfie on social media because they might not look as good as they think, and they might not receive positive comments, but social media allows them the opportunity to curate a desirable image and caption.

Research has uncovered another motive in narcissists' social media use. Not only do narcissists make themselves feel good, but they make others feel bad. Narcissism, along with the other dark traits such as sadism and psychopathy, predicts online trolling. Trolling is an odd but powerful social media strategy. The term *trolling* comes from fishing. When you troll for fish, you pull a fishing line behind your boat. What you hope to do is catch a fish that gets excited by the moving bait, hits it, and becomes hooked. This resembles social media trolling, where you post to get a reaction. It doesn't always work, but if you post enough controversial ideas in enough areas, you can hook some unlucky Internet users. An important goal of trolling is to mislead and arouse anger in victims, which is why some people believe the term *troll* came not from fishing but from the mythical Scandinavian creatures who are generally mean and aggressive, except in certain Disney movies.

A 2017 study published in the journal *Computers in Human Behavior*, for instance, linked narcissism with Facebook trolling and found that men with narcissistic tendencies were more likely to harass others online and engage in antisocial behavior such as cyberbullying, aggressively retaliating against negative comments, and creating attention-seeking posts.[5] It isn't clear if narcissists troll to get the focus of attention on themselves or to dominate others, though it is probably a bit of both, but the link with narcissism and trolling is pretty stable.

What keeps this feedback loop going is the seductive side effect of social media for narcissists—fame. It's more common now for people to become famous through their social media exploits, but this was a new idea a decade ago. This was (and still is) a radical idea: people can become famous through their own efforts. They don't need a publicist, agent, or studio supporting them. If they have a skill—from makeup to surfing—they don't need to go through a professional organization, league, or contest to become famous. They just have to grow their audience one follower at a time.

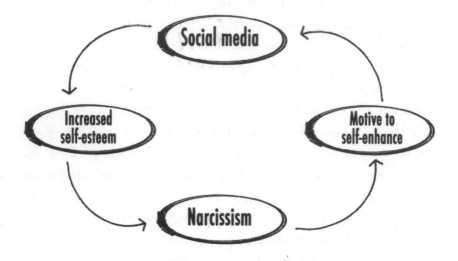

Tila Tequila was one of the early Myspace stars. She was physically attractive and had a big personality that people found appealing. Today, PewDiePie is one of the most famous people on the planet, but you probably haven't heard of him. He is a young man from Sweden with more than one hundred million YouTube subscribers. He makes goofy videos, but I can't really figure out the appeal. And that is the beauty of social media fame. If an old dude like me looked for talent, PewDiePie wouldn't be the first choice. But here we are, and PewDiePie built his fame from the ground up.

To be clear, I am not saying Tila Tequila or PewDiePie are narcissistic. I am saying that the fame they achieved on their own through social media is especially appealing to narcissists. It is yet another reason narcissists are attracted to social media. Overall, social media provides significant opportunities for self-enhancement, and this self-enhancement ranges from everyday self-promotion to serious fame. The ability to self-enhance is not an accident since it is built into these platforms. As the tech folks say: It's a feature, not a bug.

THE NARCISSISTIC CAUSE-AND-EFFECT CONUNDRUM

Does social media make people more narcissistic? If you take a nice college freshman and put him on Instagram and Facebook, for example, will using those platforms make him become more narcissistic? I wish I had a solid answer to this, but I don't. Here is what we know: Research from the past decade tells us that social media is used by narcissistic individuals in self-promoting and self-enhancing ways. The evidence for this is strong and varied.

Other studies have shown that narcissists prefer more self-promoting email addresses such as thefascinatingking@gmx.net. Based on a 2016 study, we have some evidence that this self-promotion by narcissists is self-reinforcing.[6] That is, narcissists who use social media to self-promote are able to maintain an inflated view of themselves over time. However, little consistent evidence suggests that using social media increases narcissism in an average person. For example, one study we did on Myspace found an increase in narcissism, but a similar study with Facebook didn't.[7] There's no rock-solid evidence.

My best guess is that using social media does not turn people into grandiose narcissists. To the contrary, I now think that social media is actually leading to increased insecurity in people. According to recent research in younger generations, it looks like social media use predicts less happiness. Part of this could be from the level of exposure that social media provides. Young people—and many of the rest of us—have more exposure than celebrities did in the 1920s and 1930s. This can lead to "celebrity problems" such as anxiety about looks, public perception, and reactions to public posts. People are now seeking plastic surgery and other cosmetic treatment more than before to look like their best selfie all the time.

Another issue is simply time. When people spend so much time on screens, they miss out on time spent hanging out with friends or doing outdoor activities while in the moment. Even when we participate, we're taking pictures of the concert or the group hangout to post later. This self-focused anxiety sounds suspiciously like vulnerable narcissism, but we don't have the data to know that yet.

USING SOCIAL MEDIA TO SPOT NARCISSISM

If narcissists use social media in certain ways, can we tell if someone is narcissistic by looking at their social media pages? The answer is "yes," but only sometimes. Narcissistic individuals leave traces or cues about their narcissism, such as a large follower count or use of certain words or hashtags. Although researchers can pick up on the narcissism tendencies somewhat, it is far from a perfect method. Trained computer algorithms or "narcissism detectors" could increase the ability to see narcissism on social media, but that technology doesn't work the same way as it does on TV. One episode of the crime show *Bones*, for example, used a social media page to diagnose a criminal with narcissistic personality disorder. Although it is always great to see your research used to fight crime, this is a stretch. Noticing narcissism on social media is an imperfect reflection of a person, not a secret window into their soul.

When psychologists think about spotting narcissism on social media, they see the site content as a lens that reflects the qualities of the page owner and displays them to the viewer. For the lens to work accurately, narcissism has to predict what is seen on social media. People who are narcissistic must use social media in certain ways. This might mean having an attractive profile picture, posting selfies with exposed skin, having lots of links or friends, or posting other self-promoting content. If narcissism doesn't predict social media content, then the lens doesn't work.

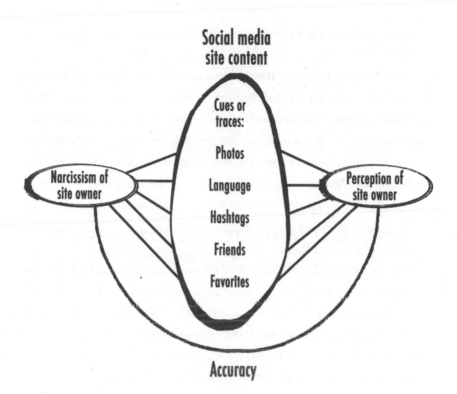

**Social media
site content**

Cues or
traces:

Photos

Language

Hashtags

Friends

Favorltes

Narcissism of
site owner

Perception of
site owner

Accuracy

Then researchers need to be able to accurately detect narcissism from the information, or cues, in the social media. For example, for a few years, psychologists thought that narcissists used more first-person pronouns such as *I*, *me*, and *mine* in their speech. It turns out from new research that this typically isn't the case, though there might be instances where it happens. However, what we do find in the research—and something most people don't know—is that swearing or cursing is associated with narcissism.

Lab studies on detecting narcissism from social media content can recognize narcissism with about 6 percent accuracy. The person's self-reported narcissism and observers' estimates correlate about .25. Today, computer algorithms could double that figure to reach up to 10 to 15 percent accuracy. To do that, we need a large training sample. This would be cool to research, and at some point estimates of narcissism and other dark traits could be built into some software such as dating apps—that might indicate "Red Flag!"—but by itself, social media is not enough to make definitive conclusions.

Another wrinkle in the detection of narcissism through social media is the professionalization of social media use in the past few years. Instagram has shifted dramatically from everyday people sharing pictures to a site for Instagram-focused models and celebrities. These models often portray an effortless beauty and desirable lifestyle. When looked at from the outside, these models appear confident, charismatic, and narcissistic. The reality, though, is that under this confident veneer often exists a large amount of anxiety and insecurity. If followers could see a video of the photoshoot, this would be clear, but all they see is the carefully curated and polished product.

This disconnect burst onto the public scene in late 2015 when Instagram model Essena O'Neill went through a psychological awakening of sorts and came clean, abruptly and publicly posting a video about leaving social media "for good." She revealed the techniques she used to get the right shot, the work it took to turn a good picture into a great one, and the effort that was involved to make it all look effortless. In short, her Instagram life was fake. O'Neill realized that she was sending out false messages to her fans and promoting the less important outer beauty over the more important inner beauty and health.

"I was lost, with serious problems so beautifully hidden. . . . If anything, my social media addiction, perfectionist personality and low self-esteem made my career," she wrote in a six-thousand-word email to her followers. "Over-sexualisation, perfect food photos, perfect travel vlogs—it is textbook how I got famous. Sex sells, people listen to pretty blondes, I just happened to talk about veganism as a trending thing on YouTube."[8]

The nineteen-year-old Australian model, who was a vegan-lifestyle enthusiast, called for followers to join her in quitting social media and seeking more from their tangible "real" lives. She launched a new website called Let's Be Game Changers, with the goal of teaching people about the destructive nature of trying to gain approval online.

A year later, however, several traditional and popular media outlets reached out to her for a follow-up. She has all but disappeared from the Internet. Her Instagram profile is wiped clean. Her Facebook profile is frozen in the past. Her new website, which at first redirected to a blank page, was overtaken by domain squatters and spam content in 2018 and is now owned by a new blogger who writes about sports, fashion, and personal growth.

In another insightful report of Instagram stars, an article appeared in *Out* magazine in 2016 about men who battled with social media pressure online titled "The Instahunks: Inside the Swelling Selfie-Industrial Complex."[9] These are attractive men with desirable and well-developed physiques. To outsiders, they seem incredibly confident, but instead, they revealed in interviews that they were insecure, felt uncomfortable taking the photos, and often felt addicted to the positive attention.

"Say I'm smoking crystal meth, and I take a hit and it feels really good," said Kyle Krieger, then age thirty-three, one of the models who was a recovering addict with nine years of sobriety. "It's similar to that feeling when you post a photo and you're getting all these 'likes.'"

Krieger, who has more than two million Instagram followers, regularly receives twenty thousand to eighty thousand hearts per photo he posts. His Instagram tagline back then? "Being popular on Instagram is like being rich in Monopoly money."

"Then your photo starts to lose engagement. Then the next day, it's like a lull in your validation," Krieger told *Out* in the 2016 article. "And the lowest you will ever feel is right before you take that next hit. Right before you post that next photo."

Unfortunately, this is one of those cases where the science doesn't help us; we just don't have data on social media stars. Hopefully that will change, but in the meantime, we have to realize that the models of narcissism and social media that apply to most of us might not hold for stars. In particular, there might be a lot more anxiety and emotional vulnerability—and less grandiosity—than we would expect.

NARCISSISTS AS SOCIAL NETWORK BUILDERS

In the end, humans are connected online, and it's likely to stay that way. The world is connected by networks of roads, train tracks, rivers, aircraft corridors, shipping lanes, and now social media. These early connectors, such as rivers and shipping lanes, were placed there by nature. People had to move to where the connections were. Most of the great cities in the world are port cities because they were connected to the social network of water. The next phase of global social connection included roads and later train networks. Ancient Rome was a center of power and was the hub for a series of roads. Today, cities such as Atlanta, Georgia, exist because they were crossroads where multiple train and highway paths intersected.

Roads are planned centrally, usually by the state or federal government. They are expensive to build out, with each paved mile costing thousands of dollars. Rails are similar. They cost a great deal of money. Currently, the Chinese government is trying to rebuild the great Silk Road connecting Asia and Europe. This will be an enormous, decades-long project.

In contrast, social networks are incredibly inexpensive to set up. You need some infrastructure, servers, programmers, and engineers. But after that, the price per connection drops dramatically and nears zero. Then all people need is an on-ramp to the social network. Years ago, this used to mean a personal computer connected to the Internet. Now it usually means a smartphone. Soon it will be something less expensive.

There wasn't and still isn't a plan to build these networks. No map was drawn to create the links between people on Facebook or any other social media platform. That's why the invention of social media was so brilliant. All it took was the ability for individuals to share content with one another—photos, thoughts, music—and the networks built themselves. John would link to Sue and Sally, Sue and Sally would link to two more friends, and pretty soon billions of people were linked up. This explosion of connection between people is similar to the real-world concept of "degrees of separation." In other words, if you wanted to deliver a note to me but had to get it to me through a series of people who know each other, how many people would it take? You might send the note to a friend in Georgia, and they would send it to a friend in Atlanta, and they would send it to a friend in Athens, and that person might know someone who knows me at the University of Georgia. In this case, you and I would be separated by four people.

When researchers, notably the great Stanley Milgram who became famous for his obedience research in the 1960s at Yale, started an experiment with this letter-sending technique, the popular conclusion became that each of us is connected to everyone else by at most six degrees of separation. That is, there are typically five or fewer people between you and me (and Kevin Bacon). Researchers later found that this conclusion isn't as rock solid as it sounds. People on the lower socioeconomic rungs of society are usually less connected than those in the upper socioeconomic rungs. Still, it is generally a smaller world than people would guess, and it is getting smaller thanks to social media. Facebook estimates that there are only three-and-a-half degrees of separation between everyone on Facebook. This is mind-blowing. It has tremendous potential for sharing ideas and information.

And here is the key point: Narcissists were central in building these networks and making the world smaller. The desire to self-promote, as shallow and self-serving as it is, has played a crucial role in connecting the world through social media. Imagine what Facebook, Instagram, or Twitter would be like without narcissists. Sure, you would have fewer trolls, humblebrags, and speedo selfies, but you also would have less action. People would talk about their families or life in general but to a lesser degree.

See for yourself. Take notice of what people post about their families. Much of it is designed to look positive. I send pictures of my daughters when they look groomed, when they have succeeded, or during a "milestone moment," such as the first day of school or homecoming. If I am in the photo, I smile, and it looks like I am part of a happy, successful family. I am not out to pump up my ego or my kids, but I'm sure not posting photos of my kids whining or myself shirtless. I'm not alone in this. My amateur narcissism, along with the more professional Kim Kardashian version, makes social media work.

NERD HERD: SELFIES AND NOSE JOBS

Believe it or not, selfies are changing the way we view ourselves—and the way we believe we should look. Plastic surgeons have begun to report an uptick in requests for cosmetic procedures from people who want to look better in selfies. In particular, the number of people under age forty who want rhinoplasty, or a nose job, has jumped in recent years. Surgeons report that patients will take out their phones during appointments and point out the parts of their selfies they don't like.

Interestingly, plastic surgery researchers at Rutgers University created an algorithm in 2018 to show that selfies distort the face, which can lead to this negative view.[10] In fact, they calculated the distortion of facial features at different camera angles and distances and found that the perceived nasal width increased as the camera moved closer to the face. At twelve inches away, selfies increased nasal size by about 30 percent. Five feet—the standard portrait distance—portrays the features at real-life scale.

That means we can use math to create the ideal selfie. Men who want to emphasize a stronger chin or chiseled jaw should position those features closer to the camera. Women who want to emphasize their eyes or deemphasize their forehead, for instance, should tilt the camera to move those features closer to the camera. Maybe narcissists have already figured this out to get their "best angle."

INSIDE SCOOP: EVOLUTION OF SELFIES

I still remember the first camera—not a smartphone—that was designed to take a picture of the photographer. I was amazed, and that was just the beginning. Several psychology and communications labs started researching the idea and found a link between selfies and narcissism. Jesse Fox at Ohio State University published some of the first findings that men with narcissistic qualities tended to post more selfies. Women edited photos more frequently, and they often felt worse after social comparison.[11]

This last aspect points to the more complex research and cultural meaning we've observed about selfies in recent years. For some, selfies can create a painful experience when it emphasizes an unfavorable body part or blemish. In addition, younger people are using secondary Instagram accounts—nicknamed "finsta" for fake Instagram—to be goofier and sillier. These more authentic images remove the social pressure to some extent, and it's an emerging form of communication rather than narcissism. Overall, my guess is that selfies will become less popular over time and be used to show association with others for friendship or status rather than abs at the gym. The status aspect may still line up with narcissism, and we may study that association next.

CHAPTER 10

Geek Culture and the Great Fantasy Migration

G eek culture has contributed to one of the biggest cultural changes in the US, although it is rarely discussed or examined in social science. A "geek" is defined as an enthusiastic fan who develops expertise on a topic through exceptional interest and effort, and it particularly applies to those in science, technology, and fictionalized realms. Although these geek interests were once marginalized in popular culture relative to athletics—sci-fi geeks were not as popular as football players—many of these geeks are now running the world. Highly successful geeks have coincided with the mainstreaming of geek culture. Instead of a negative, it's now part of everyday society, and for many, being a geek is a point of pride.

Geek culture is a mash-up of fantasy fandoms and activities, including classic Trekkies and Star Wars fans, superhero comic book collectors, people interested in Japanese cartoon styles like anime, manga, and hentai (cartoon porn), and dudes into *My Little Pony* (aka Bronies). On the activity side, people dress up as fantasy figures, which is called *cosplay* as short for *costume play*, and people who adopt animal alter egos, known as *furries* (with their furry persona being a *fursona*). More serious geeks mark their calendars to attend conventions like Comic-Con in San Diego and Dragon Con in Atlanta, which regularly draw between fifty and one hundred and fifty thousand attendees.

For the rest of us, geek culture influences our lives through popular culture. Look at the top grossing movies. They are filled with comic book superheroes, such as *Wonder Woman* and *Iron Man*, science fiction flicks such as *Star Wars* and *Ready Player One*, and fantasy adaptations such as *The Lord of the Rings* and *Game of Thrones*. Only some of these films win the top awards, but they're the major box office draws, and our kids might not be into cosplay, but they definitely dress as Wonder Woman for Halloween. In a sense, we are all kind of geeks now.

HOW PSYCHOLOGISTS STARTED STUDYING GEEK CULTURE

When I first learned about this trend in geek culture, one of my graduate students, Jessica McCain, was not only a talented social-personality psychologist, but also a bit of a geek. She told me about LARPing, or dressing up in outfits and engaging in "live action role-play" of favorite characters. Imagine playing a game of Dungeons and Dragons, but instead of imagining action on a game board, you actually dress like a halfling thief and meet with your team in person. I didn't realize until then that I had been role-playing as a nerdy ninth grader who took part in Dungeons and Dragons games.

In my younger years, geek culture was lame and seen as a subculture (hence my semi-repressed Dungeons and Dragons memories), and Jessica's research shows the terms *geek* and *nerd* were pejorative until the 1980s, when technology and computers grew in popularity and those former outcasts became more valuable. At that time, geeks and nerds adopted the terms for themselves to express pride about their subculture, and they began creating canonical lists of the best geeky media, which shared themes about larger-than-life universes, characters with extraordinary abilities, elements from history, aspects of other cultures, and the use of magic or highly advanced or futuristic technology. Knowledge about a certain world became social currency. Now this obsession with heroic and magical stories, themes, and universes is widespread, and board game cafes and video game bars dot cities and small towns across the country.

When geek culture started, different groups stuck to their favorite fandoms in cliques, with the comic book fans, the sci-fi Trekkies, and the British TV aficionados all hanging together and creating their own echo chambers. Historically, these specific geek interests were too small to create significant conventions on their own, so large events invited a full spectrum of topics that might interest geeks. That inclusion grew into mega-conventions with different "tracks," where fans mingle and pick up new interests.

The two largest US geek conventions, Comic-Con and Dragon Con, draw complicated and intricate geek cultures with involved and absorbed fans. Within one weekend, fans of popular teen vampire series such as *Twilight* or *The Vampire Diaries* mix with hardcore devotees of more obscure comics like *Tank Girl*. Beyond that, geek interests tend to cross-pollinate, and fans now mix their costumes to create new characters and inside jokes, with a zombie storm trooper mixing *Star Wars* and zombie genres, for instance. They encompass the life span of their universe, too, with today's different versions of Batman mixed among classic Batman from my childhood.

Naturally, Jessica's expertise in personality science sparked questions about this growth in geek culture and how it might relate to important trends in wider culture, including personality traits such as narcissism. She built a measure of geek cultural engagement by looking at the typical convention tracks and added a few items that were missing. From that, she also developed a Geek Culture Engagement Scale to quantify that engagement and looked for relationships to relevant personality traits.

Following is a quick list of geek-related activities, fandoms, and lifestyles that participants may find at these conventions or engage in at home.

GEEK ACTIVITIES

LARPing (live action role-playing games)

Tabletop role-playing games (Dungeons and Dragons, World of Darkness, etc.)

Computer/console gaming (*World of Warcraft*, *Half-Life*, *Minecraft*, etc.)

Cosplaying (making and wearing costumes of anime characters, superheroes, etc.)

Posting in Internet forums (4chan, tumblr, Reddit, etc.)

Attending conventions (Comic-Con, Dragon Con, etc.)

Attending Renaissance Fairs

Paranormal investigation (ghost hunting, psychic phenomena, etc.)

Puppetry (making and performing with puppets, muppets, etc.)

Robotics (making, using, and learning about robots)

Theater (acting, costuming, building sets, etc.)

Creative writing (fiction, poetry, etc.)

GEEK FANDOMS

Fantasy (*Lord of the Rings*, *Harry Potter*, etc.)

Sci-fi (Star Trek, Star Wars, Stargate, etc.)

Anime and manga (Japanese cartoons and comics)

Comic books (superheroes such as Batman or Superman, *V for Vendetta*, *Watchmen*, etc.)

Horror (writers H. P. Lovecraft, Stephen King, and Anne Rice; Korean and Japanese horror movies; *The Evil Dead*; etc.)

Alternative history (steampunk, cyberpunk, retrofuturism, etc.)

Non-anime animation (Disney, My Little Pony, Nickelodeon, Cartoon Network, etc.)

British series (*Sherlock*, *Doctor Who*, *Being Human*, Monty Python, etc.)

GEEK LIFESTYLES

Lolita (Japanese schoolgirl fashion)

Furry (dressing up as animals, fursonas)

Pagan (Wicca, Norse, etc.)

Polyamory (consensual nonmonogamous relationships)

Based on the schedule released before the 2013 Dragon Con, Jessica found more than thirty different fan tracks for the different interests and niches of geek culture. She took the listing to more than six hundred people on Amazon's Mechanical Turk, a crowdsourcing marketplace, to understand how people engaged with geek culture and how that might relate to the Big Five and other personality traits, including both grandiose and vulnerable narcissism and psychological needs such as belongingness. She asked participants to rate each geek-related item on a 5-point scale to indicate to what extent they engaged in them. Participants also completed scales related to narcissism traits, self-esteem, entitlement, and depression. Overall, the study found that geek engagement was associated with elevated grandiose narcissism, extraversion, openness to experience, entitlement, depression, and well-being.

In a second study, Jessica took the scale to the 2013 Dragon Con to test whether two hundred attendees might score higher than the non-geek-targeted groups on Mechanical Turk. Her team also took photos to examine whether outside observers' perceptions of attendees' appearance matched with their geek engagement and narcissism scores. They found that attendees scored higher on geek engagement and that higher self-reported geek engagement was associated with narcissism. An interesting point, however, is that those who appeared to put more preparation into their costumes or wore makeup, both of which can be signs of narcissism in everyday settings, weren't necessarily more narcissistic in the convention context.

In five subsequent studies, Jessica looked at personality and geek cultural engagement. Overall, she concluded that the studies presented evidence that those most engaged in geek culture are more likely to report traits associated with narcissism, especially grandiose narcissism, and fantasy proneness. They may also engage in geek cultures to maintain their narcissistic self-views, fulfill the need for belonging, and satisfy their need for creative expression. People engage in geek culture for multiple core human reasons, and narcissism seems to be an important one of them. All seven studies, involving more than twenty-three hundred survey takers, appeared in a *PLOS One* article in 2015.[1] Although no additional studies are planned with our research team at the moment, geek engagement provides a fascinating area for additional research, especially when it comes to digging into the reasons these associations might exist and how they manifest.

THE GREAT FANTASY MIGRATION AND NARCISSISM

Based on previous social norms, it seems like narcissism would be a better match with jocks than geeks, but the geek culture actually features qualities that are attractive to narcissists, including the potential for coolness and the flexibility of reality. In fact, recent research in Australia studied people who are "real-life superheroes."[2] I'm not talking about firefighters or other first responders but people who emulate comic book heroes by adopting superhero identities and helping people in bar fights or with busted tires. Read the news reports about these people if you haven't already seen them: the Rain City Superhero Movement in Seattle, the Xtreme Justice League in San Diego, and the New York Initiative in New York City. The study found that they tend to be more narcissistic than the average person, yet it also suggests that narcissism can be prosocial among these geek groups.

Great Fantasy Migration

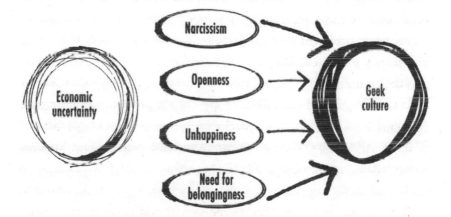

At the thirty-thousand-foot view of modern culture, we see millions of young people who were raised to believe that they were unique and important, but they now work in an economy that doesn't quite line up with that belief system. This leads to a major conflict. Across the world, a great deal of economic uncertainty exists. Economies are getting better, but employment is unstable. Professions are unstable, and the workplace is unstable. Really, there's very little stability. Young people want to be special and to matter, but they aren't and they don't. This disconnect has pushed young people into fantasy realms where they can feel special and important. A middle manager who works in a cubicle farm by day can run a guild in *World of Warcraft* by night. Those who struggled with athletics as a kid might be a legend in fantasy sports. The girl who got cut from the cheerleading squad can dress as a Klingon princess at a convention, and the men will line up.

This Great Fantasy Migration is not just about narcissism—geek culture also attracts highly interesting, creative, and unusual people, including those who are a bit neurotic and who are looking for an escape. This trend will continue as long as the economic outlook for young people doesn't match their desired need for status and success. Look to Japan to see the future: the decades-long recession there has resulted in a fantasy explosion. Many people check out of reality by not having relationships—or even sex—with humans. Instead, they're moving toward relationships with robots that do everything the owner wants them to do, and there are no self-esteem threats or awkwardness.

To be honest, reality is a little boring, which provides the perfect place for narcissism to step up. Young people no longer want to go through the motions, take a job that pays the bills, get married, have kids, and settle down forever. That doesn't sound exciting or appealing anymore. Plus, plenty of people are lonely as technology pushes us apart and social media becomes more pervasive. When we're unhappy and lacking in close relationships, connection, or meaning, we turn elsewhere. This migration isn't necessarily negative, but it's a social phenomenon, and it's happening right now.

An over-the-top but apt example is what happens in the movie *Ready Player One*, which depicts a virtual future where people spend a good portion of their lives in virtual spaces and get their esteem needs met there. Essentially, once virtual worlds exist, people migrate their social lives to inhabit them. Look at the amount of time people spend on social media, gaming, and various forms of geek culture, and it's obvious that virtual spaces are already being inhabited. Still, the Great Fantasy Migration is just ramping up. Wait until virtual reality becomes even more common-place, when visual elements can be paired with both sound and touch feedback to make everyday users feel like they're actually in another real-ity. Even further in the future, these technologies could include direct neural stimulation in the dopamine and reward centers of the brain. In terms of narcissism, this could open up new possibilities for virtual worlds for people to meet their esteem needs without physically compet-ing with others or even getting along. This could lead to more complex personality issues that we can't yet anticipate.

As part of this Great Fantasy Migration, some people who are migrating online are doing this for narcissistic ends, and it benefits both grandiose and vulnerable narcissism. For those who don't have real-world ways of expressing their superiority, success, and status, virtual worlds could offer a better way to do this. Beyond that, fantastical ways of achieving virtual success—such as making money, stockpiling resources, and killing others—could provide an even greater ego boost than every-day achievements in the real world. A fantasy world, by definition, is a user-created world, not one that's given to them. Narcissistic individuals can create a world that caters to their own narcissism. Basically, modern fantasy can support a healthy amount of ego.

FURRIES AND THEIR FURSONAS

Another group that dons different outfits and identities, a bit different from superheroes or pop culture fanatics, are called furries. Generally, furries are interested in anthropomorphic animals with human personalities, which can include human intelligence, facial expressions, speech, bipedalism, and clothing. Participants often create and wear "fursuits" for their characters, which can be simple and resemble sports mascots or more complex with animatronic parts, moving jaws, and prosthetic makeup. The most popular species include wolves, foxes, dogs, large felines, and dragons.

More than 95 percent of furries have adopted a fursona, or animal persona, which they often use online and in multiplayer online role-playing games. Some furries identify as nonhuman to some extent, with some surveys reporting about a third don't feel 100 percent human, compared with 7 percent of nonfurries. Nearly 39 percent said they wouldn't be human if they were capable of that.[3]

From a psychology standpoint, an interesting bit of work has been done on furries and fursonas. Furries tend to show more extraversion and agreeableness, and they appreciate inclusion and belongingness. Compared with other geek fandoms, furries are also more likely to identify with other furries, have furry friends, and date other furries. As a community, furries also rate themselves higher on global awareness, global citizenship, and environmental sustainability.

A 2015 study by Stephen Reysen and colleagues found that furries rate all five dimensions of the Big Five higher for their furry identity versus their own.[4] At the same time, in a following study, the research team found that sports fans also give different personality ratings when talking about their "fan identity."[5]

Overall, furries and other role-playing genres point to people's desire to seek freedom through anonymity. A classic 1976 paper talks about children dressing up for Halloween and being more likely to steal candy when in disguise and in a group.[6] Other studies since then say anonymous personas can also promote positive characteristics such as showing more personality or being outgoing—or even saving people. For narcissists, geek cultural identities can be a strategy for gaining status and esteem, even if sometimes the sex, status, and stuff isn't entirely real.

NERD HERD: IDENTIFYING AS A GEEK VERSUS A NERD

Although the terms *geek* and *nerd* are sometimes used interchangeably in popular culture, those who self-identify with these terms tend to have stronger opinions. In recent years, as people have reclaimed these identities, they've debated the categories and come up with a few guidelines. In general, a geek is a passionate fan or participant in a genre, such as the activities and fandoms mentioned above. Geeks tend to be "collection" oriented and obsess over the facts and updates related to their subject. On the other hand, a nerd is an intellectual invested in studies, sometimes of a particular topic. Nerds tend to be achievement oriented and focus on acquiring knowledge and skills.

While developing the Geek Culture Engagement Scale at the University of Georgia, we had many discussions about the distinctions and similarities between the two terms. Ultimately, there's no right or wrong answer, and one term isn't better or worse than the other. In the end, we decided, geeks are passionate participants in a genre, and nerds are generally more bookish or studious but not necessarily passionate about one topic. To answer a question that Jessica once received from a faculty member—yes, we would consider Civil War reenactors to be geeks.

INSIDE SCOOP: DEVELOPING THE GEEK CULTURE ENGAGEMENT SCALE

What I loved about Jessica's—now Dr. McCain's—geek research is that she showed how to truly operationalize a construct. Nobody had done this work on geek culture and engagement, so she had to define it, figure out how to measure it, and then validate the work by directly going to Dragon Con, which is hosted in Atlanta, about seventy miles from our campus. She recruited others to help her and carried out seven studies both in person and online.

Now her paper has been cited more than twenty times, which indicates that this area will grow. Others will continue to define it, research it, and validate it. At some point in the future, we may have an expanded scale for geek culture, which may include even more fandoms. We'll also learn more about the Big Five in relation to different types of geek cultures, such as furries, and how the Great Fantasy Migration plays into our search for an alternative outside of our everyday reality. This will become especially true as cultural identity shifts from national or ethnic ties to a more global, Disney-mediated (or at this point, Marvel-mediated) mythological system.

III

DEALING WITH NARCISSISM TODAY AND IN THE FUTURE

CHAPTER 11

Using Narcissism Strategically

Seriously, why not just be a jerk? Leadership training will help you realize that (1) there are ways to lead people that strengthen the organization, and (2) there are ways to lead people that offer the impression of strengthening the organization but focus more on the leader at the cost of followers. The former—often called *servant leadership*—works well in stable, transparent environments. The latter—let's call it *self-serving leadership*—works well in fast-paced, unstable environments. In this latter case, as in other environments mentioned earlier in this book, narcissism can be a double-edged sword. It's a mixed blessing. It has costs and benefits.

Ultimately, there are times in your life when you may want to use narcissism. Maybe you've previously used narcissism, or were acting like a bit of a narcissist, and found it was beneficial. Let's not deny that or pass over the potential positives. Instead, let's take a frank look at the times in life when narcissism could help. This is not, in any way, a call to narcissism. It's simply an acknowledgement that the narcissism trait exists, and successful narcissistic individuals are in our lives for a reason. Maybe we can learn from it.

PROS AND CONS: THE TRAGEDY
OF THE COMMONS

The easiest but most profound way to understand the benefits and costs of narcissism is through the "tragedy of the commons" dilemma. This phrase describes a shared-resource system where individuals, who act independently according to their own self-interest, behave contrary to the common good and take resources for themselves. During the enclosure movement in England in the seventeenth century, people began fencing in the shared pastures, fields, forests, and other resources, and eventually, the land became privately owned, leaving the poorest to fend for themselves. In the United States, for instance, the Boston Common used to be shared land where everyone grazed livestock.

In a functioning system, which was intended for these areas, people graze a certain amount of sheep and share equally. The grass renews itself each year, sheep graze, produce offspring, and the process continues in perpetuity. Unfortunately, what happens is that someone cheats. They graze extra sheep, believing that one or two extra won't make a difference, won't hurt anyone else, and will benefit them greatly. And then other people follow suit and sneak a few extra sheep of their own onto the land. Then more people do it. The grass doesn't come back as quickly as it did before, and everyone catches on to the scheme. Instead of backing off, restricting the cheaters, and allowing the grass to regrow, everyone jumps in and grazes all of their sheep to get the most benefit while they can. This destroys the commons completely, and there's nothing left for everyone to use.

Narcissism invokes the tragedy. At the same time, narcissists are the ones who benefit. In this exploitative rush for a precious resource, such as grazing land, gold, a fishery, a forest, or another shared property, the first person to arrive on the scene wins. They take the most and do the most damage, but they also bring home the greatest spoils.

These types of commons dilemmas demonstrate how complex narcissism can be when considering the trade-offs. Even in cases where narcissists benefit in the short-term, they destroy the commons. That means, for their strategy to succeed, they have to repeat the process again and again. They need new commons to exploit, so they move to new towns, new relationships, new jobs, and new social groups. They benefit from the short-term gains, but it's a difficult long-term strategy—and a total nightmare for everyone else.

In another scenario, the captain of a commercial fishing boat competes with other captains to catch salmon. He wants to catch more salmon than anyone else, so he cheats slightly. He starts fishing before the season begins and doesn't help other captains locate the best spots to fish. Soon enough, he catches more salmon than the others and gleefully brags about it at the bar when he returns to port. At this point in the game, narcissism was "good." He caught the most fish.

The problem, of course, is that the other captains catch on and follow suit. The culture changes from cooperation to competition. The other captains also start to fish before the season is open, and that forces the first captain to start even earlier. For a few years, the narcissism works, and he can keep bringing in a huge catch. At some point, the problems start. All of the captains are now overfishing, and the salmon are not reproducing in large numbers. Cheating even more hastens the collapse. Five years later, the first guy may still be the most successful captain, but he catches half of what he did before. The narcissism that helped him ended up hurting him in the end.

In our research on narcissism and the tragedy of the commons at the University of Georgia, we brought groups of four strangers into the lab and told them to work as "CEOs" of four forestry companies. Forestry works similarly to fisheries and other renewable resources: companies can make tons of money quickly by chopping everything down, but then the forest is depleted, and nothing is left to keep the money coming. In our study, the narcissistic CEOs started out being greedier than the others. They chopped down the most trees in the first round, and that made all of the CEOs, even the less narcissistic ones, more competitive.

As a result, the groups with more narcissistic CEOs wiped out the forests more quickly. The most narcissistic CEOs in these groups fared well because they quickly chopped down trees. However, the overall timber harvested in these narcissistic groups was less than what was harvested by more cooperative groups. In the long-term, the competitive, narcissistic strategy hurt everyone, including themselves and the forest.

The lesson here is that when you're looking for benefits from narcissism, consider what's necessary for short-term success—winning an individual competition, getting a job, finding a date, or performing in public. The use of narcissism needs to be strategic, so it's limited to the context where it actually helps (see table 11.1).

Table 11.1: Benefits and Costs of Narcissism

WHEN NARCISSISM HELPS	WHEN NARCISSISM HURTS
Initial meetings with people	Long-term relationships
Public performance	Ethical performance
Context where risk pays off (bull markets)	Context where risk hurts (bear markets)
Short-term romantic relationships	Long-term romantic relationships
Charismatic leadership	Ethical leadership
Social media connections	Meaningful friendships

There are smart ways to use narcissism, or at least to adopt a narcissistic mind-set. Let's tackle this with a listicle approach, shall we? Following are the Five Rules for Using Narcissism for Success:

Rule 1: Keep it brief. Narcissism is best in the short-term. You can use narcissism to start relationships or to get a job. This means a willingness to take risks and put yourself out there. Even some bragging can help in these situations. I heard one great story from a fellow faculty member about a professor she had in graduate school who didn't follow this advice. He mentioned during the first class that he had graduated from Harvard Divinity School. The students thought the professor must be smart and felt good about being in his class, based on the logic that if you take a class from a smart person, it suggests that you are smart. But then the professor kept mentioning it. He would say things like, "When I was at Harvard . . ." This quickly transitioned from a turn on to a turnoff for students. To avoid this, use narcissism for the introductions, and then drop it after that.

Rule 2: Keep it in public. Narcissism is great for public performance, but don't take it home with you. Imagine speaking in front of a thousand people or appearing on live television. Many people get anxious thinking about this. They think about what can go wrong or how they don't deserve the opportunity. Narcissists are different: they look at it as a way to get applause and bring what they have to offer to the audience. And guess who performs better? Narcissists do. Research shows that narcissists perform better on many public performance tasks, even the childhood game Operation, where you try to remove plastic body parts from a patient with tweezers without hitting the sides and making the buzzer go off.[1] Even with a game like this, narcissists outperform when they're in front of an audience (and underperform when the audience isn't there). In these public situations, confidence and swagger help. Just drop the attitude when around your kids or friends. They aren't your audience. In addition, don't be rude to the staff, pages, sound people, or anyone else whose sole job is to make you look good on the stage.

Rule 3: Make the first move. Be bold. One aspect of narcissism that is worth emulating is boldness. Sometimes you have to go for it and make a difference. This might mean trying something new or posting your thoughts on social media. Boldness has risks, of course, but it is an important trait to have if you want to be successful. The trick is knowing when to be bold, which is why boldness should be a tool that you have at your disposal rather than a part of your personality without an off switch.

The challenge with narcissistic boldness comes from two sides. First, you want to be bold, but you don't want to be an idiot. According to the research, real narcissism or more extreme narcissism has boldness and mistake-making without the acknowledgement that mistakes were made. Instead, strive for boldness with accountability.

Second, you need to be able to turn boldness off. On a fishing trip with my father in New Zealand, we attempted to climb a steep hillside to a fish a final pool. My dad looked at me and said, "You have kids, and I have kids, and we can't do this. We can't go on any farther." I was upset at first because it's not really my nature to give up, but my dad was right. It was a point where the need of my own ego to climb up a cliff and fish another hole, no matter what, was not as important as the need of my kids to have a father. Sometimes, others' needs should be put before your own. Some people, including myself, need to hear that message more than others.

Rule 4: Build that network. Build a broad and shallow social network. Having a few close friends is essential for well-being. As far as happiness goes, quality is always better than quantity in relationships. In the workplace, however, no matter what your job or career is, having a broad social network helps. It will help you to land a job if you are out of work or to build a sales network. Narcissists know how to do this. They look at networks as things to exploit and wonder, "What can you do for me?" To an extent, this is useful. However, this exploitative strategy can be counterproductive. It is also important to ask, "What can I do for you?" The exchange of favors is central to making a network successful.

The narcissistic secret to having broader social networks, then, is simply asking. Reach out to more people in a simple, extraverted way, and try to make a connection with them. This might mean starting the conversation with a basic "hello." It might mean exchanging business cards. It might mean having a cup of coffee. It might mean making connections on LinkedIn or other relevant social media. These broad connections can be beneficial when someone wants to ask for advice or a favor, and you might return to the connection when an opportunity pops up. People who are more introverted, more anxious, or more vulnerably narcissistic are less likely to do that.

Rule 5: Stand up for yourself. Demand what you are worth—but not what you fantasize that you are worth. One of the most interesting research findings to date is that antagonistic, disagreeable people make more money.[2] One reason for this is that they demand it. They approach their boss for a raise without doubting their worth or worrying about looking greedy or ungrateful. This is a good strategy; people should feel entitled to be paid what they are worth. The key point, however, is not demanding a fantasy equated with your importance or special brilliance. Instead, you need to make a rational business case for your worth. This accomplishes the same goals but without the antagonism of making narcissistic demands.

As part of my job, I served as the head of an academic department for eight years. During those years, I spent a great deal of time negotiating salaries and budget requests. Academics need tons of resources to run a lab—space, equipment, MRI scans, graduate student stipends, postdoc salaries, travel, and more. Essentially, a successful professor at a modern research university is running a small business that is lucrative for the university. They are chronically underpaid, often hired away by competing departments, and frequently involved in negotiations. I found over and over that the easiest people to negotiate with were those who had concrete ideas of what they wanted, gave specific justifications for what they were worth, outlined benefits that they thought they would bring to the department, and detailed evidence of what they had done in the past. Now, in all these negotiations, I already knew most of this. However, it helped that people were willing to sit down and make a good case for themselves. The important piece wasn't that they were selling me on themselves—I was already sold. What I needed was a rational business argument to take to my boss (the dean) and sell on their behalf. My boss would then need to ask a higher authority (the provost) and make a sharper business case than I had.

When you think you're bragging or making too strong a case for yourself, remember that you're actually making a business case for your interviewer's superior, and you're trying to help your interviewer build that case. The other reminder that I like to give to academics—and other professionals who don't like to brag—is that the limelight cast on them is also shared by their colleagues and students. When I attended Berkeley as an undergraduate student, we used to brag that we had more Nobel Prize winners than Russia, or some other comparison of equal merit. I never met a Nobel Prize winner at Berkeley, but I still received some residual shine from their triumphs.

DON'T FORGET: THE PERPETUAL DOWNSIDES

You know I can't end a chapter on using narcissism strategically without a final word on the potential negatives. The downside to these five narcissistic behaviors deals with the potential effect on relationships. Being more confident, bold, and assertive will destabilize your current relationships, putting close relationships at risk. This is the key risk of narcissism. You put yourself out there. You demand power, status, leadership, material, and respect. That's great, and it often works. However, in turn, you should give back more than you take. If you build networks and are a friendly person, you will help the world with that narcissism. If you demand a fair wage at your job so you can support your kid, remove stress from your life, and perform better at your work, everybody wins. If you lead a company and make millions of dollars and also build a great product and employ a large number of people, that's the way it should work.

In those cases, the ego needs are being offset by a general benefit to society itself. No matter the situation, small costs and small benefits will occur, and large costs and large benefits will occur, but that general trade-off is important ethically to conceptualize, especially when thinking about your own narcissism. Are you bringing more to the system than you're taking? Are you causing less suffering than you're creating? These questions can be tough to answer in our lives. They're hard to answer in the lab, too, but they're the ones that we need to consider.

NERD HERD: TRAGEDY OF THE COMMONS AT WORK

The tragedy of the commons affects workplaces often. If the company owns the commons, and you don't know how much grass there is, why not go for it? In social psychology research in the early 2000s, Timothy Judge and others conducted several studies about the roles that sex and agreeableness play on income.[3] Essentially, as they say, nice guys finish last. Agreeable men and women earned less—to the tune of $5,000 per year at that time—than the "disagreeable men" who were aggressive and confirmed conventional gender roles. In fact, the agreeableness-income relationship was surprisingly negative for agreeable men, who earned an average of $7,000 less than disagreeable men. Agreeableness affected future income as well. Part of this, they found, was explained by the value that disagreeable men placed on high earnings rather than relationships.

These organizational effects can extend to cultural effects as well. Social psychologist Brenda Major has written about the links among social comparison, social inequality, and personal and collective entitle-ment.[4] Essentially, those who feel entitled (such as narcissists) see what the top earner is making and want more. Those with low entitlement want to get along with others and are treated in line with "average" pay, which keeps the peace in a group but provides less. Members of disad-vantaged groups may even develop a lesser sense of personal entitlement, and what "is" has a tendency to what become what "ought" to be. This is what happened with the origins of pay gaps, including for gender and racial/ethnic groups. As people compare their situational and personal factors with advantaged groups, however, it leads them to question the discrepancies and boost their entitlement to that same pay, which creates higher levels of discontent.

INSIDE SCOOP: COMPETITION AND COOPERATION

When I was in graduate school at the University of North Carolina at Chapel Hill, Professor Chester Insko talked about cooperation and com-petition, with the big question about the best ways to make humans cooperate. Should societies simply be nice all the time, should they be totalitarian, or should there be a combination?

As part of this topic, he discussed the Mongol empire military tactic of "surrender or die," which offered enemies an opportunity to surrender instead of having their city ransacked and destroyed. Smaller settled towns often couldn't leave their possessions and rebuild effectively elsewhere, so they'd surrender and be spared, but they were required to support the Mongol army with supplies and more fighters.

In contrast, Insko also talked about the Christmas Truce of 1914 during World War I, when unofficial ceasefires sprung up across the western front. The soldiers declared their own truce in the trenches to celebrate the holidays, and the two sides greeted each other, sang carols together, and traded gifts such as cigarettes or food. However, the war resumed days later when commanders demanded it.

As a combination tactic, American political scientist Bob Axelrod created a "tit-for-tat" model that seems to work well.[5] In short, if someone cooperates with you, cooperate back. If someone competes with you, compete back. By starting off with compassion, sometimes cutting people slack if they act competitively by mistake, you have a decent recipe for a smooth and cooperative society. Entitlement and the tragedy of the commons can complicate this, but the model can work.

CHAPTER 12

Reducing Another's Narcissism

C hanging another's personality is a challenge. The key issue is motivation. In the case of changing another's personality, *you* clearly have the motivation, but the other person might not. That makes changing another person quite difficult. Still, you may be in a marriage with a narcissist, have a friend or family member who is narcissistic, or work with a boss or coworker who has narcissistic tendencies. You might even worry about your children, and they might be in a narcissistic social group at school or have a narcissistic parent. You may also be in a situation that many parents find themselves in—not wanting to pass their more negative qualities on to their children. The recent HBO series *Big Little Lies* features a struggle with a highly controlling, attractive, abusive, and narcissistic spouse played by Alexander Skarsgård. His wife (played by Nicole Kidman) tried many ways to change him, from therapy to submission, but they were only temporarily effective.

Of course, most situations that I receive questions about are not this extreme, but I always like to speak about the most extreme examples up front to be as helpful as possible. In a 2017 TEDx Talk, for instance, I spoke about the lighter side of narcissism, and people worried that I didn't speak about the serious and detrimental aspects of narcissism that can create true relationship problems. In this chapter, I'm outlining tools to help those with narcissistic traits or tendencies, not the clinical level of narcissism that needs professional diagnosis and treatment. Before I share these strategies, though, I want to address the importance of safety in the more serious cases.

As portrayed so well in *Big Little Lies*, the number one priority is helping and protecting yourself. Make sure you are not harmed physically, emotionally, or financially. It means setting firm boundaries and keeping a record of what is happening. In *Big Little Lies*, Nicole Kidman's therapist instructs her to get a secret apartment to escape to when necessary. This advice is straight out of the social psychology literature. You need to create an alternative if you want to effectively leave a relationship. This is also why shelters for battered women are so important, especially for those who aren't financially independent.

After that, it's important to remember that changing another person has a low probability of success. Every married spouse, parent, and child tries to change the other in many ways. My mom still wishes I had attended medical school, my wife still wishes I would stick to a normal diet, and my daughters still wish I wouldn't embarrass them by making bad jokes in front of their friends. I recognize these wishes are positive. I would likely be helped by having a medical degree, eating better, and not embarrassing my children (well, maybe not that one), but they remain unfulfilled. That's simply the nature of trying to change people.

Still, if you want to change another person, several strategies have some basis in research, particularly *motivational interviewing*, which is used by therapists to encourage a client to be an ally in therapy by increasing the client's intrinsic motivation for change. Essentially, the best strategy is not to change the person's narcissism directly, but instead, to change the person's desire to change. In other words, convince the narcissist to want to change, and then you can help if needed, but they must do the changing alone.

Related to this, we've started researching narcissists' desires to change. I had thought for years (and the field had thought so as well) that narcissists, especially grandiose narcissists, didn't want to change because they loved who they were. In some ways, this is still what we observe. Grandiose narcissists have high self-esteem, are happy, and feel closer to their ideal selves than the rest of us. When it comes to their more antagonistic and callous personality traits, however, such as their manipulative nature or lack of empathy, narcissists typically see these qualities as negative and want to change them.

In this research, we asked the narcissist and a friend to rate their personality traits, the positivity of these traits, and the desirability of changing them.[1] It turns out that the narcissists' self-perceptions were pretty similar to their peers' perceptions of them, as was the positivity (or lack thereof), and the desirability of changing these traits. The narcissistic individuals that I've spoken with who want to change share similar stories. They experience two important gaps in their lives: they want the close family relationships that they see others have, and they want to perform better professionally by having the positive team relationships that others have. I want to be clear: the people who discuss their narcissism with me have a high degree of self-awareness, which isn't typical, but the research suggests that some insight is often there. In this case, we want to encourage narcissistic individuals to map out the life that they want to have and then consider how their narcissistic personality interferes with that.

REDUCTION TACTICS

We can break down the areas of change into the three key ingredients of narcissism: agentic extraversion, antagonism, and neuroticism. Then we can discuss change tactics in each of those areas. The challenge is that narcissism is a trade-off, so it isn't as simple as getting rid of traits. People are complex, so when I talk about these strategies, let's also keep the benefits in mind. I provide an overview of the narcissism ingredients and aspects of change in table 12.1.

Table 12.1: Responses to Narcissistic Traits

	BENEFITS	COSTS	SOLUTIONS/ RESPONSES
AGENTIC EXTRAVERSION	Driven Socially outgoing	Work focused Infidelity	Redirect or rechannel Stop specific risks
ANTAGONISM	Aggressive Rule breaking	Aggression/ violence Cheating Antisocial Mistrust	Communal shift Gratitude Stop specific risks
NEUROTICISM	Threat detection	Suffering Anxiety Hostility	Stop hostility Anxiety reduction through diet, exercise, sleep, medication

Agentic Extraversion

First, agentic extraversion, and the drive that comes with it, is one of the most attractive features of narcissism. It captures confidence and social boldness, as well as the ability to achieve goals, ascend to leadership, and achieve other positive outcomes. At the same time, agentic extraversion itself can be bad. It can lead to some negative consequences that aren't clinically significant but can make life worse than it needs to be. One example is work-family balance. People who are highly agentic in their extraversion tend to focus heavily on tasks and projects. These people are influenced by rewards, including psychological rewards. They are drawn to success, fame, and opportunities to achieve, excel, and get recognition.

The narcissist can't turn off this energy and likely doesn't want to. Instead, you must make space for that energy within your relationship, your family, or the other important aspects of life that must be balanced. Essentially, rechannel the energy and make the new priority part of the narcissist's goals. As an example, imagine that I have a friend who is agentic narcissistic, but I want to be included more in his life. To do this, I should find a way that means my inclusion helps him to achieve his goals. With family, it may mean requiring a certain amount of time focused on family exclusively, with smartphones put away. You might need to enforce strict rules to focus the intention and energy.

Another challenge with this type of attractive agentic extraversion is that people who are socially confident and outgoing tend to have a higher risk of infidelity, including sexual infidelity. This can also mean having a large number of relationships outside of primary ones, which is important to regulate directly in a relationship with somebody who's narcissistic. If I'm in a relationship with someone, and I need a certain amount of time or a certain level of attention, this needs to be put into the relationship. It needs to be enforced, in a sense.

Antagonism

When it comes to a core trait of narcissism, antagonism is clearly much more destructive than extraversion. At the same time, it's important to remember that even antagonism has some benefits. It's useful for rule breaking. It's useful for demanding more pay. It's useful for being aggressive in sports. There are times when people need to break through a system to make change, and aggressiveness is important for that. However, aggressiveness also has a dark side. Antagonism is linked to emotional and physical abuse, cheating, numerous antisocial behaviors, rape, sexual assault, and partner abuse. If you're dealing with any of these problems at a critical threshold, the police should be involved.

You shouldn't be reading what I'm writing and trying to use these tricks. What I'm suggesting are tools for dealing with people within the normal realm of narcissism who aren't breaking the law.

When dealing with narcissistic antagonism, you have soft tools, nudges, and subtle ways of trying to bring out less antagonism, and you have hard tools, which are more direct and confrontational. Starting with the soft tools, think about narcissists as people who are wired for reward, meaning they want to feel good about themselves. If there's an opportunity to link kind, communal, or caring behaviors with feeling good, that should eventually lead to a reduction in antagonism.

We published research about this idea in 2009.[2] Imagine a group of people who are each married to a grandiose narcissist. Some of these people, during the course of their relationships, are able to bring out traits of caring and kindness in their narcissistic spouses. We sometimes call this communal activation, or a communal shift, because these communal traits are activated in the narcissist and shift in the direction of more caring traits. In those relationships, we observed, people with narcissistic partners were actually satisfied because the remaining narcissistic trait of extraversion was positive, and the harsh edges of antagonism had been softened. In other couples where that transition hadn't happened, the non-narcissistic spouse was less satisfied. In theory, that shift sounds great, but making it happen can be tough. A basic solution is a reward-based system. When narcissists act in a way that is caring or communal, compliment them and thank them. Tell them that you noticed how they were nice to a kid or loving toward their wife.

Another tactic, which is a classic cure for entitlement, is deprivation. Make a person work for something instead of having it handed to them, whether love, a business relationship, or a friendship. People can do this by putting themselves in a state of micro-deprivation, which is also known as gratitude. Intentionally setting aside a time to express gratitude, even ten minutes per day, can lead to positive feelings and happiness. Since narcissists aren't typically grateful and are more likely to blame others for their problems, getting them to switch to this gratitude mind-set can be an uphill battle. Set yourself as a role model, ask the narcissist to participate in before-meal prayers or gratitude statements, and talk about gratitude regularly in conversation.

A group of UK researchers backed up these ideas in a 2014 study that evoked empathy through perspective taking.[3] They encouraged one group of the study participants to picture themselves in another's shoes and then watch a video that prompted empathy. The perspective-taking group had reduced levels of "maladaptive" traits of narcissism such as entitlement and exploitative behavior, increased self-reported empathy, and even decreased heart rates. Overall, the researchers concluded, narcissists can be moved by someone else's suffering—if they choose to take that person's perspective.

With "harder" tactics, narcissists need to be confronted directly. From our work in narcissistic self-awareness, we've found that people who are narcissistic are aware that, at times, they can be jerks and that their antagonism can cause issues. When you confront them, however, it's best to do it privately. Don't shame or humiliate them. Instead, place the issue that you are concerned about in the context of an overall positive relationship with the desire for self-improvement. For example, among family, parents and grandparents often have disagreements about a grandchild's appearance or manners, and one way to approach a conversation with a narcissistic grandparent is to acknowledge the uncomfortable differences in opinion but explain that they can't do anything to change the child. In fact, it's helpful to mention that criticizing the child could hurt them and ruin the relationship. This type of conversation allows people to clarify, in their own minds, how important appearance is versus how important love is. If the narcissist realizes that their grandson's looks have been more important to them than love, it's often difficult for them to admit it, but once two values are pitted against each other, insight and action may reduce their antagonism.

Neuroticism

As the final trait, neuroticism is the bastion of vulnerable narcissism, and it's not positive for relationships. Neurotic people are hard to be around because they need more support, have negative thoughts about the present and the future, see more threat in the environment, and are hard to comfort. Sometimes we need people in society who are fearful, but in modern Western marriage, neuroticism is generally negative. Add the antagonism, and it's an unpleasant combination. Beyond that, the piece of neuroticism that often gets left out of the discussion is hostility and anger. When we think of neuroticism, we typically talk about sadness and depression, which is internalizing, but hostility leads to anger, which is externalizing.

The good news is that several actions can tamper neuroticism, which is at the core of many mental health problems. Lifestyle changes such as exercise, diet, sleep, meditation, and mindfulness can help greatly. The challenge, of course, is encouraging someone else to do them, but it's worth the effort, especially if you can join in those activities with them.

After that, antidepressant and anxiolytic medications such as benzodiazepines and selective serotonin reuptake inhibitors can help, particularly SSRIs, which can lead to one change that builds on another. That is, the medication reduces neurotic tendencies, which lowers depression and improves lifestyle habits that then improve neuroticism even more.

WHAT ABOUT MANIPULATION?

Of course, another way to deal with narcissism, which isn't subtle, is simply manipulating the narcissist right back. If you understand how somebody who's narcissistic is wired, you see what their goals are, allow them to get their goals met, and then benefit from that. For instance, if I want a grandiose narcissist to like me, I compliment them, make myself sound important, and talk about a future where I see them succeeding. Since we're all on the same page—page "them"—it works.

We all want authentic relationships, of course, and manipulative relationships are exhausting and unhealthy, so I urge you to only implement this idea if you have no choice in interacting with this narcissist, such as in a casual workplace relationship, and you need to find ways to work with this method so you're not impaired. In a close relationship such as marriage, instead of resorting to manipulation, consider whether you want to be in the relationship or what professional strategies, such as marriage counseling, may work.

What first alerted me to this tactic was a radio show I was on years ago that was hosted by the madam of a brothel. She said that when men come in who are clearly narcissistic, the women see them as marked targets because they're so easy to manipulate by simply fawning over them. The women know these guys are clowns, and although they show a bold, self-assured, independent, and arrogant exterior, they're just chickens waiting to be plucked when they come into a brothel.

Manipulation can have serious consequences, too. People ask me about Donald Trump and how I would deal with him. I'd do what some other countries seem to do—plan huge parades, invite him to huge dinners, and make him look like a huge deal. He loves it, and it's the best way to broker a deal with him. When people try to manipulate Trump by attacking him, it doesn't work because his level of grandiosity matches Lyndon Johnson's narcissism. He's not timid, won't back down, and is too arrogant for that to work. When Israel's prime minister Benjamin Netanyahu posted on Twitter in June 2019 about a new neighborhood in Golan Heights called "Trump Heights," for instance, he wrote: "Establishing a new community in the Golan Heights named after a friend of Israel, US President @realDonaldTrump. A historic day!" In response, Trump retweeted the post and responded: "Thank you Mr. Prime Minister, a great honor!" Now *that's* a leader who knows how to work with Trump correctly.

As another example, I did an informal consultation for a partnership lawsuit involving a powerful grandiose narcissist. The non-narcissist partner asked me for advice. When I asked him what he wanted, he said he needed a certain amount of money. So I told him to get that much money and then "lose." Although it might seem confusing, I explained that the narcissist needed to win, so the easiest route to get the money was to allow the narcissist to win publicly so that the non-narcissist could win financially.

WHAT ABOUT TALKING?

Sometimes people ask me if they can simply have a conversation with their narcissistic partner or family member about change. For instance, they ask whether they can tell the narcissist about the strategies they are thinking about using, such as giving more praise for loving behavior. In general, most advice given about narcissism suggests that direct confrontation with a person about their narcissism doesn't help. For example, when you approach your spouse about keeping the house clean, it's far more effective to have a discussion about small changes to actions and behaviors, such as doing the dishes or taking out the trash, rather than calling them a "pig" or a "mess." In the same way, calling someone a "narcissist" and describing it as a broad personality trait can be hurtful and unhelpful. Instead, focus on the specific behaviors that you want to change, and give specific examples that will help them see how their actions affect others. If they simply don't realize what they're doing, they may be able to anchor their motivation in a new behavior, such as the motivational interviewing technique described above.

Beyond that, a few recent studies show us that many narcissists seem to have at least some awareness of their behaviors and agree that some of their actions are negative. Given this newer research, it may be worth having a conversation if your partner has self-awareness around their actions and seems open to this type of discussion. Even then, it's important to be careful with the words that you use to talk to them about their actions and behaviors. Again, nobody wants to be tagged with a negative label, especially a narcissist whose motivation stems from being superior and special. To do this, talk about broad trait profiles, such as antagonism, and explain how that is hurting the relationship. If the conversation goes well, they may be able to open up and talk about the ways that their antagonism hurts other areas of their life as well.

WHAT ABOUT PARENTING?

People ask me about narcissism and parenting all the time. People want to know how they can raise a child who is not narcissistic. People don't want to have a child who is a spoiled brat, who seems selfish, or who is cruel. This makes total sense. But to be extremely honest, I don't worry that much about parenting. Parenting matters but doesn't make much of a difference. Overall, I feed my daughters, tell them I love them, and go on adventures with them, so they develop a sense of agency. Beyond that, I don't try to shape their personality because it doesn't work within the normal range of parenting.

I want to make two important points before people call me crazy. Yes, you can mess up your children. If you put them in a box and raise them there, they'll be horribly traumatized. Second, parenting matters in the sense that feeding and clothing your children and protecting them from harm is important, but think about the families you know with two children. Unless they're identical twins, even fraternal twins, siblings are extremely different from each other, and they could never be changed into the other one. Beyond ensuring that your kids are fed and behaving in line with society, you don't have that much control. I couldn't switch one daughter's personality with the other's, even if I had the resources of an entire psychiatric hospital, Facebook, and the CIA.

All that said, people want a strategy or method to know they're making the right decisions and taking the correct actions. One strategy I recommend for parents is the CPR method for narcissism control. The

C stands for compassion and caring. One of the biggest buffers against narcissism is having warm, empathetic relationships. Model those relationships in your own life and reward your children for them.

The *P* is for passion. When you approach anything with passion and joy, including sports, music, work, and love, the ego drops away. You don't brag about what you are doing—you share your excitement with others. In fact, studies show that people can't experience deep passion when they're reflecting on their awesomeness. Share your passion with your children and encourage their own.

The *R* is for responsibility. It's easy to take responsibility for success, but it's hard to take responsibility for failure. Taking responsibility for both outcomes is key to keeping the ego in check. This is a practice. For example, I've studied the self-serving bias, or the tendency to take credit for success and blame others for failure, for years. I am aware of the issue. I know that it's smarter in the long-term to learn from mistakes rather than to pretend they are someone else's fault, and I still make excuses when I screw up.

CPR Method

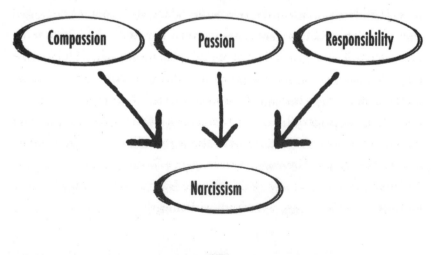

Let's extend the CPR concepts further and the reasons they buffer against narcissism. Compassion, of course, has to do with connection, love, and belonging. The research on attachment, even among nonhuman primates and other mammals, shows that love is a foundational experience. Early attachment experiences are vital, as well as later friendships. As an example, I frequently invite my daughters' friends over for food, and then I make them a meal or at least scrounge up something in our kitchen, which shows my support of them and also creates a welcoming environment for their friends. I can't provide friendships for my daughters, but I can support them.

Next, people don't think about passion as much when it comes to battling narcissism, but it's one of the most important tools. If you do work that you love and engage in activities daily that you enjoy, you teach your kids what's possible and that they, too, can have passion in their lives. On the other hand, if you spend most of your time on tasks to get attention, not be punished, or not be looked down on, your child will observe that as well. Plus, when people act from states of flow and become engaged in that perfect harmony at their fullest potential, ego and narcissism fall away. That feeling draws energy from the creative process rather than a specific accomplishment, which means your greatest performance comes from letting go of ego. Your children will mirror that.

Related to this, responsibility is about taking ownership of one's life, one's mistakes, and one's successes in equal measure. The best way to encourage this with your kids is to reward them for doing it. If they make a mistake, tell them it was a good try, it didn't work, but it didn't mean anything about their identity. It also helps to tell them that you respect when they take responsibility for their actions. When you reward success and punish failure, you end up with dishonesty, shame, and guilt rather than responsibility. Instead, celebrate their efforts even as you mourn the failure, which will boost their ability to bounce back from failures in adulthood and keep moving forward with integrity.

Reducing Your Own Narcissism

The reality is that many of us struggle with some aspects of narcissism. Even if we aren't worried about a clinical diagnosis of narcissistic personality disorder, we might realize that our need for attention gets us into trouble, or our sense of entitlement causes us to get angry when it isn't useful. I notice my sense of entitlement when I travel and, as often happens, things go haywire. I can be stuck in an airport with literally thousands of people, yet I can still manage to become angry that I'm the one who's inconvenienced. I also struggle with turning off my ambition and focusing on my family. I would like to have an ego-switch that I can control, but unfortunately, positive changes have taken me years of practice.

About a hundred years ago, at the birth of personality science, researchers believed that adult personality didn't change. Freud believed that personality became fixed in the first six years of life, and a person's way of coping with challenges made the difference in life from that age. If you were resistant to toilet training as a child, for instance, you would become "anal retentive" as an adult—inflexible, greedy, and uptight. If you were a little too into breastfeeding, you would become "orally fixated" as an adult—addictive, pleasure-seeking, and always with something in your mouth like a cigarette or pencil. If you were into your genitals, you would become "phallic" as an adult male—aggressive, competitive, and domineering. Although these personality traits live on, and we still call people anal, oral, or dicks (since "phallocentric" doesn't quite have a ring to it), Freud was wrong about both the root and flexibility of these traits.

The great American psychologist William James was more optimistic about personality change, but even he thought personality could change when people were young but then hardened into an inflexible state. He wrote that "in most of us, by the age of thirty, the character has set like plaster, and will never soften again."[1] This is closer to what we know today but still incorrect.

CHANGING WHAT WE CAN

Personality can change, and it typically changes throughout life. In research on the Big Five, extraversion and openness often decrease over time while agreeableness increases. As we get older, the pattern is to become less curious, driven, and sociable, but we also become kinder. This pattern suggests that narcissism (high extraversion and low agreeableness) should lessen as we age. Although there is less research on narcissism than personality overall, the best guess is that, on average, narcissism decreases as we age. It doesn't mean that narcissism declines in all cases, and narcissism in advanced age can become a bigger problem in some people who experience cognitive impairment and loss of emotional self-control. These individuals lose some ability to regulate their narcissism and can become even more angry and judgmental over time.

Even so, if personality can change as we age, the question remains as to whether we can intentionally accelerate those changes in our personality by strategically putting ourselves in certain situations, having certain experiences, or taking certain medicines. One way to answer this is to look at the research that measures personality change following interventions, such as psychotherapy and psychedelics, and fortunately, Brent Roberts and colleagues did this in a systematic review that was published in 2017.[2] They analyzed more than two hundred studies that tracked changes in personality traits during interventions.

First, most of what we know about personality change comes from research into psychotherapy, and most people are in psychotherapy for traits involving neuroticism. In that regard, we know much more about change in neuroticism than the other traits. With that said, there does seem to be a reliable change in personality following intentional interventions, which can include drugs such as psilocybin or certain antidepressants, psychodynamic or cognitive behavioral therapies, or experimental interventions. The results are relatively similar across those choices in terms of personality change. When it comes to the Big Five traits themselves, the biggest area of change occurs in neuroticism, meaning people become less neurotic or more emotionally stable over time using these treatments, Roberts and colleagues found. There's also evidence, though, of smaller change in the other traits. People increase slightly in extraversion, agreeableness, conscientiousness, and openness.

The next question to test is whether people can volitionally or intentionally change their personality traits. One way researchers Chris Fraley and Nathan Hudson tested this in 2015 was by asking people at the beginning of a sixteen-week experiment which of the Big Five traits they wanted to change.[3] Then they would create plans to implement change. The researchers found that people moved in the direction they wanted to go, though only slightly. The easiest trait to change, which is great in general but not good news for narcissism, was increasing extraversion.

This area of research is new, but there is promise. For example, another study published in 2018[4] followed a ten-week coaching program designed to encourage volitional personality change. The results indicate that the program resulted in increases in conscientiousness and extraversion and significant decreases in neuroticism, and the changes were maintained three months after the program, particularly for neuroticism and extraversion.

At the same time, change can backfire. One of the more interesting examples involves self-esteem intentions. In a 2011 study where college roommates at Ohio State University were instructed to boost either their self-esteem or connection, those who focused on connection had greater connection, but those who focused on self-esteem ended up with increased mistrust and isolation.[5] What I observe naturally, which falls outside of scientific data but seems to ring true, is that narcissistic individuals desire change as they mature and watch changes in the social world around them. Many young people start out young and ambitious and don't see much value in family life, which is seen as boring and expensive in terms of time and lifestyle. What happens to some of these more self-focused young people as they grow up and see their friends start families is that they realize they are missing out on that life experience. It is hard to understand at first because being narcissistic is fundamentally about being intentionally out of balance, emphasizing "self" over "other." However, when someone has the foundational insight that building a life on something as fleeting as social status is a poor investment, they want something more meaningful or substantial.

New findings are coming out about this aspect of change. A study released in 2019 looked at narcissism over time.[6] Called "You're Still So Vain," the article discusses how narcissism tends to decline with age from the twenties to the forties, particularly related to narcissism's facets of leadership, vanity, and entitlement. Narcissism decreased over time, but it occurred with complexity. For instance, study participants who were supervisors in their jobs had smaller decreases in leadership, which makes sense. In addition, those who had unstable relationships or were physically healthy had smaller decreases in vanity. These findings make sense because the young adults with higher leadership levels were more likely to be in a supervisory position by middle age, and those with higher vanity levels had fewer children and were more likely to be divorced by middle age. Altogether, people tend to become less narcissistic as they age, but this depends on the particular career and family pathways they pursue during their lives.

The specific suggestions that follow are aimed at the larger goal of reducing narcissism by expanding the capacity for love at a personal level. To get to that larger goal, you need to use the Trifurcated Model.

CHANGING NARCISSISM

The first question to ask is: What aspects of narcissism should change? We can break these into agentic extraversion, antagonism, and neuroticism, as we did in chapter 12, and think about them like the intervention studies mentioned there. Ideally, this is how it would be done in scientific studies. Given the limits of what we know, however, I want to delve into specific issues that I see frequently that can be matched with practical responses. We need to figure out what gives us the most trouble in our lives and then implement an appropriate practice. I'll discuss these on a spectrum from the classically grandiose problems, such as risk-taking, to the classically vulnerable ones, such as fragile self-esteem.

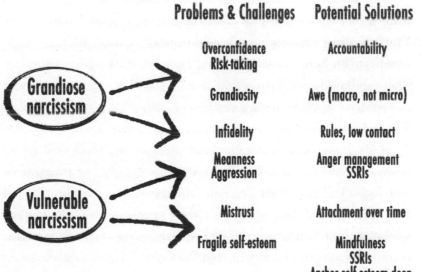

Problems & Challenges	Potential Solutions
Grandiose narcissism	
Overconfidence Risk-taking	Accountability
Grandiosity	Awe (macro, not micro)
Infidelity	Rules, low contact
Meanness Aggression	Anger management SSRIs
Vulnerable narcissism	
Mistrust	Attachment over time
Fragile self-esteem	Mindfulness SSRIs Anchor self-esteem deep

Overconfidence

Overconfidence and risk-taking are benefits of grandiose narcissism in many instances, but they can also lead to catastrophic consequences. In the infamous 1990s takedown of Barings Bank, one of the most prestigious banks in the United Kingdom since the 1700s, a twenty-eight-year-old trader named Nick Leeson defrauded the company out of about $1.3 billion, which was twice the bank's available trading capital. His risks led to a major collapse. In reality, even though one trader became the face of the downfall, there's often a risk-supportive CEO involved in this type of event. In a 2016 study of the 2007–2009 financial crisis, for instance, overconfident CEOs were more likely to weaken lending standards and up their leverage.[7] This ultimately made their companies more vulnerable to the economic downturn, and during the crisis, they had more loan defaults, greater drops in operating and stock return performance, greater increases in default probability, and higher likelihood of CEO turnover.

In these cases, the trouble with risk-taking is that people believe they can get away with it, make up for it if they fail, or take a bigger risk to cover up the earlier risk. Narcissists, in general, take risks, observe the feedback (or lack thereof), don't learn from those risks, and take more. When gambling becomes a problem, for instance, people take money from their loved ones, go into debt, and destroy their lives in an attempt to correct an original streak of bad luck. They're convinced the whole time that they have the scheme, trick, or inside advantage to win.

How do you account for this level of overconfidence? One of my words to live by is, "Reality always wins," meaning that no matter what we believe or what we fantasize, reality will set the record straight. To deal with this overconfidence, reality needs to intervene. Research suggests finding this through accountability and transparency with a supervisor, machine, or peer. Then people are less likely to overreport or self-enhance their performance. I'm not advocating for in-house corporate spying by any means, but in terms of your own life, having some mechanism for accountability will help reduce narcissism.

Personally, my favorite mechanism for accountability is natural consequences. The simplest example is when a child burns their hand on a stove. They burn their hand once, realize they shouldn't do it, and then don't try it again. It's the magic of learning without teaching. In many activities involving nature, these consequences pop up. If you practice any sport, including one that can cause physical harm, such as football, surfing, or skiing, you've likely gotten hit on the head, wiped out, or fallen down. This doesn't mean you quit, but it does mean that you will be more cautious as your skills develop.

Grandiosity

Second to overconfidence is grandiosity, or generally thinking you're a big deal. Almost everyone inflates how they are and how they see themselves, and it isn't necessarily troubling. When it interferes with work or relationships, though, it may be time for a change. One way to reduce the self-enhanced view is to ask specific questions about those qualities. If you think you're a "great" student, then what is your grade point average? If you're a "great" leader, then what specific leadership roles have you taken, and how have you motivated and mentored others? When you think about the specifics, you might find it becomes more challenging to come up with answers. This marks the boundary between talking a good game and having a good game.

In contrast, another way to attack grandiosity is by showing the "self" how big the world is, which is known as an experience of awe. When the world is vast, the ego is small. It can be an uncomfortable experience, but it's also a powerful experience. Studies suggest that experiences of awe, such as standing in a majestic forest, can reduce entitlement and increase humility. In virtual environments, simulating the Earth as a small blue dot in the universe uses the same idea to provoke awe.

What doesn't seem to work, unfortunately, is what I've called "micro-awe" in everyday life. At the University of California, Irvine, Paul Piff and colleagues researched this by instructing participants to notice bits of grandeur, such as a beautiful sunset over the rim of the Pacific Coast Highway.[8] You'd imagine that might change someone, and in the work they've done, it boosts prosocial behavior, but it doesn't last. People appreciate it but then move on with their day without long-term effects.

Infidelity

Another variable associated with grandiose narcissism in infidelity. When most people think about someone who is unfaithful is a relationship, they consider it a hurtful act, and it is, but research shows that it's driven by the extraverted side of narcissism. It's attention-seeking and reward-seeking behavior. The best way to stop this type of behavior is to avoid the reward—even the temptation of it. People believe they have will-power, but the general rule with self-control is that if you don't want it, stay away from it. If I don't want ice cream in my diet, I don't keep it in the freezer. If I don't want to drink, I don't go to bars. If I don't want to cheat on my wife, I don't hang out with women who aren't my wife late at night when I'm drinking at bars. If you follow this guideline, it reduces the reward-seeking possibility of infidelity by a huge amount.

People jumped all over Mike Pence when he was running for vice president because he said he doesn't spend time alone with women who aren't his wife. This might lead to all sorts of challenging political and social issues, but what it does is protect Pence from cheating on anybody, being caught cheating on anybody, or even being accused of cheating on anybody.

Aggression

Meanness and aggression are obviously profound problems with narcissism. In our work, I've seen that narcissistic people can be aware that their aggression is harmful and pushes people away and can lead to bullying and physical violence. In the largest review that I've found looking at anger treatment, which is a large meta-analysis published by the American Psychological Association, there's essentially no difference in the effectiveness of the different treatments.[9] Group therapy for anger management, self-help treatment, and a few others work, but the method that doesn't work is catharsis. This is the old idea that aggression is pent-up energy that needs to be released. Previously, people were told to punch pillows or print out the image of the person they hate and throw darts at it. What this actually seems to do is reinforce aggression even more. It makes aggression rewarding.

Plus, depression can look like aggression, especially in men. When some men are depressed, they become hostile, which appears to be callousness, but really, it's neuroticism or suffering. When depression is externalized rather than internalized, people are snappy, critical, and irritable, and it can be misinterpreted and misdiagnosed.

Mistrust

Mistrust occurs with both grandiose and vulnerable narcissism, but it's more pronounced with more vulnerable forms. This mistrust is linked to basic attachment, particularly basic parental attachment. According to attachment theory, children who are raised in less stable environments, or less secure environments with parents who are not present, are more likely to have mental disorders or substance abuse problems. Since these children grew up in that environment, they learn to be less trusting of others and guarded in their relationships with other people. This is a rational response, and it's adaptive as children but less so later.

The problems occur when that child grows up and wants to enter a healthy environment where trust works, but their tendency to mistrust others hinders close relationships. Researchers have spent time on relationship attachment styles, especially among children, and some research indicates that change can occur in moving mistrust to trust. In some cases, the treatment for mistrust is simply dealing with it, meaning you form a relationship with someone you want to trust and get comfortable with your mistrust until you learn to move past it over time. This is tough, but therapy can help with it, and it seems to be the most effective approach.

Fragility

Finally, there's the issue of self-esteem fragility, or the idea that if someone says something negative or unflattering about you, you become reactive or destabilized by it. To give you an example, after video of my 2017 TEDx Talk on narcissism was posted online, I made the mistake of looking at the comments. People said I looked fat. Those viewers could have made plenty of negative comments about me that I wouldn't have cared about, but for some reason, reading that I looked fat created a narcissistic wound. That fragility I felt caused me suffering. This type of suffering then triggers a reaction. The natural inclination in these instances is to go on the offensive and attack back or go on the defensive and say you're not fat. I generally try not to feed the trolls, but that is not satisfying in the short-term.

The easy solution is to not listen to *any* feedback because everyone else is an idiot. Of course, that isn't effective because you would never learn anything about yourself. Instead, you need a system to learn from the outside by taking in both positive and negative information, not get dysregulated by it, and move forward with what you know. Mindfulness can help with this.

A more specific practice, though, is self-compassion, which is defined as an ability to treat yourself like a loving friend would treat you. This includes seeing yourself as a common member of humanity, being present in the moment, and not beating yourself up for mistakes in the past. This practice of self-compassion, particularly thinking about how your friend would respond, can be really useful. Friends would likely tell us to relax, take a breath, brush off the negative comment, and move on as a human being like everyone else.

That inner voice of self-compassion takes away the sting that comes with negative feedback. Over time, you can develop that capacity to receive feedback and be able to evaluate it as relevant or irrelevant. Some relevant feedback comes from people you care about, and you want to listen to it. Other feedback comes from Internet trolls, and you really don't want to listen to that. The short version is that you remove the ego from the equation.

BIG SOLUTIONS

We'll end with a big-picture vision of how to tackle your own narcissism in terms of society. In personality research, social investment theory is based on the idea that society is an integrated unit that combines work, volunteering, religion, and community. It involves helping those older than us and younger than us in this dynamic system. To invest in a community, your personality must be shaped in certain ways, which form the axis of stability in the Big Five.

To be a stable member of a community, you need to be agreeable, conscientious, calm, emotionally stable, kind, and hardworking. To the extent that you're willing to invest yourself in the community, you're naturally going to shift in the direction of being more disciplined, conscientious, agreeable, and cooperative. You'll also form more friendships and more social connections, and you'll feel better about yourself. You'll feel more stable and less lonely. When psychologically committed to these roles in a community, you're more likely to shift in this positive direction, according to a 2007 meta-analysis of social investment research done by Jennifer Lodi-Smith and Brent Roberts at the University of Illinois at Urbana-Champaign.[10]

It is the exact same principle with exercise. I practice yoga daily, so my body has adjusted to a body that can practice yoga every day. If I were a long-distance runner, my body would adjust to being a distance runner. It's the same with how you treat your social life. If you invest yourself in the community, you will become a community-focused person—with the personality traits of a community-focused person. At the individual level, changing narcissism is about opening up to love. At the social level, it's about connecting to the community more broadly.

CHAPTER 14

Psychotherapy
for Narcissism

I have some good news and some bad news. The good news is that despite what you might have read, narcissistic personality disorder, or NPD, *can* be treated in psychotherapy. The bad news is that there is no gold-standard treatment. No clinical trials have focused on NPD or compared different treatments. Rather, mental health professionals who have had some success in treating narcissism have filed clinical reports, and NPD has been included secondarily in clinical trials focused on other disorders.

For instance, the Research Domain Criteria project, or RDoC, is a National Institute of Mental Health initiative that started in 2010 to find new approaches for investigating mental disorders. By integrating biology, behavior, and context, the aim is to explore basic processes of human behavior across the range from normal to abnormal. Essentially, the goal from the modern scientific medicine angle is to break down diseases, such as NPD, into their most basic neurochemical processes, study them in a lab, and then test treatments on rodents before humans. As you can imagine, this is helpful at the basic level—there are rodent models for depression, dementia, and other mental illness—but it's not useful for complex human psychological processes that aren't shared with rodents, which include most personality disorders. Even if you could build a rodent model of narcissism, such as rat dominance and mating, and test treatments, it wouldn't likely be productive or helpful.

Plus, the US government doesn't consider NPD to be a major health concern. Far more research funding goes into studying border-line personality disorder because of the clear self-harm and potential for prevention. The harm caused by NPD, for instance, falls between the mental health and criminal justice systems, so research on NPD typically drops to a secondary goal or priority. Often a treatment study on borderline personality disorder can also assess and capture data on vulnerable NPD. Likewise, a study on group therapy might include narcissism as one of the several disorders diagnosed among the participants.

Because there isn't a specific study to point you to or a gold standard for treatment, I can't definitively say how to treat NPD. I will try to do the next best thing by offering a general overview of what the research indicates and filling in the holes with some speculation about what could work.

POTENTIAL BARRIERS TO NPD TREATMENT

Before explaining the three avenues that might work—psychodynamic, cognitive behavioral, and psychiatric—it's important to point out the barriers that may get in the way when treating NPD, which could determine the most effective option. In psychotherapy, of course, motivation is a major factor, and for it to be successful, the person who enters treatment must want to be there in the first place and be able to stick with it. Narcissists typically have low motivation for seeking treatment, especially those with the more grandiose forms. Vulnerable narcissists seek treatment because they're suffering, but the grandiose narcissists' spouses are the ones who are more likely to seek help. This is what I see as an expert as well. More often than not, people ask me how to deal with or understand a loved one with narcissism rather than their own narcissism.

Narcissists also have a high dropout rate in therapy. In a 2008 study on narcissism and attrition, John Ogrodniczuk and colleagues in British Columbia analyzed 240 patients admitted to a formal, full-day inpatient treatment program designed to make them feel happier, improve interpersonal problems, and reduce general psychiatric distress.[1] The dropout rate was 63 percent for narcissism patients and 32 percent for others. Those narcissists who stayed improved like everyone else in the study. They still had intrusive behavior such as domineering and vindictive attitudes, but they had fewer interpersonal difficulties, the study authors concluded.

The positive here is that a psychologist who is skilled in treating narcissistic personality disorder will know this and can use techniques to keep people in therapy. This often means playing into the client's narcissism by saying, "You have so many talents that could benefit the world. We need to control your NPD, so you can have the impact that you deserve." Wendy Behary, a clinical social worker who has made a career out of treating NPD and wrote *Disarming the Narcissist: Surviving and Thriving with the Self-Absorbed*, describes it as a dance. The therapist needs to shift between lifting up the clients at some points and helping them face less-flattering realities at other points.[2]

Well-trained psychotherapists also use *motivational interviewing* to engage narcissistic clients, which came from research on substance abuse treatment. Narcissism, like doing cocaine, is a mixed blessing, so the goal of motivational interviewing is to encourage the client to see the downsides of narcissism clearly and come to the conclusion that change is necessary. To do this successfully, a psychotherapist empathizes with the narcissist's struggles and praises the narcissist's gifts while tying these to the narcissist's newly strengthened desire to change. Just like coaching a friend through a destructive romantic relationship, it's important to support them so they don't feel pushed away, but also support their decision to leave the relationship.

FOUR WAYS PSYCHOTHERAPISTS VIEW NPD TREATMENT

Although no definitive standard exists, psychotherapists line up on a few aspects of treating NPD. In a 2015 study of pathological narcissism, a group of researchers at Canadian universities asked thirty-four psychotherapists to explain to the researchers how they'd classify several descriptions of disorders.[3] The descriptions included a grandiose version of NPD, a vulnerable version of NPD, and a panic disorder. Overall, the research team wanted to check whether therapists would approach narcissistic disorders in a different way than panic disorders. The research team found four ways that psychotherapists talked about NPD treatment.

First, therapists talked about introspective and relational approaches to NPD. They hoped the patients would be willing to look inward to deal with foundational childhood issues that may have affected current relationships, including the relationship with the therapist, which is called *transference*. As people develop and find ways to relate to others in life, they may transfer feelings from early in life to those relationships. Therapy, in this case, investigates the idea of transference itself and the analysis of transference as a way of digging to the root of issues.

A second theme emerged with classic cognitive behavioral therapy. Although several types of cognitive behavioral therapy may help narcissism, this group focused on a homework-based, directed manualized therapy, which is more commonly used with a panic disorder and not narcissism. With a panic disorder, a therapist might encourage a patient to induce a panic attack by inhaling and exhaling in a paper bag and then train them in the moment to decondition it. This approach works for a specific situation such as a panic attack, but the therapists in the study converged on the conclusion that it isn't likely applicable for the broader personality aspects of narcissism.

Then the group split between their recommended treatments for the grandiose and vulnerable tendencies. For more vulnerable narcissists, the therapists said they'd be more likely to provide support during therapy since this type of client tends to be more needy, sad, or shy. They would also adopt a supportive stance with those who express a lack of self-worth, shame, or inferiority. They would say more positive statements such as "You're a good person" to contradict the patient's fragile self-esteem.

The fourth theme in the study, which becomes more of an issue in therapy, focused on the "angry, provocative patients," or the grandiose narcissists who blame others for their problems. These patients test the limits in therapy, tend to be abusive, and aren't fun to treat. The therapists said it would be best to be consistent in analyzing the patients' behaviors by repeatedly showing them how their patterns affect their lives. In these cases, the therapists noted the need to be conscientious about setting boundaries and being direct with the client.

Overall, as the study indicates, psychotherapists may treat narcissism by talking about the past, dealing with self-esteem and self-loathing, and connecting negative patterns or behaviors with ongoing issues such as relationship problems.

THREE BASIC THERAPIES FOR NARCISSISM

Following, I'll outline three broad classes of therapies that are popular now for treating NPD: psychodynamic, cognitive behavioral, and psychiatric medication (see table 14.1). These contain subcategories, and new treatments are constantly being developed, but this is a reasonable way to see the similarities and differences.

Table 14.1: Basic Therapies for Narcissism

	EXAMPLE	PRINCIPLES
PSYCHODYNAMIC	Transference-focused psychotherapy	Focus on early relationships and ego defense
COGNITIVE BEHAVIORAL	Schema therapy Dialectical behavior therapy Acceptance and commitment therapy	Focus on relational schema and representation Focus on impulse and affect regulation Buddhist/stoic acceptance of life and let it go
MEDICATION	SSRIs Ketamine	Stabilize elevated levels Serotonin activation

Psychodynamic

A range of therapeutic approaches has been reported to help with narcissism. The original—and still common—is psychodynamic treatment, which can take several forms. Each shares an interest in understanding unconscious processes, discussing the childhood roots of the disorder, and working to establish client insight. This is a fancy way of saying the client "gets it." Psychodynamic therapy for NPD tends to focus on identifying hidden feelings of rejection or anger, uncovering the roots of these feelings in childhood, and helping the client to understand how those childhood traumas translated into becoming a narcissistic adult.

As mentioned at the beginning of the book, psychodynamic therapies came from the psychoanalytic therapy first laid out by Freud, which was later developed in the 1960s and 1970s by Austrian psychoanalysts Otto Kernberg and Heinz Kohut. Known for their theories on borderline personality and narcissistic pathology, the two studied the causes, psychic organization, and treatment of the disorders in different ways. Kernberg focused more on Freud's theories about people's struggle between love and aggression, and Kohut split from Freud's ideas by talking about people's need for self-organization and self-expression. Kernberg insisted on being neutral rather than supportive during therapy, always challenging a narcissist's tendency to aim for control, which aligns with Freud's thinking. On the other hand, Kohut saw narcissistic illusions as a way to focus on the "self" and introspection, and he encouraged transference to help the patient self-cure.

The science has progressed beyond both of these early approaches, and modern psychodynamic therapies integrate the two ideas. Transference-focused therapy, for instance, looks at the interaction between the patient and therapist to understand how the therapist reacts. If anger or attraction arises, for instance, that could indicate how the patient views and interacts with the world. The modern psychodynamic therapies are typically short, not five days per week on an analyst's couch for years. Although those old-school treatments still exist, they're not necessarily considered the most effective, both for time and the wallet. Even today, this type of psychodynamic therapy is most popular around New York City, and new research is being done at Columbia University. At the same time, various groups in different locations have developed different therapies that borrow from psychodynamic therapies but are usually shorter in duration.

Cognitive Behavioral Therapy

More contemporary approaches use cognitive behavioral therapy, or CBT, which looks at the thoughts and actions that cause personal challenges in the present day. The CBT approach is rational, and the goal is to change destructive thoughts and behaviors. For instance, a client may experience trouble at work because he is a tyrant and creates a toxic environment. He knows he is a talented salesperson, but the company wants to let him go. The psychologist might identify the narcissist's explanation for the tirades, such as, "The staff members are stupid and get in my way."

and then compare that to the client's goal of "I want to be the number one salesperson in the company." The process of therapy then examines how the destructive behavior damages the client's goal and then pulls out the specifics of why the staff members are "stupid." The psychologist will encourage the client to try new thoughts, such as, "The staff isn't trained, and they need me to help them to help me." CBT is designed to be a shorter-term treatment, which aims to solve specific problems rather than try to rebuild the narcissist.

Cognitive behavioral therapy is the standard model taught in research-based academic training centers, as we have at the University of Georgia. Started by American psychiatrist Aaron Beck in the 1970s, cognitive therapy investigates behaviors, thoughts, and representations of the self, others, relationships, and the past. It has been most widely used for depression, where it became a go-to model to focus on negative views of the future, why those views exist, how to confront those views, and how to potentially change some of them. It can be a specific, directed process that works effectively, especially with depression.

Since the early work by Beck, new cognitive therapies developed for personality disorders, in particular, including schema therapy by Jeffrey Young, which was intended for those who relapsed or failed to respond to other therapies such as traditional CBT. It focuses on self-beliefs as they relate to current and past relationships. Clinically, analysts observe that narcissistic clients have extremely positive self-views alongside extremely negative self-views, which are triggered by different environments. Schema therapy pinpoints those triggering moments, uncovers the thought or behavioral pattern that occurs, and then tries to modify them to be less harmful and more positive. This approach has been tested successfully in large groups of people with different personality disorders but not specifically with narcissism.

Another popular and well-studied therapy is dialectical behavior therapy, or DBT, typically aimed at borderline personality disorder. Started by University of Washington psychologist Marsha Linehan, the technique pairs cognitive behavioral tools with mindfulness to focus on learning how to cope with thoughts without acting on them impulsively. Linehan originally developed DBT to treat suicidal behaviors, which has extended to other mental disorders, particularly those related to emotion dysregulation. In my own experience, when I was angry with a superior at my university, the DBT group in my department advised me to put a cold compress on my face to stop the feedback loop of blood rushing in my cheeks. Another tactic in DBT is to use the "wise mind" to make decisions, rather than the emotion-filled mind that might make impulsive choices in the moment. It helped in the moment; I didn't get fired. Although few studies have researched the therapy's effect on narcissism, a case study done by Sarah Fischer at the University of Georgia (now at George Mason University in Virginia) showed that scores on the Narcissistic Personality Inventory dropped after DBT. Vulnerable narcissists could benefit especially, it seems.

A third cognitive therapy that's growing in popularity is acceptance and commitment therapy, or ACT, which extends Buddhist ideals of acceptance. More than a mindfulness practice, ACT relies on the acceptance of situations for good or ill. Essentially, suffering happens in life, and it's important to accept it. This therapy makes sense historically and is what Buddha taught in the mustard seed parable—a woman who is suffering because she lost a loved one asks the Buddha for help, and he agrees to make a magic potion if she collects a mustard seed from everyone who hasn't lost a loved one. Of course, she searches for the seeds and can't find anyone who hasn't lost someone. She realizes this and returns to follow the Buddha's practices. The point here is not nihilistic acceptance but that everyone deals with difficult situations, and that's part of life as a human being. As far as I know, no work has combined ACT with narcissism, but I suspect it may work better for the more neurotic piece of NPD. At the same time, some heavy truth in the right context could treat more callous and grandiose aspects of NPD.

Medication

Questions always come up about psychopharmacological therapies, or medications, for narcissism and NPD. There are no real recommendations available. However, some antidepressants or selective serotonin reuptake inhibitors (SSRIs) are recommended for borderline personality disorder. Related to that, if a patient's NPD includes lowered self-esteem, high neuroticism, and unstable sense of self, an SSRI may be a reasonable approach.

Researchers are exploring possibilities of new medications for depression, particularly treatment-resistant depression. The hot topic right now—outside of the classic psychedelics—is ketamine, a dissociative drug used for starting and maintaining anesthesia. It induces a trance-like state to provide pain relief, sedation, and memory loss. Also known as "K" or "Special K," ketamine has been used illicitly as a club drug or a hallucinogenic aid. Yale University psychiatrists are the pioneers of current ketamine research, and in March 2019, the Food and Drug Administration approved a nasal spray containing esketamine, derived from ketamine, to treat major depression. It activates the serotonin system, which seems to work on depression in the studies that Yale has released.[4] To be clear, this is unlikely to affect grandiose aspects of narcissism. In the future, it may be able to help with irritability that can come across as antagonism, basically giving people a little longer fuse, but we need more research to know for sure.

FINDING THE RIGHT THERAPIST

If you think you have NPD or are trying to advise someone who has NPD, it's important to find the treatment and therapist who might work best for the situation. Although I've been asked for advice on selecting the best therapist for NPD many times, I can't give an exact answer. Different types of therapists provide different types of treatments, and it can be tough to tell them apart at first. The types and availability also differ by county and state. In these situations, I typically offer a few thoughts to steer the search.

In general, I suggest looking for a trained clinical psychologist or psychiatrist who was educated at a major research university, such as the University of Georgia, University of Minnesota, or University of California at Los Angeles. Any large university in any state will contain a flagship clinical psychology program, especially ones that are accredited by the American Psychological Association (APA) and the Psychological Clinical Science Accreditation System (PCSAS). Graduates from these programs will have the best training and will be the smartest people with that training. This doesn't mean they're the best therapists, but at least you can count on basic quality control if you work with someone from one of these programs. They're also likely trained in the latest therapies, well-versed in cognitive behavioral techniques, and skilled at breaking down problems.

Psychodynamic therapies and psychoanalysts tend to do their work in New York City and East Coast and West Coast hubs. If you are highly intelligent and introspective, psychoanalytic therapy might be helpful because it gives you the option to look inward, learn, and grow, which could be motivating. This tends to be more expensive and a limited option, depending on where you live.

Beyond that, you can look for psychotherapists who specialize in personality disorders. This will also depend on location, but if you live in a larger city, you should be able to find clinics and professionals with this specialty. Many of them will focus on borderline personality disorder and DBT or related therapies, but they're a good place to start since training is specific and targeted. Plus, these therapies require a process that is taught to the professionals, so it's often consistent and reliable regardless of location.

In the end, picking a psychotherapist is like investing. You can talk all day about the best investment—equity percentages, bonds, real estate, or gold—but you have to invest to get a return. Some investments go sideways, some are disasters, and some are home runs. The action of investment matters most, and the different methods simply tweak the basic model of socking away more money for better eventual returns. The same is true for psychotherapy and narcissism. In the end, the biggest challenge will be committing to the therapy, so if you can find one that will work and you feel you're making progress (or others in your life are noticing it), then that's the therapy for you. And if it doesn't work, try another one. As a final note: I'm not saying you should burn through every therapist in town to find someone who agrees with you that there's someone to blame other than yourself. Instead, if you invest in yourself over time with psychotherapy, there is a decent chance for improvement—despite everything we once thought about NPD.

FINDING REFUGE FROM NARCISSISM'S EFFECTS

As a final note in this chapter, it's necessary to speak to those who want help if they're involved with narcissists at work or at home and want to make themselves less vulnerable to the upset they experience. This is difficult. The key is seeking help, but there's no "anti-narcissism" therapy. In a situation with lawbreaking behavior, such as violence, assault, and defamation, legal remedies can be used. If you're suffering from clinical outcomes, such as depression, clinical treatments may work best. There are online blogs like One Mom's Battle, which focuses on divorcing a narcissist, but no ideal therapeutic approach that I am aware of as a professional.

Overall, those who deal with narcissists need sanity checks in their life, which I think of as reality testing. The idea is that you need someone you trust—a therapist, pastor, parent, spouse, or friend—who can support your view of reality rather than that of the narcissist. If you want help moving beyond the relationship, multiple people should be enlisted as allies, whether that comes from friends, family, or doctors.

Social support helps. I wish there were a body of scientific research on this, but there really isn't.

NERD HERD: PSYCHOTHERAPY BY LOCATION

People often ask me why psychodynamic models are found in New York City and certain other cities on either side of the country. Psychology and its variants spread across the United States at different times and in different ways. Psychoanalysis was and still can be an elite, expensive form of therapy. When it came from Europe, it took root in major cities, especially New York City. Freud's ideas reigned there. In New England, William James found Freud's ideas a little dark and favored willpower and good character, and a new approach to mental health bloomed there that downplayed diagnoses and supported community living, including church and work. The West Coast is a different story, where more humanistic and Gestalt psychology flourished. California was the heart of the human potential movement and the self-esteem movement. The Midwest was the birthplace of industrial psychology, and the South has great psychology research labs, but generally, there's less interest in psychotherapy and more emphasis on religion.

INSIDE SCOOP: FOR THOSE SEEKING HELP

Part of the motivation for writing this book was to get as much information out there as I can. I receive dozens of emails from people who are desperate for a solution to narcissism. They are so desperate that they email a stranger who presented a TEDx Talk and wrote the script to a TED-Ed lesson. Of those who contact me, there are few who are personally struggling with NPD. Instead, most are struggling with a narcissistic spouse, child's spouse, or boss.

People are looking for the best answer, but they end up emailing me because there are no easy or obvious answers out there. Think about it this way: If there is someone with strong narcissistic tendencies in your life, they have hurt or alienated many people. Some people cut them off, some people sue them, some people try to appease them, and some people think they are awesome—there is no specific effect of narcissism to treat. For that reason, I think the best starting point is general counseling or therapy. Figure out what is going on with you and then follow the path that is best for your own well-being.

CHAPTER 15

Future Science Around Narcissism

S cience always progresses with new theories, tools, and research methods, which makes the scientific study of narcissism fun. When psychologists, psychiatrists, and psychoanalysts first started trying to understand narcissism, they had only their observations and insights, which are important first steps but prone to bias and error. We often end up seeing what we want to see. Science is still prone to bias and error, but we are making progress.

In this final chapter, I want to look at the future—and the science and related treatments that will change how we see and treat narcissism, as well as personality more generally. Some of these ideas will take off on their own, some will be monetized and pushed on people, and some will be kept illegal and remain held from people. In addition to those ideas, I want to call out the massive wave that is genetics. The birth of genetically modified babies to patients under the care of He Jiankuiin, a biophysics researcher in China, means I might even live to see that procedure go mainstream, although the decision by the Chinese government to imprison Dr. He for three years will slow this work.

Technology and statistical advances are making it more possible to study people in real time and with the richest context possible. In a sense, we are moving from still pictures to movies. For instance, smartphones can be used for "ambulatory assessment," which covers a range of assessment methods being used to study people in their natural environment, including observational data, self-report information, and biological/behavioral/physiological numbers. Data analysis of words and images are being powered by computers, and we have lab tools that can read emotions from faces and spoken language. Beyond that, trace data can capture information from our credit cards, cookies, and digital armbands. Finally, neuroimaging with functional MRI is allowing us to see the brain circuitry that underlies personality in specific situations.

FIRST LOOK: ADVANCES IN GENETICS

In general, the latest in molecular genetics will advance current knowledge about the nuances of personality. Scientists have known for decades that personality is heritable—and that it comes, in part, from our biological parents. Researchers learned this by studying twins. Because identical twins are more genetically similar than nonidentical twins, they could assume that at least some of the similarities were inherited. They furthered that by studying twins who were raised by different families to understand how much of the differences between them is due to parenting. Now the latest science might uncover the genes involved in intelligence, the Big Five traits, and personality, including narcissism.

Researchers know that personality isn't the result of one or two genes but scores of genes that each account for a tiny bit of personality. Because there is no "narcissism" or "extraversion" gene (or known cluster of genes), we need to look at the genomes for hundreds of thousands of people who have taken personality tests. This large-scale research is called a genome-wide association study, or GWAS. Tests can map a genome now for about $1,000, which is incredible given that the first genome map cost more than $2.5 billion. The price will eventually hit $100. Today, scientists have a good idea of the many genes that make up height. In ten to twenty years, we may have the same information for narcissism. It's simply a matter of cost and interest to use the data to detect a pattern in the noise.

Based on that information, clinical psychologists will want to know how to change those genes and personality traits. This could mean finding a way to avoid expressing those genes. For instance, a patient who learns she has a genetic predisposition for heart disease is likely advised to take preventive measures through diet, exercise, and stress reduction. With personality, that could be different. An incredible new procedure called CRISPR, or clustered regularly interspaced short palindromic repeats, has been developed for direct gene editing in living animals by using DNA fragments to destroy specific DNA. Scientists have already used CRISPR to edit DNA in babies with a disabled CCR5 gene, which is responsible for two types of HIV resistance. Editing the gene, in theory, should protect these babies from HIV. The initial work was done in China, and now a group in Russia is said to be working on it.

My guess is that a variant of CRISPR will catch on as a preventive practice in fertility clinics. For personality, any first targets will likely be broadly aimed at anxiety reduction. At the same time, I don't know if genetic intervention will get to the point where it can reliably change personality in a desirable way. That would mean drawing a decent map between complex genes at birth and personality at a later date, which may not be predictable with much precision. This would take a large amount of data, complex science, and intricate math models. Plus, computer power—most cutting-edge psychological science today relies on computer scientists, statisticians, and physicists to capture and model the data.

NEXT STEPS: NEW SCIENCE

The massive technological changes of the last several decades have made their way into psychological science. It has taken some time to harness these tools, but the effort is starting to bear fruit, and it's where the most exciting breakthroughs will occur in the next decade. Since the developments are overlapping and becoming interwoven, the future of narcissism research will look different and more complex. Table 15.1 provides an overview of some promising new methods.

Table 15.1: New Science of Personality Studies

	EXAMPLE	ISSUES
AMBULATORY ASSESSMENT	Wireless body area network connected to smartphone to collect pulse	Data, batteries, sensors
LINGUISTIC AND VIDEO DATA ANALYSIS	Computational linguistics Facial recognition software	Extracting meaning from text and videos
NEUROIMAGING	fMRI MEG EEG	Sample size, expense, building more complex human models
TRACE DATA	Social media	Privacy, validity

Ambulatory Assessment

The possibilities are endless with ambulatory assessment, as described at the beginning of this chapter, in terms of electronic sampling, experiential sampling methods, and electronic momentary assessment. In the old days, researchers conducted diary studies where participants would fill out a diary on paper. Next, researchers hooked people up with pagers (remember those?) and beeped them five times a day and said, "How do you feel?" to get an idea of how people felt over time. Now ambulatory assessment can collect a large amount of information about people and in a passive, noninvasive way that doesn't interfere with everyday actions. Timothy Trull from the University of Missouri has discussed the possibilities of using smartphones, e-diaries, and physiological monitoring to assess symptoms, predict future occurrences, monitor treatments, prevent relapses, and understand new interventions. One of the coolest examples of this idea is a wireless body area network (WBAN) that surrounds a smartphone as the hub of data collection and measurement. Think about what it can collect now—elevation, movement, spatial location, and even voice, not just words, but the intonations and speed of speech. Smartphones can also connect with other devices, such as a wristband that measures pulse or steps.

Beyond that, the quantified self, or self-tracking, movement has become popular for people to record their "stats" or movements over time. In recent years, psychologist Ryne Sherman has strapped video cameras to people that record every minute of their day to understand the situations people encounter in their lives and how they navigate those situations. This creates a pretty decent measure of somebody's life, especially when capturing how their voice changes, what words they use, and what they see at intervals of time. The data can also map to location and time. The challenge, of course, is that this creates so much data that it's tough to know how to analyze it and make sense of it at first.

Additional issues, which engineers bring up often, include reliable battery power and sensors. Batteries are improving, but they still don't last long enough. Sensors are getting smaller, but they could be smaller still. Breakthroughs in areas such as sleep studies, where sleep bands can measure data, however, show that science is getting there. These tools will change entirely how research is approached.

Linguistic and Video Data Analysis

Next to the physical issues, psychology researchers face questions around the science of language and vision, or the study of video data. Previously, scientists would analyze emotions from videos using average ratings or impressions from a group of humans. This is labor-intensive and time-consuming. Now we can make better sense of linguistic and video data with computers alone. At the University of Texas at Austin, psychologist James Pennebaker created the Linguistic Inquiry and Word Count (LIWC), a text analysis program that at first simply tallied the presence of words but later found that certain words "hung together," such as pronouns or words with an aggressive tone. In May 2019, a group of researchers across the country, led by Nicholas Holtzman at Georgia Southern University, released a LIWC analysis of narcissistic words. They found that the strongest correlates of narcissism were swear words, second-person pronouns, and words related to sports.[1] The negative correlates included tentative words, anxiety/fear words, and words related to sensory or perceptual processes. Although this is fascinating, these programs don't pick up on context or tone, such as the use of sarcasm. The new wave of research will search for the context and extract the meaning by looking at a network of words.

After text analysis, researchers are looking to video recognition and machine learning to detect emotional facial expressions from the psychology science perspective. A simple example of this is Duchenne smiles versus non-Duchenne smiles. Sometimes people smile with their mouth but not their eyes. It looks phony and sometimes predatory because it looks like a deceptive smile. Instead, a full smile involves engagement of both the mouth and eyes, which is the Duchenne smile, or what is popularly called "smizing" now. Computer programs can recognize this, and once these programs are reliable enough to match real-time videos and linguistic coding, researchers will uncover interesting data to understand narcissism.

Almost considered the inverse of ambulatory assessment, trace data provides observations based on aggregated data in the connected world. For instance, smartphones hold concert tickets, airplane flights, online purchases, GPS maps, and selfies. People leave these breadcrumbs—these traces—in company databases around the world. At a university, for instance, students use their ID cards to check out library books, go to the gym, enter the dorm, visit the health center, and eat at the dining hall. If administrators pulled the data together and matched it with grades, they might be able to see when students begin to face issues on campus, whether that's staying in the dorm all the time or falling off their exercise plan. In the future, as data analysis becomes even more sophisticated, this trace data could be used in psychology science to study addictions, such as tracking gamblers who travel to Las Vegas.

Related to this, "Big Data" research is making headway in personality science, as it is in many other fields. In 2018, researchers at Northwestern University used complex, quantitative models to define new personality clusters, and they came up with four: reserved, role models, average, and self-centered.[2] Their findings seem to follow the Big Five model well. Those in the "role model" group were high in every trait but neuroticism, and those in the "self-centered" group were high in extraversion but below average in agreeableness, conscientiousness, and openness. This may be a new model to study narcissism.

Many other areas of research will grow in the next decade, including social network analyses that map out narcissists' social networks and how they change over time. This "ego-mapping" data could also track narcissism within an environment, including which area of town has the highest density of narcissism and at what time. Many techniques will be developed to help us understand and lower narcissism.

Neuroimaging

Although it's more difficult to see the cost curve in this area than with genetics or behavioral genetics, neuroimaging will be another major area for new research. Functional neuroimaging, in particular, allows people to move and interact, albeit constrained, which gives an idea of how oxygen or oxygenated blood moves through the brain during the imaging. Scientists use sophisticated tools to analyze the images and create interesting stories, but the biggest challenge still is obtaining enough samples to take reliable measurements and make sense of the data.

Structural MRI (like the kind you'd get on your knee) and functional magnetic resonance imaging (fMRI) allow psychology researchers to look at structural processes, the shape of the brain, the morphology of the brain, and the oxygen and iron flows in the brain. To date, researchers do this by showing study participants certain images or asking them to complete certain tasks and then measuring the differences in the activated areas of the brain during that time. There have only been a couple studies of narcissism with imaging, but the potential to measure narcissistic differences is there, especially when scientists are able to use bigger sample sizes and apply machine-learning techniques.

Since fMRI measures blood and oxygen flow, it's slow, and it doesn't capture rapid brain changes. For that, researchers use the electroencephalogram (EEG), which measures brain waves, even in milliseconds. The challenge with the EEG, however, is that it doesn't pinpoint where activity happens in the brain. Although speed can be measured well, the location is not precise.

The magnetoencephalogram (MEG) measures the magnetic field around the brain with such sensitivity that it picks up nuance in the field in response to stimuli immediately. It's less common and quite expensive. It doesn't localize as well as an fMRI but can pinpoint better than an EEG, and when combined, these tools can provide interesting results. Neuroimaging of narcissism is in its infancy. The studies are small, and there aren't many of them because of the cost, but the hope is that as this technology develops and the price comes down, scientists will gain clear insights into narcissism and the brain circuitry activated in certain key situations such as risk-taking, self-enhancement, and aggression.

To give one example of what the science may look like, a research team in China recently sent me a draft of a study using machine-learning techniques to predict individual narcissism from MRI scans. Imagine taking an fMRI scan of two hundred people and then using that data to predict each person's narcissism score. Instead of coming up with theories about where narcissistic brains differ, raw computing power could look at thousands of correlations and see what aspects of the brain scans predict narcissism. Using this machine-learning approach in a small, single sample doesn't work well, but as soon as researchers can train these models on several large datasets, they will do a decent job of predicting narcissism. This process has worked well for companies such as Netflix, which uses my viewing data alongside the data of millions of others to predict what I would like to watch next. Personality's seat in the brain circuitry is a more complex question than what movies a person likes, but the math is pretty much the same.

THE FINAL FRONTIER: NEW TREATMENTS

In terms of new treatments, four are currently in various levels of use. Either they're at the beginning stages of use but haven't been widely adopted, in late-stage clinical trials, or in the translational stage that could become the next big treatment. Table 15.2 provides a selection of these new therapies to give you an idea of what is coming, including the drawbacks or current concerns that may hinder progress.

Table 15.2: New Treatment

	EXAMPLE	ISSUES
BRAIN STIMULATION	Transcranial magnetic stimulation (very low ECT)	Efficacy, harm, more anxiety
PSYCHEDELICS	MDMA Psilocybin	Illegal in US, not tested on narcissism, psycholytic vs. psychedelic vs. shamanic
VIRTUAL REALITY	Virtual acquisition Proteus effect	Virtual rather than in person Efficacy

Brain Stimulation

Brain stimulation therapies, which are some of the most interesting, are designed to directly affect areas of the brain. The most common example is transcranial magnetic stimulation, sometimes described as low-level electroshock therapy, or electroconvulsive therapy (ECT). This therapy seems to scramble the neurons, and when they reset and start firing again, people feel better. Done under general anesthesia, ECT is most commonly used in patients with severe major depression or bipolar disorder. At the moment, ECT isn't used for narcissism because scientists can't link it to those specific traits. In his book *The Psychopath Test*, Jon Ronson writes about transcranial techniques being used to deactivate areas in the frontal cortex, which make people act more like impulsive and psychopathic individuals.[3] In this case, the ECT treatment shifts people more toward psychopathic rather than narcissistic, but this technique could have potential for neurotic symptoms associated with vulnerable narcissism as well.

The truly cutting-edge work, however, deals with anesthetizing deep nerve bundles to stop the effects of anxiety, which is particularly relevant for extreme post-traumatic stress disorder. In June 2019, Medal of Honor recipient and Marine veteran Dakota Meyer had this treatment and said it felt like "a million pounds was taken off."[4] Called stellate ganglion block (SGB), the anesthetic injection numbs nerves at the base of the neck, dulling the area associated with the body's fight-or-flight response. Developed by Eugene Lipov, who works at the Service-Disabled Veteran-Owned Small Business program in collaboration with the Department of Defense and Veterans Affairs, the injection was first used to treat women experiencing menopausal hot flashes and now helps to diminish PTSD symptoms such as depression, anxiety, and insomnia.

Meyer compared his experience of the treatment to being in downtown New York City during rush hour and, all of a sudden, driving down a quiet country road. Meyer had served in the Kunar Province in

Afghanistan in 2009 when a patrol was ambushed by more than fifty enemy fighters. He made five trips into the ambush zone for six hours to save as many people as he could. Since then, he hadn't been able to "get the war out of his head." A 2014 study found that a week after the first SGB injection, about 70 percent of the 166 veterans who participated in the study experienced relief, and for many of them, the relief lasted for several months.[5] The Department of Defense gave the Army a $2 million grant to conduct a randomized, three-year study on the effects among 240 veterans with PTSD, which wrapped up in 2019, so we should know more as soon as the results are released publicly. These treatments hold promise for anxiety, depression, and hostility but not necessarily narcissism or antagonism in general.

Psychedelics

Interest and research around psychedelics are also exploding. Via serotonin activation, psychedelics create an altered state of consciousness and differences in thought, vision, and hearing. The nature of these effects depends a great deal on the set and setting of the experience, but there is not a specific psychedelic effect. Major psychedelic drugs include mescaline, LSD, psilocybin (mushrooms), ecstasy (MDMA, or molly), and DMT. The latter drug has drawn extensive attention recently, particularly in plant medicine forms such as ayahuasca that are given by a shaman or experienced healer.

Although people have reported profound visions while using DMT, the research on this plant medicine is too new to be conclusive right now. The ayahuasca plant isn't illegal in the United States, per se, but the active ingredient, DMT, is banned as a Schedule I drug. It can be used as a ceremonial plant medicine under the First Amendment, but it's illegal in research settings outside of religious use. Plus, DMT hasn't been tested in narcissism, though psychedelics tend to lead to lowered neuroticism, greater openness, and an overall change in ego.

In the 1950s, psychedelic treatments were tested through psycholytic therapy, where the patient would undergo psychoanalysis by talking about their childhood, fears, and dreams while taking a dose of LSD or another psychedelic. Taking a psychedelic drug would loosen up patients and help them recover memories and make connections that they might otherwise miss. In modern studies, ongoing clinical trials are testing MDMA as a treatment for PTSD in veterans, in combination with cognitive behavioral tools.

Early psychological researchers also experimented on themselves. Havelock Ellis, who first used the concept of narcissism scientifically, was also the first academic to bring peyote from cactus buttons to England and write about his experiences. Like ayahuasca, peyote is used in shamanic psychedelic ceremonies that create a safe space where the shaman can chant away negative energy, invite in intervening spirits, and clear blocks or trauma. Rather than a psychoanalytic or psychotherapeutic practice, the ceremony occurs on a mystical or spiritual plane, which is tough to discuss from a scientific perspective.

Overall, psychedelic therapies may be the most powerful potential medicines available. Although most are safe, especially when people are properly screened for mental illness and the experiments are conducted in a controlled environment, the legal issues make testing tough. Since these therapies lead to a "decoupling" from self that isn't typically possible under normal states of consciousness, they may offer a more unique opportunity for psychological change. It's a powerful tool, but researchers don't know how to harness it or use it yet. I hope that by the time this book is published, we will have some personality data from groups using ayahuasca in traditional ceremonies.

Virtual Reality

The final area of mind-blowing science, which hasn't hit as quickly as I thought it would but will soon, is virtual reality. You may have played with one of the new video game models that are available to the public, and some of those are great, but the research models available to scientists are game-changing. At the University of Georgia, the psychology building sits next to the journalism building, where Dr. Sun Joo "Grace" Ahn started a virtual reality lab to conduct communications research as well as collaborative research with other departments across campus.

When I toured the lab around 2014, one of her students put me in a helmet and instructed me to walk across the dark bridge in front of me. In reality, it was a board on the ground, but I couldn't see the board, and I felt like I was really on a bridge. I was so scared that I almost reached down to grab the board. It was one of the most immersive, amazing experiences I've had. As I left, I had a thought that this new technology would change the world and that its power would be akin to the ego-changing experience of psychedelics.

Fast-forward a few years, Dr. Ahn and my student Jessica McCain developed a project with a virtual Kim Kardashian, which prompted the user to see themselves as Kim and choose attractive material items versus less attractive items. What we thought, based on psychological theory, was that participants would experience the Proteus effect, which is the tendency for people to take on the characteristics of their avatar or digital representation. For instance, if I play an online basketball game as Michael Jordan, I should play a little better in the game—and maybe even outside the game—because I internalize beliefs about his (and thus, my) ability. In this case, interestingly, we didn't find that. It seems that participants felt somewhat negative to be seen as narcissistic, and they reacted by being less narcissistic.

Again, this is an incredibly preliminary look at how virtual reality may change the way we view and study ego. At the moment, though, the virtual reality money is being funneled into football. During an academic meeting years ago, I visited a virtual reality cave in Michigan, and the focus was on teaching people to play better football, which will likely lead the way in developing this science. I'm hopeful that virtual reality will give people the opportunity to try out perspective-taking, which may be one mechanism to change narcissism, by allowing narcissists to see both the negative effects that narcissism can have on others as well as the positive value that others give to them when they aren't narcissistic. Beyond that, virtual reality should be able to give us those "awe" experiences that let us see how small we are compared to the world and realize that our personal lives don't matter as much as we think they do.

NEW TRENDS IN RESEARCH

Although it may seem contrary to what you'd expect, new research is beginning to show a drop in narcissism in the population. In truth, our society is in a complicated phase with a shift in culture. At the same time that we're seeing a rise in populist, narcissistic leaders across the world, people are also growing tired of the narcissistic sense of self that we're seeing online. People are beginning to call out influencers and the fake posts of online marketing ninjas standing next to private jets they've rented by the hour to appear rich and famous. I don't know what will happen for sure, but my guess is that the kids who are growing up with social media right now are already seeing the downsides of the narcissistic self in the same way that some of us saw the downsides of disco and cocaine and moved away from that trend. Instead of celebrating a more narcissistic self, they're shifting to a restrained ego.

We're already seeing this on platforms like TikTok, where young users are posting everyday videos of practical jokes and dance routines. Instead of previously viral YouTube videos where people featured grandiose displays of their "haul of the day," or cool and expensive stuff, TikTok posters are interested in vulnerable, "real" conversations about life or simple entertainment to make their days fun or funny. As I sit with my teens and watch them laugh at TikTok posts, I see a new world less focused on status and more focused on creativity. This is pure speculation, but I have hope. It's time to focus our research on this new generation.

EPILOGUE

FACING THE FUTURE WITH HOPE

At this point in the book, you now know far more about narcissism than any researcher did in the 1990s and even the early 2000s. You've seen that narcissism is grounded in basic personality and that narcissism plays a role in social media, relationships, and leadership. You know that narcissism can be used and minimized, and that, if it is a personality disorder, it can be treated. Importantly, you also learned what we don't know—but hopefully will learn soon.

Remember that scientific knowledge is always shifting and changing. Some of the insights in this book may prove to be incorrect. With that caveat in mind, I do think that we have made some real progress in the last couple decades in the research on narcissism. And I hope that you have also picked up some useful ways to apply this knowledge in your own life.

A benefit of understanding narcissism is that it becomes less scary. When we turn on the TV or open news apps and see stories related to political corruption or new cases in the #MeToo movement, one impulse is to rid the world of narcissism. That gut instinct is understandable given what's happening in today's world. Others want to throw in the towel and believe this is the reality today and what we will always face. But I see another way forward: create (or recreate) systems that provide transparency and accountability for those in positions of public trust. This includes politicians but also professionals such as academics and those running public corporations. I'm not talking about *Black Mirror* spying but instead reinvigorated accountability. In science, this is the "open science" movement, which has washed away several careers built on sand.

In other areas, we need to support active, investigative journalism that reports the news—and that people trust. Narcissism thrives in a post-truth world, which developed with the rise of social media, "fake news," and a changing news industry where local news publications are closing their doors. New media organizations are developed each year to fill these gaps, and one way to combat the negative aspects of narcissism in our world is to support these efforts.

Beyond that, I'm a big believer in natural consequences and the reality principle, where narcissism thrives in the short-term but fails in the long-term. Under our current "American Dream," where many people feel compelled to build a personal brand to survive, we've created a system that almost demands some aspects of narcissism in order to thrive. People base their success on initial flash and charisma, and that works fine if you're a child who is trying to show off and jump off a cliff into the lake below. But if you're the person who has the nuclear codes, society doesn't benefit from your narcissism. Fortunately, I believe we're beginning to shift to a moment where narcissistic leaders aren't able to rely on their dishonesty and manipulative nature because society as a whole is beginning to see through the façade.

On social media, for instance, content is already shifting away from promotion and brand-building to entertainment and information sharing. The most successful businesses and solopreneurs are teaching others and providing true value through learning, and brand is becoming secondary. In addition, we're seeing a boom in podcasts and long-form content. Although studies show that our attention spans continue to shrink, we're spending more time on longer videos, audios, and articles that we think are worth our time.

In all, I bet on optimism and the long-term outlook. I just got a puppy, have my money in the stock market, and am eager to see my daughters grow up and start their careers. I have positive feelings about the world and the next ten to fifteen years. More people are turning away from materialism and consumerism and turning toward meditation, yoga, mindfulness, and the deeper benefits of spirituality. They're asking more questions about ego than ever before.

The growth of interest in narcissism research boosts this optimism rather than detracts from it. When I started studying narcissism, relatively few people understood it or knew what it was. In fact, many people struggled to pronounce it. But today, think about how many articles are written about it and how many conversations we're having about it. Overall, we're pushing back against global brands, and microcelebrities are reducing the centralized focus on megacelebrities who, in general, support more grandiose ideas of fame, wealth, and "status" linked with narcissism. Now that we know how to talk about narcissism, we can recognize it and account for it in our lives—both the positive and negative aspects.

During this next decade, I envision the pendulum swinging back. The prolific 2000s-era narcissism will fade as more people recognize and reject the phoniness of our narcissistic leaders who rose to power and failed in their leadership. Fame is more fleeting now than ever, and people are waking up to that fact.

We're turning back to self-care, renewal, and smaller communities built on personal connections. We're seeking happiness, and true happiness is ultimately built on love and genuine relationships. The fact that we're seeking the new, the different, and the authentic means we have the ability to shift away from harmful behaviors and lifestyles. Although this shift may take time, it's heading in the right direction.

It's complicated, of course, but I think over time the things that add value to the world will expand, and those that don't, won't. If we focus on what brings actual value to us and our communities—simply love and meaningful work—and avoid being distracted by uncontrollable fear or greed, we should be okay.

QUICK-START GLOSSARY

Big Five: The main personality traits, remembered as OCEAN or CANOE (openness, conscientiousness, extraversion, agreeableness, neuroticism). In general, people want to score higher in the first four and lower in neuroticism.

Correlation: The association, or co-relationship, between two variables. Correlations can range from 1 (a complete positive relationship) to −1 (a complete negative relationship). Most personality research deals with correlations around .2 or .3.

Grandiose narcissists: These ambitious, driven, and charming individuals have high self-esteem and generally feel good about themselves. These are the narcissists you will see most often in your life. We are often drawn to their boldness but are later repelled by their self-centeredness and lack of empathy.

Narcissism: Expressing the core traits of self-importance, antagonism, and a sense of entitlement.

Narcissistic personality disorder (NPD): The extreme and inflexible variant of narcissism that leads to clinical-level impairment in love and work.

Personality disorders: Psychological disorders that are based in extreme and inflexible personality characteristics that lead to significant impairment in life.

Personality traits: Descriptions of people that are stable across different situations and time.

Randomized controlled trial: When testing a treatment, one group is selected at random to receive the treatment and another group to receive the control (such as a placebo pill).

Reliability: How consistently a personality measure works. A reliable measure will work the same way across items and time.

Self-regulation: The ability to control oneself in the interest of achieving long-term goals.

Trifurcated Model of Narcissism: New model of narcissism that includes both grandiose and vulnerable narcissism, which share a core of disagreeableness, self-importance, and self-entitlement.

Validity: How well a personality test measures what it is supposed to measure (for example, does a test of extraversion measure extraversion, not something else?).

Vulnerable narcissists: Introverted, depressed, and easily hurt by criticism. They report having low self-esteem, but despite that, they see themselves as deserving of special treatment.

NOTES

Chapter 1

1. Ben Candea, "Santa Barbara Killer Claimed He Was Victim in 'Twisted Life' Memoir," ABC News, May 24, 2014, abcnews.go.com/US/santa-barbara-killer-claimed-victim-twisted-life-memoir/story?id=23861753.

Chapter 2

1. Seth Rosenthal et al., "The Narcissistic Grandiosity Scale: A Measure to Distinguish Narcissistic Grandiosity from High Self-Esteem" (published online ahead of print, July 3, 2019), *Assessment* (2019), www.ncbi.nlm.nih.gov/pubmed/31267782.

Chapter 3

1. Lewis Goldberg, "The Structure of Phenotypic Personality Traits," *American Psychologist* 48, no. 1 (1993): 26–34, psych.colorado.edu/~carey/Courses/PSYC5112/Readings/psnStructure_Goldberg.pdf.
2. Paul Meehl, "Why Summaries of Research on Psychological Theories Are Often Uninterpretable," *Psychological Reports* 66 (1990): 195–244, citeseerx.ist.psu.edu/viewdoc/download?doi=10.1.1.392.6447&rep=rep1&type=pdf.
3. Jochen Gebauer et al., "Agency and Communion in Grandiose Narcissism," chapter 8 in *Agency and Communion in Social Psychology*, ed. Andrea Abele and Bogdan Wojciszke (Abingdon, UK: Routledge, 2017), doi.org/10.4324/9780203703663-8.
4. Michael Ashton et al., "Honesty-Humility, the Big Five, and the Five-Factor Model," *Journal of Personality* 73, no. 5 (October 2005): 1321–1354, doi.org/10.1111/j.1467-6494.2005.00351.x.
5. Angela Book et al., "Unpacking Evil: Claiming the Core of the Dark Triad," *Personality and Individual Differences* 101 (October 2016): 468, doi.org/10.1016/j.paid.2016.05.094.

Chapter 4

1. Mandy Cantron, "To Fall in Love with Anyone, Do This," Modern Love, *New York Times*, January 9, 2015, nytimes.com/2015/01/11/style/modern-love-to-fall-in-love-with-anyone-do-this.html.

Chapter 5

1. American Psychiatric Association, *Diagnostic and Statistical Manual of Mental Disorders (DSM-5)* (Washington, DC: APA Publishing, 2013), xxx.

Chapter 6

1. Erin Buckels et al., "Behavioral Confirmation of Everyday Sadism," *Psychological Science* 24, no. 11 (2013): 2201–2209, doi.org/10.1177/0956797613490749.
2. Erich Fromm, *The Heart of Man: Its Genius for Good and Evil* (New York: Lantern Books, 1964).
3. Mila Goldner-Vukov et al., "Malignant Narcissism: From Fairy Tales to Harsh Reality," *Psychiatria Danubina* 22, no. 3 (2010): 392–405.
4. Delroy Paulhus, "Toward a Taxonomy of Dark Personalities," *Current Directions in Psychological Science* 23, no. 6 (2014): 421–426, doi.org/10.1177/0963721414547737.
5. Linda Rodriguez McRobbie, "Why a Little Evil Is Good—And a Lot of Empathy Is Bad," *Boston Globe*, October 27, 2018, bostonglobe.com/ideas/2018/10/27/why-little-evil-good-and-lot-empathy-bad/IsJyWqUrkHWrYLcTtnTQyI/story.html.
6. Josh Miller et al., "A Critical Appraisal of the Dark Triad Literature and Suggestions for Moving Forward," PsyArXiv Preprints, Cornell University, February 14, 2019, psyarxiv.com/mbkr8/.
7. H. Unterrainer et al., "Vulnerable Dark Triad Personality Facets Are Associated with Religious Fundamentalist Tendencies," *Psychopathology* 49, no. 1 (2016): 47–52, doi.org/10.1159/000443901.
8. B. Edwards et al., "Dark and Vulnerable Personality Trait Correlates of Dimensions of Criminal Behavior Among Adult Offenders," *Journal of Abnormal Psychology* 126, no. 7 (2017): 921–927, doi.org/10.1037/abn0000281.
9. Scott Kaufman et al., "The Light vs. Dark Triad of Personality: Contrasting Two Very Different Profiles of Human Nature," *Frontiers in Psychology* 10 (March 12, 2019), doi.org/10.3389/fpsyg.2019.00467.
10. Lane Siedor, "Narcissism and Hypomania Revisited: A Test of the Similarities and Differences in Their Empirical Networks," *Current Psychology: A Journal for Diverse Perspectives on Diverse Psychological Issues* 35 (2016): 244–254.

Chapter 7

1. Keith Campbell, "Narcissism and Romantic Attraction," *Journal of Personality and Social Psychology* 77, no. 6 (1999): 1254–1270, doi.org/10.1037/0022-3514.77.6.1254.
2. C. S. Hyatt et al., "The Relation Between Narcissism and Laboratory Aggression Is Not Contingent on Environmental Cues of Competition," *Personality Disorders: Theory, Research, and Treatment* 9, no. 6 (2018): 543–552, doi.org/10.1037/per0000284.

3. Brad J. Bushman et al., "Narcissism, Sexual Refusal, and Aggression: Testing a Narcissistic Reactance Model of Sexual Coercion," *Journal of Personality and Social Psychology* 84, no. 5 (2003): 1027–1040, doi.org/10.1037/0022-3514.84.5.1027.

4. Kelly Dickinson et al., "Interpersonal Analysis of Grandiose and Vulnerable Narcissism," *Journal of Personality Disorders* 17, no. 3 (2003): 188–207, pdfs.semanticscholar.org/8db5/d181e5ec85fd61de162d3c43e70611eaf4a4.pdf.

5. Avi Besser et al., "Grandiose Narcissism Versus Vulnerable Narcissism in Threatening Situations: Emotional Reactions to Achievement Failure and Interpersonal Rejection," *Journal of Social and Clinical Psychology* 29, no. 8 (2010): 874–902, college.sapir.ac.il/sapir/dept/hrm/katedra/Besser_Priel_(2010b).pdf.

6. Linda Jackson et al., "Narcissism and Body Image," *Journal of Research in Personality* 26, no. 4 (1992): 357–370, doi.org/10.1016/0092-6566(92)90065-C.

7. Marsha Gabriel et al., "Narcissistic Illusions in Self-Evaluations of Intelligence and Attractiveness," *Journal of Personality* 62, no. 1 (1994): 143–155, doi.org/10.1111/j.1467-6494.1994.tb00798.x.

8. Richard Robins et al., "Effects of Visual Perspective and Narcissism on Self-Perception: Is Seeing Believing?" *Psychological Science* 8, no. 1 (1997): 37–42, simine.com/240/readings/Robins_and_John_(10).pdf.

9. Nicholas Holtzman et al., "Narcissism and Attractiveness," *Journal of Research in Personality* 44, no. 1 (2010): 133–136, doi.org/10.1016/j.jrp.2009.10.004.

10. Nicholas Holtzman and Michael Strube, "People with Dark Personalities Tend to Create a Physically Attractive Veneer," *Social Psychological and Personality Science* 4, no. 4 (2013): 461–467, doi.org/10.1177/1948550612461284.

11. Mitja Back et al., "Why Are Narcissists So Charming at First Sight? Decoding Narcissism-Popularity Link at Zero Acquaintance," *Journal of Personality and Social Psychology* 98, no. 1 (2010): 132–145, doi.org/10.1037/a0016338.

12. Marius Leckelt et al., "Behavioral Processes Underlying the Decline of Narcissists' Popularity Over Time," *Journal of Personality and Social Psychology* 109, no. 5 (2015): 856–871, doi.org/10.1037/pspp0000057.

13. Joanna Lamkin et al., "An Exploration of the Correlates of Grandiose and Vulnerable Narcissism in Romantic Relationships: Homophily, Partner Characteristics, and Dyadic Adjustment," *Personality and Individual Differences* 79 (2015): 166–171, doi.org/10.1016/j.paid.2015.01.029.

14. Michael Grosz et al., "Who Is Open to a Narcissistic Romantic Partner?" *Journal of Research in Personality* 58 (2015): 84–94, doi.org/10.1016/j.jrp.2015.05.007.

15. E. A. Krusemark et al., "Comparing Self-Report Measures of Grandiose Narcissism, Vulnerable Narcissism, and Narcissistic Personality Disorder in a Male Offender Sample," *Psychological Assessment* 30, no. 7 (2018): 984–990, doi.org/10.1037/pas0000579.

16. Anna Czarna et al., "Do Narcissism and Emotional Intelligence Win Us Friends? Modeling Dynamics of Peer Popularity Using Inferential Network Analysis," *Personality and Social Psychology Bulletin* 42, no. 11 (2016): 1588–1599, doi.org/10.1177/0146167216666265.

17. W. K. Campbell et al., "Narcissism and Commitment in Romantic Relationships: An Investment Model Analysis," *Personality and Social Psychology Bulletin* 28, no. 4 (2002): 484–495, doi.org/10.1177/0146167202287006.
18. Mitja Back et al., "Narcissistic Admiration and Rivalry: Disentangling the Bright and Dark Sides of Narcissism," *Journal of Personality and Social Psychology* 105, no. 6 (2014): 1013–1037, doi.org/10.1037/a0034431.
19. E. H. O'Boyle et al., "A Meta-Analytic Review of the Dark Triad–Intelligence Connection," *Journal of Research in Personality* 47, no. 6 (2013): 789–794, doi.org /10.1016/j.jrp.2013.08.001.
20. E. Grijalva et al., "Narcissism: An Integrative Synthesis and Dominance Complementarity Model," *Academy of Management Perspectives* 28, no. 2 (2014): 108–127, doi.org /10.5465/amp.2012.0048.

Chapter 8

1. Bandy Lee, *The Dangerous Case of Donald Trump: 37 Psychiatrists and Mental Health Experts Assess a President* (New York: Thomas Dunne Books, 2017).
2. Keith Campbell, "Trump, Narcissism and Removal from Office per the 25th Amendment," Medium, May 19, 2017, medium.com/@wkcampbell/trump-narcissism -and-removal-from-office-per-the-25th-amendment-cd30036a799.
3. Timothy Judge et al., "Personality and Leadership: A Qualitative and Quantitative Review," *Journal of Applied Psychology* 87, no. 4 (2002): 765–780, doi.org/10.1037 //0021-9010.87.4.765.
4. Susan Cain, *Quiet: The Power of Introverts in a World That Can't Stop Talking* (New York: Broadway Books, 2012).
5. Glenn Ball, "Clergy and Narcissism in the Presbyterian Church in Canada" (DMin diss., Trinity Theological Seminary, 2014), academia.edu/8945796/clergy_and_narcissism _in_the_presbyterian_church_in_canada.
6. J. T. Cheng et al., "Pride, Personality, and the Evolutionary Foundations of Human Social Status," *Evolution and Human Behavior* 31 (2010): 334–347.
7. Ashley Watts, "The Double-Edged Sword of Grandiose Narcissism: Implications for Successful and Unsuccessful Leadership Among US Presidents," *Psychological Science* 24, no. 12 (2013): 2379–2389, doi.org/10.1177/0956797613491970.
8. Scott Lilienfeld et al., "The Goldwater Rule: Perspective from, and Implications for, Psychological Science," PsyArXiv Preprints, Cornell University, last updated July 2, 2018, psyarxiv.com/j3gmf/.

Chapter 9

1. "Selfie Is Oxford Dictionaries' Word of the Year," *Guardian*, November 19, 2013, theguardian.com/books/2013/nov/19/selfie-word-of-the-year-oed-olinguito -twerk.
2. Jung-Ah Lee et al., "Hide-and-Seek: Narcissism and 'Selfie'-Related Behavior," *Cyberpsychology, Behavior, and Social Networking* 19, no. 5 (2016): 347–351, doi. org/10.1089/cyber.2015.0486.

3. Jessica McCain et al., "Narcissism and Social Media Use: A Meta-Analytic Review," *Psychology of Popular Media Culture* 7, no. 3 (2016): 308–327, doi.org/10.1037/ppm0000137.

4. Samuel Taylor, "An Experimental Test of How Selfies Change Social Judgments on Facebook," *Cyberpsychology, Behavior, and Social Networking* 20, no. 10 (2017): 610–614, doi.org/10.1089/cyber.2016.0759.

5. N. Ferenczi et al., "Are Sex Differences in Antisocial and Prosocial Facebook Use Explained by Narcissism and Relational Self-Construal?" *Computers in Human Behavior* 77 (2017): 25–31, doi.org/10.1016/j.chb.2017.08.033.

6. Jessica McCain et al., "Narcissism and Social Media Use: A Meta-Analytic Review," *Psychology of Popular Media Culture* 7, no. 3 (2018): 308–327, doi.org/10.1037/ppm0000137.

7. Brittany Gentile et al., "The Effect of Social Networking Websites on Positive Self-Views: An Experimental Investigation," *Computers in Human Behavior* 28, no. 5 (2012): 1929–1933, doi.org/10.1016/j.chb.2012.05.012.

8. Megan McCluskey, "Instagram Star Essena O'Neill Breaks Her Silence on Quitting Social Media," *Time*, January 5, 2016, time.com/4167856/essena-oneill -breaks-silence-on-quitting-social-media/.

9. Chadwick Moore, "The Instahunks: Inside the Swelling Selfie-Industrial Complex," *Out*, August 17, 2016, out.com/out-exclusives/2016/8/17/insta-hunks-inside-swelling -selfie-industrial-complex.

10. Brittany Ward et al., "Nasal Distortion in Short-Distance Photographs: The Selfie Effect," *JAMA Facial Plastic Surgery* 20, no. 4 (2018): 333–335, doi.org/10.1001 /jamafacial.2018.0009.

11. Jesse Fox et al., "The Dark Triad and Trait Self-Objectification as Predictors of Men's Use and Self-Presentation Behaviors on Social Networking Sites," *Personality and Individual Differences* 76 (2015): 161–165, doi.org/10.1016/j.paid.2014.12.017.

Chapter 10

1. Jessica McCain et al., "A Psychological Exploration of Engagement in Geek Culture," *PLOS One* 10, no. 11 (2015): e0142200.

2. Vladislav Iouchkov, "'The Hero with a Thousand Graces': A Socio-Criminological Examination of the 'Real-Life Superhero' Phenomenon" (PhD diss., Western Sydney University, 2017), researchdirect.westernsydney.edu.au/islandora/object/uws:46253 /datastream/PDF/view.

3. Jakob W. Maase, "Keeping the Magic: Fursona Identity and Performance in the Furry Fandom" (master's thesis, Western Kentucky University, 2015), digitalcommons.wku .edu/theses/1512.

4. Stephen Reysen et al., "A Social Identity Perspective of Personality Differences Between Fan and Non-fan Identities," *World Journal of Social Science Research* 2, no. 1 (2015), doi.org/10.22158/wjssr.v2n1p91.

5. Catherine Schroy et al., "Different Motivations as Predictors of Psychological Connection to Fan Interest and Fan Groups in Anime, Furry, and Fantasy Sport Fandoms," *The Phoenix Papers* 2, no. 2 (2016): 148–167.
6. E. Diener et al., "Effects of Deindividuation Variables on Stealing Among Halloween Trick-or-Treaters," *Journal of Personality and Social Psychology* 33, no. 2 (1976): 178–183, doi.org/10.1037/0022-3514.33.2.178.

Chapter 11

1. Harry Wallace et al., "The Performance of Narcissists Rises and Falls with Perceived Opportunity for Glory," *Journal of Personality and Social Psychology* 82, no. 5 (2012): 819–834, doi.org/10.1037/0022-3514.82.5.819.
2. Ellen Nyhus et al., "The Effects of Personality on Earnings," *Journal of Economic Psychology* 26, no. 3 (2004): 363–384, doi.org/10.1016/j.joep.2004.07.001.
3. Timothy Judge et al., "Do Nice Guys—and Gals—Really Finish Last? The Joint Effects of Sex and Agreeableness on Income," *Journal of Personality and Social Psychology* 102, no. 2 (2012): 390–407, doi.org/10.1037/a0026021.
4. Brenda Major, "From Social Inequality to Personal Entitlement: The Role of Social Comparisons, Legitimacy Appraisals, and Group Membership," *Advances in Experimental Social Psychology* 26 (1994): 293–355, doi.org/10.1016/S0065-2601(08)60156-2.
5. Robert Axelrod, *The Evolution of Cooperation* (New York: Basic Books, 1984).

Chapter 12

1. J. D. Miller et al., "Personality Disorder Traits: Perceptions of Likability, Impairment, and Ability to Change as Correlates and Moderators of Desired Level," *Personality Disorders: Theory, Research, and Treatment* 9, no. 5 (2018): 478–483, doi.org/10.1037/per0000263.
2. Eli Finkel et al., "The Metamorphosis of Narcissus: Communal Activation Promotes Relationship Commitment Among Narcissists," *Personality and Social Psychology Bulletin* 35, no. 10 (2009): 1271–1284, doi.org/10.1177/0146167209340904.
3. Erica Hepper, et al., "Moving Narcissus: Can Narcissists Be Empathic?" *Personality and Social Psychology Bulletin* 40, no. 9 (2014): 1079–1091, doi.org/10.1177/0146167214535812.

Chapter 13

1. William James, *The Principles of Psychology* (New York: Henry Holt, 1890), 121, gutenberg.org/ebooks/57628.
2. Brent Roberts et al., "A Systematic Review of Personality Trait Change Through Intervention," *Psychological Bulletin* 143, no. 2 (2017): 117–141, doi.org/10.1037/bul0000088.

3. N. W. Hudson et al., "Volitional Personality Trait Change: Can People Choose to Change Their Personality Traits?" *Journal of Personality and Social Psychology* 109, no. 3 (2015): 490–507, doi.org/10.1037/pspp0000021.

4. Jonathan Allan et al., "Application of a 10-Week Coaching Program Designed to Facilitate Volitional Personality Change: Overall Effects on Personality and the Impact of Targeting," *International Journal of Evidence Based Coaching and Mentoring* 16, no. 1 (2018): 80–94, doi.org/10.24384/000470.

5. Amy Canevello et al., "Interpersonal Goals, Others' Regard for the Self, and Self-Esteem: The Paradoxical Consequences of Self-Image and Compassionate Goals," *European Journal of Social Psychology* 41, no. 4 (2011): 422–434, doi.org/10.1002 /ejsp.808.

6. E. Wetzel et al., "You're Still So Vain: Changes in Narcissism from Young Adulthood to Middle Age," *Journal of Personality and Social Psychology* (advance online publication; 2019), doi.org/10.1037/pspp0000266.

7. Po-Hsin Ho et al., "CEO Overconfidence and Financial Crisis: Evidence from Bank Lending and Leverage," *Journal of Financial Economics* 120, no. 1 (2016): 194–209.

8. Paul Piff et al., "Awe, the Small Self, and Prosocial Behavior," *Journal of Personality and Social Psychology* 108, no. 6 (2015): 883–899, doi.org/10.1037/pspi0000018.

9. Michael Saini, "A Meta-Analysis of the Psychological Treatment of Anger: Developing Guidelines for Evidence-Based Practice," *Journal of the American Academy of Psychiatry and the Law* 37, no. 4 (2009): 473–88.

10. Jennifer Lodi-Smith et al., "Social Investment and Personality: A Meta-Analysis of the Relationship of Personality Traits to Investment in Work, Family, Religion, and Volunteerism," *Personality and Social Psychology Review* 11, no. 1 (2007): 68–86, doi.org /10.1177/1088868306294590.

Chapter 14

1. John Ogrodniczuk et al., "Interpersonal Problems Associated with Narcissism Among Psychiatric Outpatients," *Journal of Psychiatric Research* 43, no. 9 (2009): 837–842, doi.org/10.1016/j.jpsychires.2008.12.005.

2. Wendy Behary, *Disarming the Narcissist: Surviving and Thriving with the Self-Absorbed* (Oakland, CA: New Harbinger Publications, 2013).

3. David Kealy et al., "Therapists' Perspectives on Optimal Treatment for Pathological Narcissism," *Personality Disorders: Theory, Research, and Treatment* 8, no. 1 (2015): 35–45, dx.doi.org/10.1037/per0000164.

4. John Krystal et al., "Ketamine: A Paradigm Shift for Depression Research and Treatment," *Neuron* 101, no. 5 (2019): 774–778, doi.org/10.1016/j.neuron.2019.02.005.

Chapter 15

1. Nicholas Holtzman et al., "Linguistic Markers of Grandiose Narcissism: A LIWC Analysis of 15 Samples," *Journal of Language and Social Psychology* 38, nos. 5–6 (2019): 773–786, doi.org/10.1177/0261927X19871084.

2. Martin Gerlach et al., "A Robust Data-Driven Approach Identifies Four Personality Types Across Four Large Data Sets," *Nature Human Behavior* 2 (2018): 735–742, doi.org/10.1038/s41562-018-0419-z.
3. Jon Ronson, *The Psychopath Test: A Journey Through the Madness Industry* (New York: Riverhead Books, 2011).
4. J. D. Simkins, "Medal of Honor Recipient Praises Revolutionary Neck Injection Treatment for PTSD," *Military Culture, Military Times*, June 18, 2019, militarytimes.com/off-duty/military-culture/2019/06/18/medal-of-honor-recipient-praises-revolutionary-neck-injection-treatment-for-ptsd/.
5. Sean Mulvaney et al., "Stellate Ganglion Block Used to Treat Symptoms Associated with Combat-Related Post-Traumatic Stress Disorder: A Case Series of 166 Patients," *Military Medicine* 179, no. 10 (2014): 1133–1140, doi.org/10.7205/milmed-d-14-00151.

SUGGESTED READINGS

The goal of this book is to give you the information and tools you need to understand narcissism from a scientific perspective. To that end, I am providing a list of key readings. These are the broad reviews or conceptual papers on key topics, and I've also included some of the classic readings in the field.

Academic research is published in academic journals. If you try to find an article in one of these journals, you need to have access through a library, or you'll be charged a large sum of money—and none of that money goes to the authors. Here is how I navigate the academic literature: if I wanted to look at narcissism and extreme sports, for example, I use the Google Scholar search engine and type in "narcissism extreme sports." A long list of articles appears, sorted by relevance, which can be filtered.

Then what? Ideally, one of those articles would be a review or meta-analysis, which is a statistical review of several studies in one paper. In this example, however, no luck. Another option is to find the most highly cited article (e.g., "cited by 120") and start there. Citations mean the article is referenced by other researchers, so a highly cited article is important because it "matters" in an academic sense. You can then search for articles that cited this article to find more recent research. Basically, you can move in different directions in the academic network until you're satisfied with what you find.

Another option, which is how many academic fields work, is to look at an individual research lab. Certain researchers in the narcissism field are mentioned frequently, so you can search for them on Google Scholar and see everything they have written. Heck, follow them on Twitter and you can see the latest work get handed around. Science is incredibly social and tribal; you'll find any interesting topic has opposing camps.

Once you find an article on Google Scholar, the pdf or link will be next to the title, if one exists. Plenty of academic research is posted online for free. If the article isn't posted, there is often a preprint version available on a server somewhere, especially for new articles. As an example, my student writes a paper and posts it online on Open Science Framework (OSF). If the paper is published in an official journal, he might upload the noncopyedited version online. This "gray market" literature is growing quickly. Since my student is also tech savvy, he may upload the code and sample data as well.

If an article is not online, academics may use a gray area site started by a woman in Kazakhstan to make science open. I won't name it here because I don't know what the legal issues might be, but go look for it. I will cheer when she gets a Nobel Prize.

When you read articles in psychology, an opening abstract tells you what's in the paper in one hundred to two hundred words. This makes skimming fast but doesn't substitute for a full reading. Beyond the abstract, journal articles have four main parts: an introduction that includes the hypotheses being tested, methods, results, and discussion. Often, the easiest place to get the heart of the paper is the beginning of the discussion and the figures/tables. You look at the images while reading the researchers' recap of the study in a paragraph or two. Since research articles share the same structure, you can read what you want quickly but also get a broad background if you want.

With all that said, following are some key readings in narcissism. There are hundreds of studies out there, but these are good starting points.

Trait Models of Narcissism

Several groups have converged on the three-factor model of narcissism in somewhat different ways. This gives me more confidence that we are onto something with the Trifurcated Model.

Krizan, Z., and A. D. Herlache. "The Narcissism Spectrum Model: A Synthetic View of Narcissistic Personality." *Personality and Social Psychology Review* 22, no. 1 (2018): 3–31.

Rogoza, R., M. Żemojtel-Piotrowska, M. M. Kwiatkowska, and K. Kwiatkowska. "The Bright, the Dark, and the Blue Face of Narcissism: The Spectrum of Narcissism in Its Relations to the Metatraits of Personality, Self-Esteem, and the Nomological Network of Shyness, Loneliness, and Empathy." *Frontiers in Psychology* 9 (2018): 343.

Weiss, B., W. K. Campbell, D. R. Lynam, and J. D. Miller. "A Trifurcated Model of Narcissism: On the Pivotal Role of Trait Antagonism." In *The Handbook of Antagonism: Conceptualizations, Assessment, Consequences, and Treatment of the Low End of Agreeableness*, edited by Joshua Miller and Donald Lynam, 221–235. San Diego, CA: Elsevier, 2019.

People also love the Dark Triad research, so here is Paulhus's classic paper. A recent meta-analytic review by Vize doesn't find much difference between psychopaths and Machiavellians. This is a debate that will keep going.

Paulhus, D. L., and K. M. Williams. "The Dark Triad of Personality: Narcissism, Machiavellianism, and Psychopathy." *Journal of Research in Personality* 36, no. 6 (2002): 556–563.

Vize, C. E., D. R. Lynam, K. L. Collison, and J. D. Miller. "Differences Among Dark Triad Components: A Meta-Analytic Investigation." *Personality Disorders: Theory, Research, and Treatment* 9, no. 2 (2018): 101–111.

This was our team's first effort to systematically analyze the nomological networks of grandiose and vulnerable narcissism. You'll see we found tons of data.

Miller, J. D., B. J. Hoffman, E. T. Gaughan, B. Gentile, J. Maples, and W. K. Campbell. "Grandiose and Vulnerable Narcissism: A Nomological Network Analysis." *Journal of Personality* 79, no. 5 (2011): 1013–1042.

Dynamic Models of Narcissism

Morf's paper was the most influential dynamic model in the social psychological work in narcissism. This is a classic.

Morf, C. C., and F. Rhodewalt. "Unraveling the Paradoxes of Narcissism: A Dynamic Self-Regulatory Processing Model." *Psychological Inquiry* 12, no. 4 (2001): 177–196.

Here is a more recent dynamic approach to narcissism by Back and colleagues. There is a lot of work in this area.

Back, M. D., A. C. Küfner, M. Dufner, T. M. Gerlach, J. F. Rauthmann, and J. J. Denissen. "Narcissistic Admiration and Rivalry: Disentangling the Bright and Dark Sides of Narcissism." *Journal of Personality and Social Psychology* 105, no. 6 (2013): 1013–1037.

This is my dissertation, which describes a self-regulatory model of attraction.

Campbell, W. K. "Narcissism and Romantic Attraction." *Journal of Personality and Social Psychology* 77, no. 6 (1999): 1254.

Foster has done several papers looking at the role of approach orientation in narcissism. This is a good one to start with.

Foster, J. D., and R. F. Trimm IV. "On Being Eager and Uninhibited: Narcissism and Approach–Avoidance Motivation." *Personality and Social Psychology Bulletin* 34, no. 7 (2008): 1004–1017.

This is our team's recent dynamic model of narcissistic organizational leadership.

Sedikides, C., and W. K. Campbell. "Narcissistic Force Meets Systemic Resistance: The Energy Clash Model." *Perspectives on Psychological Science* 12, no. 3 (2017): 400–421.

Clinical Debates

A few papers look at the debates in narcissism as it crosses from a clinical disorder into a trait, and from grandiose to vulnerable.

Cain, N. M., A. L. Pincus, and E. B. Ansell. "Narcissism at the Crossroads: Phenotypic Description of Pathological Narcissism Across Clinical Theory, Social/Personality Psychology, and Psychiatric Diagnosis." *Clinical Psychology Review* 28, no. 4 (2008): 638–656.

Miller, J. D., D. R. Lynam, C. S. Hyatt, and W. K. Campbell. "Controversies in Narcissism." *Annual Review of Clinical Psychology* 13 (2017): 291–315.

Wright, A. G., and E. A. Edershile. "Issues Resolved and Unresolved in Pathological Narcissism." *Current Opinion in Psychology* 21 (2018): 74–79.

Cool Studies

The "cool" factor is apparent in the title of these—and they make an appearance in this book.

Back, M. D., S. C. Schmukle, and B. Egloff. "Why Are Narcissists So Charming at First Sight? Decoding the Narcissism–Popularity Link at Zero Acquaintance." *Journal of Personality and Social Psychology* 98, no. 1 (2010): 132–145.

Brummelman, E., S. Thomaes, S. A. Nelemans, B. O. De Castro, G. Overbeek, and B. J. Bushman. "Origins of Narcissism in Children." *Proceedings of the National Academy of Sciences* 112, no. 12 (2015): 3659–3662.

Campbell, W. K., C. P. Bush, A. B. Brunell, and J. Shelton. "Understanding the Social Costs of Narcissism: The Case of the Tragedy of the Commons." *Personality and Social Psychology Bulletin* 31, no. 10 (2005): 1358–1368.

Gebauer, J. E., C. Sedikides, B. Verplanken, and G. R. Maio. "Communal Narcissism." *Journal of Personality and Social Psychology* 103, no. 5 (2012): 854.

Hyatt, C., W. K. Campbell, D. R. Lynam, and J. D. Miller. "Dr. Jekyll or Mr. Hyde? President Donald Trump's Personality Profile as Perceived from Different Political Viewpoints." *Collabra: Psychology* 4, no. 1 (2018): xx.

McCain, J., B. Gentile, and W. K. Campbell. "A Psychological Exploration of Engagement in Geek Culture." *PLOS One* 10, no. 11 (2015): e0142200.

Tracy, J. L., J. T. Cheng, R. W. Robins, and K. H. Trzesniewski. "Authentic and Hubristic Pride: The Affective Core of Self-Esteem and Narcissism." *Self and Identity* 8, no. 2–3 (2009): 196–213.

Vazire, S., L. P. Naumann, P. J. Rentfrow, and S. D. Gosling. "Portrait of a Narcissist: Manifestations of Narcissism in Physical Appearance." *Journal of Research in Personality* 42, no. 6 (2008): 1439–1447.

Watts, A. L., S. O. Lilienfeld, S. F. Smith, J. D. Miller, W. K. Campbell, I. D. Waldman, and T. J. Faschingbauer. "The Double-Edged Sword of Grandiose Narcissism: Implications for Successful and Unsuccessful Leadership Among US Presidents." *Psychological Science* 24, no. 12 (2013): 2379–2389.

Young, S. M., and D. Pinsky. "Narcissism and Celebrity." *Journal of Research in Personality* 40, no. 5 (2006): 463–471.

Reviews

Here's a selection of the broader reviews out there.

Bosson, J. K., C. E. Lakey, W. K. Campbell, V. Zeigler-Hill, C. H. Jordan, and M. H. Kernis. "Untangling the Links Between Narcissism and Self-Esteem: A Theoretical and Empirical Review." *Social and Personality Psychology Compass* 2, no. 3 (2008): 1415–1439.

Campbell, W. K., B. J. Hoffman, S. M. Campbell, and G. Marchisio. "Narcissism in Organizational Contexts." *Human Resource Management Review* 21, no. 4 (2011): 268–284.

Gnambs, T., and M. Appel. "Narcissism and Social Networking Behavior: A Meta-Analysis." *Journal of Personality* 86, no. 2 (2018): 200–212.

Grijalva, E., and D. A. Newman. "Narcissism and Counterproductive Work Behavior (CWB): Meta-Analysis and Consideration of Collectivist Culture, Big Five Personality, and Narcissism's Facet Structure." *Applied Psychology* 64, no. 1 (2015): 93–126.

Grijalva, E., D. A. Newman, L. Tay, M. B. Donnellan, P. D. Harms, R. W. Robins, and T. Yan. "Gender Differences in Narcissism: A Meta-Analytic Review." *Psychological Bulletin* 141, no. 2 (2015): 261–310.

Holtzman, N. S., and M. J. Strube. "Narcissism and Attractiveness." *Journal of Research in Personality* 44, no. 1 (2010): 133–136.

Liu, D., and R. F. Baumeister. "Social Networking Online and Personality of Self-Worth: A Meta-Analysis." *Journal of Research in Personality* 64 (2016): 79–89.

McCain, J. L., and W. K. Campbell. "Narcissism and Social Media Use: A Meta-Analytic Review." *Psychology of Popular Media Culture* 7, no. 3 (2018): 308–327.

O'Boyle, E. H., D. Forsyth, G. C. Banks, and P. A. Story. "A Meta-Analytic Review of the Dark Triad–Intelligence Connection." *Journal of Research in Personality* 47, no. 6 (2013): 789–794.

Samuel, D. B., and T. A. Widiger. "A Meta-Analytic Review of the Relationships Between the Five-Factor Model and DSM-IV-TR Personality Disorders: A Facet Level Analysis." *Clinical Psychology Review* 28, no. 8 (2008): 1326–1342.

Some Common Scales

Here are citations for some of the more commonly used narcissism scales.

NARCISSISTIC PERSONALITY INVENTORY (NPI)

Gentile, B., J. D. Miller, B. J. Hoffman, D. E. Reidy, A. Zeichner, and W. K. Campbell. "A Test of Two Brief Measures of Grandiose Narcissism: The Narcissistic Personality Inventory-13 and the Narcissistic Personality Inventory-16." *Psychological Assessment* 25, no. 4 (2013): 1120–1136.

Raskin, R., and H. Terry. "A Principal-Components Analysis of the Narcissistic Personality Inventory and Further Evidence of Its Construct Validity." *Journal of Personality and Social Psychology* 54, no. 5 (1988): 890–902.

PATHOLOGICAL NARCISSISM INVENTORY (PNI)

Pincus, A. L., E. B. Ansell, C. A. Pimentel, N. M. Cain, A. G. Wright, and K. N. Levy. "Initial Construction and Validation of the Pathological Narcissism Inventory." *Psychological Assessment* 21, no. 3 (2009): 365.

HYPERSENSITIVE NARCISSISM SCALE (HSNS)

Hendin, H. M., and J. M. Cheek. "Assessing Hypersensitive Narcissism: A Reexamination of Murray's Narcism Scale." *Journal of Research in Personality* 31, no. 4 (1997): 588–599.

FIVE-FACTOR NARCISSISM INVENTORY (FFNI)

Miller, J. D., L. R. Few, L. Wilson, B. Gentile, T. A. Widiger, J. MacKillop, and K. W. Campbell. "The Five-Factor Narcissism Inventory (FFNI): A Test of the Convergent, Discriminant, and Incremental Validity of FFNI Scores in Clinical and Community Samples." *Psychological Assessment* 25, no. 3 (2013): 748–758.

Sherman, E. D., J. D. Miller, L. R. Few, W. K. Campbell, T. A. Widiger, C. Crego, and D. R. Lynam. "Development of a Short Form of the Five-Factor Narcissism Inventory: The FFNI-SF." *Psychological Assessment* 27, no. 3 (2015): 1110–1116.

NARCISSISM ADMIRATION AND RIVALRY QUESTIONNAIRE (NARQ)

Back, M. D., A. C. Küfner, M. Dufner, T. M. Gerlach, J. F. Rauthmann, and J. J. Denissen. "Narcissistic Admiration and Rivalry: Disentangling the Bright and Dark Sides of Narcissism." *Journal of Personality and Social Psychology* 105, no. 6 (2013): 1013–1037.

Leckelt, M., E. Wetzel, T. M. Gerlach, R. A. Ackerman, J. D. Miller, W. J. Chopik, and D. Richter. "Validation of the Narcissistic Admiration and Rivalry Questionnaire Short Scale (NARQ-S) in Convenience and Representative Samples." *Psychological Assessment* 30, no. 1 (2018): 86–96.

NARCISSISTIC GRANDIOSITY SCALE (NGS)

Crowe, M., N. T. Carter, W. K. Campbell, and J. D. Miller. "Validation of the Narcissistic Grandiosity Scale and Creation of Reduced Item Variants." *Psychological Assessment* 28, no. 12 (2016): 1550–1560.

NARCISSISTIC VULNERABILITY SCALE (NVS)

Crowe, M. L., E. A. Edershile, A. G. Wright, W. K. Campbell, D. R. Lynam, and J. D. Miller. "Development and Validation of the Narcissistic Vulnerability Scale: An Adjective Rating Scale." *Psychological Assessment* 30, no. 7 (2018): 978–983.

PSYCHOLOGICAL ENTITLEMENT SCALE (PES)

Campbell, W. K., A. M. Bonacci, J. Shelton, J. J. Exline, and B. J. Bushman. "Psychological Entitlement: Interpersonal Consequences and Validation of a Self-Report Measure." *Journal of Personality Assessment* 83, no. 1 (2004): 29–45.

INDEX

Page numbers in italics refer to figures and tables.

aggression, 119, 126–27, 218–19
agreeableness, 47–49, 53, 61, 74, 93, 98
   income, 193
   leadership, 139–40
alpha. *See* stability
ambulatory assessment, 240–41
antagonism, 6, 49, 53–54, 98, 107, 114,
   119, 126, *200*, 201–3
antisocial personality disorder, 85–86, 92
anxiolytics, 67
approach and avoidance, 66–68
assertiveness, 52
attachment theory, 219
average (being "average"), 80–82
awe, 217–18

Barnum Effect, 23–24
beta. *See* plasticity
Big Five traits, 47–50, 52, 61–62, 97
   agreeableness, 47–49, 53, 61, 74, 93,
     98, 139–40, 193
   change, 212–13
   conscientiousness, 48–50, 108
   extraversion, 48, 50, 52–54, 107,
     139–40, 200–1
   neuroticism, 24, 47, 49–50, 81, 127,
     131, 139, 200, 204, 213, 219
   openness, 48–50, 139
Big Little Lies (TV show), 197–98
bipolar personality disorder, 86–87, 246

boldness, 53, 106–7, 189–90
borderline personality disorder, 85–86,
   92, 102, 224, 230, 232
Bradley, Omar, 141–42
brain stimulation, 246–47
Brandon, Nathaniel, 27

Cain, Susan, 139
change. *See* reducing narcissism in others;
   reducing your own narcissism
chocolate cake model, *129*, 130
Columbine shooting, xi
compassion, 208–9, 220–21
conscientiousness, 48–50, 108
cooperation, 194–95
CPR (compassion, passion, responsibility)
   method, 208–9

depression, 8, 54, 79, 94, 204, 219, 230,
   232, 246
*Diagnostic and Statistical Manual of
   Mental Disorders (DSM)*, 13, 40, 94
   arguments concerning content,
     95–96
   narcissistic personality disorder
     (NPD), 83–88
domination, *117*, 119
drugs and drug abuse, 67, 87, 232, 247–48
   see also medication
Duckworth, Angela, 108

empathy, 11, 84, 88, 203
Energy Clash Model, 148, *149*, 150
enthusiasm, 52
entitlement, 6, 49, 88, 194, 202, 211, 217
evolutionary psychology, 14, *15*
extraversion, 48, 50, 52–54, 200–1
    Energized Triad, 106–7
    enthusiasm and assertiveness, 52
    hypomanic extraversion, 107
    leadership, 139–40
    responses to, *200*

face validity, 30
fading goal problem, 73
fragility, 220–21
Freud, Sigmund, 11, 95, 211–12, 228–29
furries, 179–80

Galton, Francis, 46
gaslighting, 128
geek culture, 171–80
    furries, 179–80
    geek and *nerd*, meanings of, 172,
        180–81
    Geek Culture Engagement Scale,
        173–75, 181
    Great Fantasy Migration, 176–79
genetics, 238–39
goals. *See* motivation
Goldwater Rule, 151
grandiose narcissism, 6, *7*, 64, 66, 74,
    98, 115
    extraversion, 53–54, 131
    hypomania, 107
    infidelity, 218
    measuring, 33–36
    overconfidence, 216
    selfies, 155
    vulnerability, 91
    and vulnerable narcissism, 8–10
    see also leadership and narcissism
grandiosity, 217–18
    as feature of NPD, 84–85, 87, 90
    and hypomanic extraversion, 107
    Narcissistic Grandiosity Scale (NGS),
        35–36, 41

Great Fantasy Migration, 176–79

HEXACO Personality Inventory, 61–62
homophily, 124–25
Hypersensitive Narcissism Scale (HSNS),
    36–37
hypomania, 86, 107, 109

impairments, 82–83
infidelity, 218
introversion, 48, 96, 139

James, William, 26, 212, 235
Jobs, Steve, 49, 133
Jung, Carl, 11, 95–96

Kaufman, Scott Barry, 103–4
Kernberg, Otto, 228–29
Kohut, Heinz, 228–29
Kraepelin, Emil, 93, 95

leadership and narcissism, 136–50
    benefits and costs, *188*
    competition and cooperation,
        194–95
    double-edged sword of narcissistic
        leaders, *146*
    effectiveness, 137, 143–48
    emergence, 137–43; dominance
        versus prestige, 140–42
    extraversion and introversion, 139
    networks, building of, 190–91
    organizational change, 148–50
    public performance, 189
    self-serving leadership, 185
    servant leadership, 185
    standing up for yourself, 191–92
    successful use of, 188–92
    tragedy of the commons dilemma,
        186–88, 193–94
    U.S. presidents, 146–48
    using narcissism strategically, 185–93
lexical hypothesis, 46
Likert, Rensis, 29
love, 71, 77, 113–14, 209, 222
    see also relationships and narcissists

love bombing, 127–28

Machiavellianism, 99–100
Maslow, Abraham, 11, 26
McCain, Jessica, 172–73, 175–76, 181
medication, 204, 213, *228*, 232
    psychedelics, 247–48
    SSRIs (serotonin reuptake inhibitors),
        94, 204, *228*, 232
    see also therapy and treatment
Miller, Josh, 41, 101–2, 151
mistrust, 219–20
motivation, 66–69
motivational interviewing, 198, 225
Murray, Henry, 33

narcissism
    aggression, 119, 126–27, 218–19
    antagonism, 6, 49, 53–54, 98, 107,
        114, 119, 126, *200*, 201–3
    approach and avoidance, 66–68
    assertiveness, 52
    basic trait ingredients of, *54*
    benefits and costs, *188*
    criminality, association with, 101–3,
        127
    communal narcissism, 60–61
    culture, 15
    decreasing as we age, 214
    defining, ix–x, 4–10
    diagnosing, 83–91; criteria, 87–88;
        personality disorder clusters,
        91–93; public figures, 150–51;
        specifier, 90
    extraversion, 48, 50, 52–54,
        200–1; Energized Triad, 106–7;
        enthusiasm and assertiveness, 52;
        hypomanic extraversion, 107;
        leadership, 139–40; responses
        to, *200*
    fading goal problem, 73
    grandiosity, 217–18; feature of
        NPD, 84–85, 87, 90; and
        hypomanic extraversion, 107;
        Narcissistic Grandiosity Scale
        (NGS), 35–36, 41

    healthy use of, 188–92
    impairments, 82–83
    intelligence, association with, 132–33
    malignant narcissism, 100–1
    measuring. *See* personality tests and
        scales
    mistrust, 219–20
    motivation, 66–69
    nesting dolls analogy, 19–20
    neurochemistry, 20–21
    neuroticism, 24, 47, 49–50, 204,
        213; and aggression, 219;
        extremely low levels of, 81;
        leadership, 139; relationships,
        127, 131; responses to, *200*
    online searches of, ix
    overconfidence, 216–17
    public performance, 189
    reality principle problem, 74–75
    recipe, 53–55
    reducing narcissism in others,
        197–209
    reducing your own narcissism,
        211–22
    risk-taking, 216
    scales/tests, 33–37, *38*
    self-esteem and self-regulation,
        69–76, 214, 220
    sexual aggression, 119
    social media, 156–68
    "sex, status, and stuff," 68, 72–73,
        116, 158
    testing yourself, 42–44
    Trifurcated Model of Narcissism, 10,
        28, 114, 130
    types, 4–10: combination of types, 7;
        grandiose narcissism, 6, *7*, 8–10,
        33–34, 53–54, 61, 64, 66, 74, 91,
        98, 107, 115, 131, 155, 216, 218;
        positive and negative associations
        related to narcissist types, *9*;
        vulnerable narcissism, 6, *7*, 8–10,
        36–38, 54, 65–66, 69, *98*, 102–3,
        115, 120, 127–28, 138–39, 155,
        204, 219
    using strategically, 185–93

narcissism *(continued)*
  willing accomplice problem, 74
  workplace relationships, 133,
    148–50, 194–95
  see also leadership and narcissism;
    narcissistic personality disorder
    (NPD); personality; personality
    tests and scales; relationships
    and narcissists; therapy and
    treatment; traits
The Narcissism Epidemic (Campbell and
  Twenge), 15, 20
Narcissistic Grandiosity Scale (NGS),
  35–36, 41
narcissistic personality disorder (NPD),
  79–96
  diagnosing, 83–91; criteria, 87–88;
    personality disorder clusters,
    91–93; public figures, 150–51;
    specifier, 90
  distinction from narcissism, 79–80
  distinction from other personality
    disorders, 85–87
  evolution of classification, 94
  extreme/inflexible, 82
  gender, 84
  impairments, 82–83
  impulsivity, 85–86
  malignant narcissism, 100–1
  prevalence in general population, 84–85
  see also narcissism
Narcissistic Personality Inventory (NPI),
  34–35, 40, 42–43
Narcissus (Greek myth), 113–14, 120
nerd and *geek*, meanings of, 172, 180–81
networks
  building, 190–91
  organizational networks, 150
  research, 243
  social media, 156–68, 250
  see also social media and networks
neurochemistry, 20–21
neuroimaging, 243–45
neuroticism, 24, 47, 49–50, 204, 213
  and aggression, 219
  extremely low levels of, 81

leadership, 139
  relationships, 127, 131
  responses to, *200*
nomological network, 13, *15*, 55–57
normal (being "normal"), 80–82, 95

openness, 48–50, 139
organizational change, 148–50
overconfidence, 216–17

Patton, George, 140–41
parenting, 207–9
Paulhus, Del, 98, 100–1
personality, 10–14
  average/normal, 80–82, 95
  changing, 211–14
  extreme/inflexible, 82
  Freudian model, 211–12
  impairments, 82–83
  levels of analysis, 20
  models: biopsychological, 12–13;
    cultural, 14–15; evolutionary, 14,
    15; humanistic, 11–12; as maps,
    18–19; nomological network,
    13, *15*, 55–57; psychodynamic,
    11; self-regulatory, 13–14, *15*;
    standard psychological model, 12
  nesting dolls analogy, 19–20
  new science of personality studies, *240*
  scientific advancements and research,
    239–50
  see also personality disorders;
    personality tests and scales; traits
personality disorders
  antisocial, 85–86, 92
  bipolar, 86–87, 246
  borderline, 85–86, 92, 102, 224,
    230, 232
  clusters, 91–93
  diagnosing, difficulty and subjectivity
    of, 93
  evolution of classification, 93–94
  narcissistic personality disorder
    (NPD), 79–96
  see also narcissistic personality
    disorder (NPD)

personality tests and scales
 Barnum Effect, 23–24
 creating new scales, 108
 defining traits to be measured, 25–28
 forced-choice scales, 40
 Geek Culture Engagement Scale,
  173–75, 181
 Grit Scale, 108
 Likert/Likert-type scales, 29, 40
 limits, 38–39
 measurement, challenges of, 28–32
 positive and negative scale
  comparisons, 30
 Rosenberg Self-Esteem Scale, 31–32
 scale types, 33–37, 38, 61
 testing yourself, 42–44
 reliability, 30–31
 validity, 30–31
plastic surgery, 20, 161, 168
plasticity, 50–51
psychedelics, 247–48
psychological models of personality
 biopsychological model, 12–13
 cultural model, 14–15
 evolutionary psychology, 14, 15</ital
 humanistic model, 11–12
 as maps, 18–19
 nomological network, 13, 15
 psychodynamic model, 11
 self-regulatory model, 13–14, 15</
  ital
 standard psychological model, 12
 see also personality
psychopathy, 98–99, 101, 103, 107, 159
public performance, 189

Quiet, 139

Raskin, Robert, 34, 40
reality principle problem, 74–75
reducing narcissism in others, 197–209
 manipulation, 204–6
 motivational interviewing, 198, 225
 narcissist's desire to change, 197–99
 parenting, 207–9
 responses to narcissistic traits, 200

tactics for reducing, 200–7; agentic
  extraversion, 200–1; antagonism,
  201–3; neuroticism, 204
 talking, 206–7
reducing your own narcissism, 211–22
 aggression, 218–19
 challenges and solutions, 215
 community, 221–22
 fragility, 220–21
 grandiosity, 217–18
 infidelity, 218
 love, 222
 mistrust, 219–20
 overconfidence, 216–17
relationships and narcissists, 113–32
 afteraffects, 131
 attractiveness of narcissists, 120–25
 benefits for the narcissist, 116–20;
  admiration, 118–19; association,
  117–18; consolation, 120;
  domination, 119
 chocolate cake model, 129, 130
 downsides/negative effects, 125–28
 effective adornment, 121–22, 123
 gaslighting, 128
 homophily, 124
 love bombing, 127–28
 patterns, 128–32
 reducing narcissism in others,
  197–209
 strategies, 117, 118–20, 123
 workplace relationships, 133, 148–50
reliability, 30–31
research. See personality tests and scales;
 scientific advancements and research
Research Domain Criteria project, 223
Rodger, Elliot, 2–4, 10, 16–18
Rosenberg Self-Esteem Scale, 31–32
Rosenthal, Seth, 35, 41

sadism, 100–1, 159
scales. See personality tests and scales
scientific advancements and research,
 239–50
 ambulatory assessment, 240–41
 genetics, 238–39

scientific advancements and research
  (continued)
    linguistic and video data analysis,
      241–43
    neuroimaging, 243–45
    new science of personality studies, *240*
    new trends, 250
    treatments, *245*; brain stimulation,
      246–47; psychedelics, 247–48;
      virtual reality, 248–50
self-esteem, 26–28, 31, *32*, 70–75, 214,
  220
selfies, 153–56, 168–69
self-regulation, 69–76
self-serving bias, 76–77
"sex, status, and stuff," 68, 72–73,
  116, 158
Siedor, Lane, 108–9
The Six Pillars of Self-Esteem (Brandon), 27
social media and networks, 156–68, 250
    fame, 159–60, 164–65
    identifying narcissism from social
      media posts, 162–63
    insecurity, 161
    negative effects of, 164–65
    self-enhancement, 158, 161
    selfies, 153–56, 168–69
    social networks, development of,
      166–67
    trolling, 159
specifiers, 90
SSRIs (serotonin reuptake inhibitors), 94,
  204, *228*, 232
stability, 50–51
standing up for yourself, 191–92

therapy and treatment, 219–20, 223–35
    approaches to treating NPD, 226–27
    basic therapies for narcissism, 227,
      228, 229–32; cognitive behavioral
      therapy (CBT), 229–31;
      psychodynamic, 228–29
    barriers to treatment, 224–25
    finding the right therapist, 232–35
    geographical differences in popularity
      of various approaches, 235

medication, 204, 213, *228*, 232;
    psychedelics, 247–48; SSRIs
    (serotonin reuptake inhibitors),
    94, 204, *228*, 232
motivational interviewing, 198, 225
scientific advancements and research,
    239–50
see also reducing narcissism in
    others; reducing your own
    narcissism
Thurstone, Louis Lean, 29
"To Fall in Love with Anyone, Do This,"
  (*New York Times* "Modern Love"
  article), 77
tragedy of the commons dilemma,
  186–88, 193–94
traits, 46
    antagonism, 6, 49, 53–54, 98, 107,
      114, 119, 126, *200*, 201–3
    aspects, 52–53
    assertiveness, 52
    boldness, 53, 106–7, 189–90
    Big Five, 47–50, 52, 61–62, 97;
      agreeableness, 47–49, 53, 61, 74,
      93, 98, 139–40, 193; change,
      212–13; conscientiousness,
      48–50, 108; extraversion, 48,
      50, 52–54, 107, 139–40, 200–1;
      neuroticism, 24, 47, 49–50, 81,
      127, 131, 139, 200, 204, 213,
      219; openness, 48–50, 139
    Big One, 50
    Big Six, 61
    Big Two, 50–51
    defining, 25–28
    enthusiasm, 52
    extreme/inflexible, 82
    facets, 52–53
    faith in humanity, 104–5
    hierarchy, *51*
    honest-humility, 61–62
    humanism, 104–5
    humility, 61–62, 104
    hypomania, 86, 107, 109
    impairments, 82–83
    as ingredients, 46–47

Kantianism, 104–5
levels, 52–53
Machiavellianism, 99–100
measuring, 28–32
nomological network, 13, *15*,
    55–57
plasticity, 50–51
psychopathy, 98–99, 101, 103,
    107, 159
sadism, 100–1, 159
stability, 50–51
trait cousins, 97
triads, 97; Energized Triad, 106–9;
    Light Triad, 103–5; Dark Triad,
    97–103, 121
see also narcissism; personality
treatment. *See* therapy and treatment
triads, 97
    Energized Triad, 106–9
    Light Triad, 103–5
    Dark Triad, 97–103, 121
Trifurcated Model of Narcissism, 10, 28,
    114, 130
trolling, 159
Trump, Donald, 50–59, 195–96,
    149–50, 205

U.S. presidents, 146–48
    see also Trump, Donald

validity, 30–31
virtual reality, 248–50
vulnerable narcissism, 6, *7*, 54,.65–66,
    98, 115, 120
    extrinsic motivators, 69
    and grandiose narcissism, 8–10
    leadership, 138–39
    measuring, 36–38
    mistrust, 219
    neuroticism, 204
    relationships, 127–28, 204
    selfies, 155
    Vulnerable Dark Triad, 102–3

When You Love a Man Who Loves Himself
    (Campbell), 113, 129
willing accomplice problem, 74
Woodworth Personal Data Sheet, 24
workplace issues, 133, 148–50
    competition and cooperation, 194–95
    tragedy of the commons dilemma,
        186–88, 193–94
    see also leadership and narcissism

ABOUT THE AUTHORS

W. Keith Campbell, PhD, professor of psychology at the University of Georgia, is the author of more than one hundred and fifty scientific articles, a personality textbook, and the books *When You Love a Man Who Loves Himself: How to Deal with a One-Way Relationship*; *The Narcissism Epidemic: Living in the Age of Entitlement* (with Jean Twenge), and *The Handbook of Narcissism and Narcissistic Personality Disorder: Theoretical Approaches, Empirical Findings, and Treatments* (with Josh Miller). His work on narcissism has appeared widely. He has been interviewed on the topic by most major news outlets and was the author of the popular TED-Ed lesson "The Psychology of Narcissism." Dr. Campbell holds a bachelor's degree from the University of California, Berkeley, a master's degree from San Diego State University, and a doctorate from the University of North Carolina at Chapel Hill, and he did his postdoctoral work at Case Western Reserve University. He lives in Athens, Georgia, with his wife, daughters, and dog, Murphy.

Carolyn Crist is an internationally published independent journalist who has reported stories in the United States, Mongolia, South Korea, and elsewhere. She worked as a staff reporter for daily newspapers and decided to go solo after earning a master's degree in health and medical journalism from the University of Georgia.

You can now find her work in consumer and trade publications such as AARP, the *Atlanta Journal-Constitution*, *Parade*, Reuters, *U.S. News & World Report*, and *Wired*. Crist is a board member of the American Society of Journalists and Authors and the freelance correspondent for the Association of Health Care Journalists. She also owns Crist Media, a media consulting firm, and runs the Freelance Writing Roadmap website and podcast, where she helps others learn how to write and work for themselves. She lives in Athens, Georgia, with her fiancé, Drew, and two adorable black-and-white cats, Jesse and Vanya.

ABOUT SOUND TRUE

SOUNDS TRUE is a multimedia publisher whose mission is to inspire and support personal transformation and spiritual awakening. Founded in 1985 and located in Boulder, Colorado, we work with many of the leading spiritual teachers, thinkers, healers, and visionary artists of our time. We strive with every title to preserve the essential "living wisdom" of the author or artist. It is our goal to create products that not only provide information to a reader or listener but also embody the quality of a wisdom transmission.

For those seeking genuine transformation, Sounds True is your trusted partner. At SoundsTrue.com you will find a wealth of free resources to support your journey, including exclusive weekly audio interviews, free downloads, interactive learning tools, and other special savings on all our titles.

To learn more, please visit SoundsTrue.com/freegifts or call us toll-free at 800.333.9185.

sounds true
WAKING UP THE WORLD